CATCH A
FALLING
STAR

CATCH A FALLING STAR

A Story About Growing Up With Jeanne Little

KATIE M LITTLE

For Mum, who always said, 'Just have a go.'

CONTENTS

PART 1

My Generation • 9
The Jean Genie • 15
Born to Be Wild • 21
Stayin' Alive • 31
Everybody Wants To Rule The World • 39
Wake Me Up Before You Go-Go • 45
Money Changes Everything • 53
Living Doll • 63
Dancing Queen • 69
Owner Of A Lonely Heart • 79
Like a Virgin • 83
Little Lies • 89
Love Is a Stranger • 95
The Killing Moon • 105
Streets of Your Town • 107
There Is a Light
That Never Goes Out • 113
Blue Monday • 121
Barracuda • 125

PART 2

Every Little Thing She Does Is Magic • 135
Burning Down the House • 141
I Touch Myself • 147
I See Red • 171
Heart of Glass • 173
Damn It, Janet • 177
Kiss Me, Kiss Me, Kiss Me • 181
The Unguarded Moment • 185
Talk Of The Town • 189

I Want To Break Free • 193
Hungry like the Wolf • 199
Party Girl • 203
The Future's So Bright,
I Gotta Wear Shades • 209
Don't You
(Forget About Me) • 215

PART 3

You'd Be so Nice to Come Home To • 227
Time Heals Everything • 231
Falling in Love Again • 237
Pistol Packin' Mama • 243
Anything You Can Do
I Can Do Better • 249
Tap Your Troubles Away • 255
Everything's Coming Up Roses • 261
I've Got You Under My Skin • 267
I Wanna Be Loved By You • 271
There's No Business
Like Show Business • 275
Love and Marriage • 279
Thanks for the Memory • 283
I'm Always Chasing Rainbows • 287
Dancing with Tears in My Eyes • 291
A Spoonful of Sugar • 295
After You've Gone • 299
Run Rabbit Run • 303
I'll Be Here Tomorrow • 309
Life Is Just a Bowl of Cherries • 315
Sing A Song Of Sixpence • 321

PART 1

MY GENERATION

Apparently I was a quiet child, or so Dad tells me, but really, with a mum like Jeanne Little, who was famous for talking a mile a minute, it was hard to get a word in edgewise. Mum was a weekly regular on *The Mike Walsh Show*, the number one daytime television show in the 1970s and early '80s that everyone in Australia watched. Every weekday a ninety-minute show was filmed in front of a packed studio audience and broadcast to millions of viewers across the nation. These were the heady vaudevillian days of television where magic was made. In a studio the size of a small aircraft hanger, it was 'Lights! Camera! Action!' The smell of hairspray and foundation, adrenaline and perspiration sizzling under high-voltage lights, the music of a live band, the excitement and unpredictability of broadcasting live.

Mum 'fell onto television', as she liked to say, when she was pregnant with me, and I grew up backstage, taken everywhere with her. In my mind I can retrace our steps as I held her hand and followed her into the labyrinth of the Channel 9 studios. Down the long corridors lined with huge, glossy posters of the top-rating stars of the network – Paul Hogan, Tony Barber, Jana Wendt, Don Lane and Brian Henderson, who all had enormous eighties hair and shoulder pads, brilliant smiles and eyes that would follow me down the corridor, like paintings in a haunted mansion. My mother's image would eventually be hung along this hallowed wall of fame as well, complete with her trademark false eyelashes and bleached blonde hair.

Our steps would echo as we took the stairs down the glass-walled fire escape, which overlooked the helipad and the great antenna, which stretched way up high into the clouds like Jack's magic beanstalk, the tip pulsating with red warning beacons. If I was really lucky a helicopter would be landing and the whole building would reverberate with the THWUMP, THWUMP, THWUMP of the blades as people ran from the chopper in a crouch, sometimes clutching their toupee for dear life.

But there was never any time to stand and watch. Television ran to a strict schedule and we would be ushered quickly to one of the backstage rooms where Mum could get ready. A laminex counter stained with coffee rings and cigarette burns, above which was one long mirror framed with frosted light bulbs. The bare room was furnished with thin carpet and maybe a plastic chair if we were lucky, a few hooks on the wall littered with a collection of odd coathangers; backstage television studios are rarely glamorous places.

Mum would invariably be carrying a gigantic black duffel bag over her shoulder with some amazing outfit that she'd created tucked away inside, as well as maybe a white styrofoam head with a wig pinned to it, and always her enormous, soft black leather handbag which rattled with lipsticks and bobby pins, hairnets and deodorant cans loaded with ozone-thinning CFCs, nail polish and hair rollers – anything and everything she might need as she transformed herself backstage from humble 'plain Jane' into the persona millions came to adore.

I knew once we reached this room to keep out of her way; I was Mum's helper and took my job as seriously as any magician's assistant. Despite my young age I knew how to pull off the rubbery old eyelash glue while Mum did her make-up and was always at the ready to fasten a clasp or yank a zipper up. Jeanne, who loved noise, who was always talking loudly, or singing, or even whistling, was rarely silent except for when she was sewing or preparing backstage. And it would be in silence that I would watch her transform herself: treading on the backs of her white canvas sneakers and peeling off her old stonewashed jeans, slipping each of her long legs into the toes of pantyhose, stepping carefully into her latest creation – a dress sewn with squares of toast or rubber gloves or hot pink balloons (which I was strictly forbidden to touch until after the show), an ankle-length gown sewn with double-sided tape, glittering with freshly minted two-dollar coins, a white bridal gown made of plastic sandwich wrap, each outfit more incredible and outrageous than the last.

She always did her own make-up, so going to the make-up room where the stars were prepped was really just a formality, to give her a final last blast of hairspray and check her foundation. The air was always so heavy with spray everyone was dizzy from lack of oxygen, rows of golden cans lined up against another long mirror with more bare light bulbs, before which sat four enormous, black padded chairs. The make-up girls always shrieked with joy to see what Mum was wearing but if Mike

Walsh, the great Wizard of Oz himself was occupying one of the big padded chairs, his collar protected by a ring of tissue-paper petals, they knew better than to divert their attention away from him.

After the make-up room, Mum would be taken to sit and wait her turn in the 'green room', the lounge where the show's guests waited backstage to go on, clutching styrofoam coffee cups and watching the show as it was being aired on a special little television that didn't show the commercials, just static and a loud beeping sequence of numbers counting down at the end of each ad break. Sometimes though she would have to go out to talk to the stage manager about her spot before the show started, or later, when they learnt she had a singing voice, she'd be brought out to do a sound check with the band. I'd follow her onto the floor, through the sacred, sealed airlock that would soon be lit up with the words 'ON AIR' in bright red neon.

'Don't touch anything!' Mum would whisper, and we would step our way carefully through the pretend wooden stages, tiptoe across the platform floors (Mum always walked on tiptoes whether she was wearing sneakers or heels), and push our way past the heavy velvet curtain, weighed down with a hem of lead weights, into the blaring heat and glare of the stage lights. Holding me by the hand, she would lead me across the thick, glossy linoleum that snaked with inch-thick cables, linking up the enormous half-dozen cameras that glided over the floor like giant black creatures with one huge bulging eye each, all trained on Mike's seat.

Perhaps some of the studio audience were already being seated, filing their way up into the tiered, stadium-style seats. The majority were women, hair freshly permed for the occasion; housewives who had managed to escape into this fantasy land for a day, who were about to be taken on their very own magic carpet ride. Perhaps the person whose job it was to 'warm up' the audience was already working them, getting them up to speed for the show, firing their synapses like crackerjacks in preparation for Mike Walsh's snappy delivery, telling them stand-up jokes and one-liners, getting them ready to play their part, in readiness for when the sign lit up saying 'APPLAUSE!'.

'There's Jeanne!' they'd whisper if they caught a glimpse of my mum, trying not to draw attention to herself, creeping around the edge of the stage like a tall, elegant gazelle, and a ripple of excitement would run through the crowd like electricity. 'We love you Jeanne!' someone might yell, to which she would flap her hands and wave at them, 'Ooah Dahling, aren't you divine!'

Some days, in fact most days, it was like a circus, with Mike Walsh the ringmaster himself, exuding charisma and charming the guests with his resounding baritone voice, leading the show from serious acts to outright hilarity with his naughty-boy charm and quick Irish wit that paired perfectly with my mother's innocent antics and dippy personality. If ratings were up, the guests were entertaining and Mike was in a good mood the place sang with productivity and everyone back-slapped and laughed along for the ride, but if the guests were dull or the audience felt a little limp, everyone tiptoed around him like a landmine.

Under the incredible heat of the stage lights, dressed in jacket and tie, Mike's forehead would bead with sweat. The make-up girls would sit offstage watching with horror as the oily make-up curdled with his hair dye – their necks were on the line if a rivulet of inky liquid trickled down in plain sight of the camera, and in the breaks they would scurry on with fans and sponges and spray, dabbing along his brow, tweaking at his sparse, overworked hair, poised to leap back to safety. Mike's mood kept everyone on their toes and the show at the forefront of the ratings for nearly a decade.

So how did my mother, the humble daughter of a Scottish immigrant, who grew up in hand-me-downs from her seven siblings in a little two-bedroom house in Brighton-Le-Sands, end up being a regular on *The Mike Walsh Show*, with millions of people across Australia tuning in hoping to catch her spot each week? Jeanne Little. Everyone knew her name; most people outright adored her and mobbed her in the street, a few utterly loathed her – 'That voice!' – and a few odd ones even stalked her. She won a Gold Logie for Most Popular Television Personality in 1976 then two Silver Logies later on and was a household name across Australia. Even today I'm often introduced as 'Jeanne Little's daughter', which always makes people stop to look twice and usually their faces light up before they start telling me a fond memory. It seemed that *everybody* knew my mother.

It was only when I went to live overseas at eighteen that I got a taste of what it felt like to not be part of a famous family and live in complete anonymity. I found myself working in a girls boarding school way out in the English countryside, where the little girls in red dungarees teased me about my Australian accent and called me a convict. But that was nothing compared to the outright bullying I'd endured in primary school at the bus stop, where older girls would hang out of the bus windows as it pulled up at my stop, all piling on top of each other to scream out 'HELLLLLLOOOOO DAAAAAAAAAARLING!!!' like a pack of strangled cockatoos. Overseas, however, the British headmaster's wife was a thin, pale woman who barely acknowledged me; she thought of me only as the hired help sent out from the colonies until the day she discovered my mother was very famous in Australia. 'How wonderful!' she exclaimed. 'Do tell me, what is it she's famous for?'

Inwardly I rolled my eyes. 'I should have known,' I thought to myself, but I was well practised in answering these sorts of questions so I just smiled at her and said gaily, 'Making dresses out of garbage bags!' That shut her up.

Aussies, of course, who remember my mum, will laugh heartily at this – the most popular spot she did on *The Mike Walsh Show* was a segment with clothes made out of dish-washing cloths and garbage bags. Mum had no idea it was going to be so successful but it skyrocketed into a huge, nationwide competition to make a wedding dress out of disposable plastic garbage bags. Thousands upon thousands of home dressmakers were inspired to create the most fantastical gowns; work that would have taken hours and hours with detail usually reserved only for the most expensive fabrics, from smocked bodices and hand-stitched frills to metres of veils cut into delicate lacework and trains to rival the wedding dress of Diana the Princess of Wales. The entries piled in, photographs of dresses each more incredible than the last, a display of unrivalled talent and creativity that culminated in a televised fashion parade watched by millions.

Of course that wasn't really all my mother was famous for, but in some ways the Glad Bag competition summed up the essence of my mother's persona – a little bit of fun and frivolity in an otherwise dull world, and what every ordinary, stay-at-home woman dreams of, a chance to try on the glass slipper and escape the everyday.

On a visa entry or official document my mum would fill in her occupation as 'entertainer' and I guess that's as good a description as any for what she was famous for. It's hard to sum her up in only a few words, but I suppose, first and foremost, she absolutely loved sewing and had the most wonderful talent for dreaming up amazing outfits that would evoke delight and pure joy in people. But she was also such a naturally funny person, saying and doing things in her own unique way that others found hilarious. She was a welcome celebrity on television chat shows and panels such as *Beauty and the Beast* and then turned out to be a wonderful singer as well, starring in a hit musical and a number of theatre productions and then later doing her own cabaret shows that my parents worked on together. Dad would write them and research the songs and Mum would make all the incredible outfits and costumes, then Mum would perform while Dad manned the lighting and sound. Mum far surpassed most people's estimations.

THE JEAN GENIE

I must have heard her tell it a thousand times or more, usually to journalists who sat entranced in our lounge room, waiting on her every word with pen and pad at the ready, too captivated by her story to even drink the coffee set before them that would usually be stone cold by the time they remembered to take a sip. This is the story of how Mum 'fell onto television'.

'Well Dahling …' she would start, the way she started all stories. 'Poor Barry and Katie, having to hear this tired old story again!'

Dad would make an excuse to go off to the kitchen and I would go about doing whatever I was doing, but we couldn't ever really avoid hearing the story because Mum had an incredibly loud voice and even with the three of us living in an enormous, four-storey terrace, there was no escape. Her voice, a mash up of her mother's Scottish brogue, father's Swedish lineage and corrugated-iron-pure-Aussie-rasp, made her accent distinctive. She would talk until her throat was hoarse and only ever knew one volume, so loud you could hear her a block away. If she had to do a phone interview the neighbours three doors down wouldn't have to bother reading the article. When she phoned me I had to hold the receiver two inches away from my ear and shout over her to lower her voice, then she'd stop and whisper, 'Oh! Sorry! Was I shouting? Is that better?'

Mum had such high energy that she could hardly sit for a moment, and it would take all her willpower to sit on the couch and stay still long enough to be interviewed. Dressed to the nines, blonde hair pinned back or hidden beneath a wig, with larger than life eyelashes stuck on and tonnes of make-up she would hold court in her own uniquely bold yet bashful manner, her long, angular arms flapping about as she retold the story, her chunky silver rings clicking and jingling along with her unstoppable movements. No wonder she was as 'thin as a bee's wing' – even sitting down she probably burned more calories than the average person running a marathon.

Journalists positively adored her; she was such a flamboyant personality and always had wonderfully funny stories to recount with a minimum of probing on their part. 'How did you get onto television Jeanne?' was the question they usually started right off the bat with and the story would begin, the only problem being they had to condense the whole anecdote down into one teeny little paragraph if they wanted to write anything else in their article about her. But this is the story as I remember it being told, the story that journalists would marvel over, as familiar to me as any one of my favourite childhood fairytales. The story went like this.

Years ago, when Mum was pregnant with me, she decided to open a little sewing business. Tucked away in a loft in Five Ways Paddington, she ran up dresses for an eclectic bunch: retired showgirls and wealthy dames who adored her over-the-top fashion and fabrics – sequins, feathers and chiffon en masse. She worked hard at realising her dream but never made any money because the ladies she sewed for always made a million alterations or changed their minds all the time, and Mum was too nice to charge them more money. Women would get a dress designed then put on a tonne of weight right before the final fitting, or ask for a plunging neckline and turn up with silicone implants.

'Oh, I was hopeless Dahling, it was a failing business! But I always loved sewing you see …'

'How did you learn to sew, Jeanne?'

Her mother – Nan – had been a tailor. One of Mum's earliest memories was of the time she received a little miniature working sewing machine as a child for Christmas. This was nothing short of a miracle, and undeniable proof that Santa Claus really did exist because she was the youngest of seven children and they were 'as poor as church mice'. As a baby her father had dropped her on her head coming back from the pub and this had been the final straw for Nan who had finally said enough was enough and packed up and left him, putting all her savings down as a deposit on a little two-bedroom house by the water at Brighton-Le-Sands, in the south of Sydney.

Nan was a hard worker and firm believer that anything you set your mind to you could achieve and wasted no time in renovating the little house herself. It wasn't uncommon to find her up on the roof replacing tiles or hidden under the kitchen sink fixing the plumbing. Mum's two brothers slept in the garage and her four sisters shared one of the bedrooms, leaving Mum and her mother to share a double bed in the other room.

'We'd both go to bed every night holding onto the sides because there was a dip in the middle but as soon as we fell asleep we'd roll in together and wake up in the morning squeezed together like a sandwich Dahling!'

'Little Jeanne' was the baby of the family and Nan's favourite. I suppose her mother had to be tough on the older kids to keep them all in line, but with Mum Nan could afford to be a bit softer, and so because of this, when she cried going to school for the first time Nan brought her home again and told her not to worry, she could stay home for another year. Mum would always tell this bit as if it was the most outrageous thing she'd ever heard, with a 'Fancy that!' tone and exclamation point after it. 'She said I could just stay home for ANOTHER YEAR!' she'd scream, then collapse into a fit of giggling.

Little Jeanne was incredibly shy with an awful stutter and was quite content to just stay at home alongside her mother, who worked as a seamstress from home. Nan, now the sole parent of seven children with no help from the children's father, who had vanished without trace, worked day and night, her sewing machine rattling along as she worked her job and did extra sewing and alteration work for neighbours and friends. As if all of this wasn't enough on top of running a house, she turned her hand to assisting Mum's two older brothers to run a successful foundry, drawing up magnificent full-sized patterns on the kitchen table for their wrought iron lacework, which I guess wasn't so dissimilar to the clothing patterns she worked with, drawn up on tracing paper.

'Really Jeanne?'

'Yes Dahling, the University of Sydney's gates were designed by my mother. Isn't that remarkable! She also designed the big gates that went all around the Rozelle Mental Institution but that was when my father was still around working with the boys. Mumma always said it was surprising they didn't mistake him for an inmate and keep him locked away in there forever!'

Nan was, by all accounts, a force to be reckoned with and lived a glorious life, making the most of every opportunity that came her way. Like a true Scott she didn't let a thing go to waste and saved every penny. Every cent she earned she put into the house, then as soon as she could scrape together another deposit she put it straight down on more real estate and steadily began to build up her assets; as well as any one of Australia's most admired colonial emancipists.

Enticed by her sister's success, Nan's sister Lottie and her husband soon moved out from Scotland and into one of Nan's houses. And then their father moved into the already crowded house at Brighton-Le-Sands – since every bedroom was claimed the old grandpa took up residence on the lounge!

When one of Mum's sisters became engaged there was a big party. Everyone was very excited, mainly because it meant the house would become less crowded, but particularly Mum, who was thrilled to be moving out of her mother's bed at last and into the bedroom with her older sisters. But after the wedding her sister's new husband still hadn't managed to secure a job and so the newlyweds stayed put and nine months later added a baby to the house as well.

'Grandpa was a very sweet old thing Dahling, but his Scottish accent was so thick no-one other than Mumma could understand what he was saying. He finally died one night sitting on the toilet. Mumma said it was probably the only place the poor old thing could be alone!'

Being an only child, I could barely imagine what it was like to grow up in a house like that, full of noise, bursting with people and constant chaos. I pictured the house like the dormitory in *Oliver Twist* – 'Please Sir, I want some more' – or pictured Mum and her mother wedged into a little antique bed together like Charlie Bucket's grandparents in *Willy Wonka & the Chocolate Factory* who ate watery cabbage soup for every meal. Mum would tell the journalists they were so poor she grew up in nothing but hand-me-downs and wore shoes with so many holes they had to be lined with newspaper.

One Christmas Nan's brother came to visit, which was always a cause of great celebration because he kept lollies in his pockets and loved to spoil the children. Hearing him whistling as he walked down the side path of the house the kids would rush to greet him and Nan would put the kettle on and serve up one of her famous cakes. When all the kids were sitting down he went around asking them what special things they were hoping Santa Claus would bring them for Christmas.

'I was too shy to speak when he asked me and then my older sister Margie piped up and said "Jeanne wants a sewing machine!" and I was mortified! I had seen a tiny sewing machine in the window of a shop and knew I could never have it.'

But on Christmas morning, like magic, there was the tiny sewing machine Mum had wished so hard for, sitting at the end of her bed. She couldn't believe her eyes! She started making doll's clothes using any little scraps of fabric left over from her mother's tailoring work and then secretly began to squirrel items out of the linen closet.

'One day I made a smart little playsuit for myself out of two brightly coloured tea towels I found at the back of the closet. Mumma raised one eyebrow but didn't say a word about the tea towels that she'd probably been saving to use for a special occasion, but I think she was secretly thrilled I loved to sew. Next I made a pair of smart grey slacks. "Where did you get those?" Mumma asked, and I had to admit to her I'd made them out of the ironing board cover.'

Having nothing much to work with, Mum had to be resourceful and inventive. As she got older she made dresses for parties from off-cuts and anything she could get her hands on, experimenting with cheap materials to create looks she'd seen in magazines. Shredding organza to look like ostrich feathers, or even sewing plastic to look like leather, stretching her wages by painting shoes to match her outfit or dying her own hair to complete the look.

'Yes Dahling, I just loved going to parties and dressing up. One time I made a whole jacket out of tinfoil and it looked wonderful! That's where I got the idea so many years later to do the garbage bag outfits that were such a big hit.'

It was at one of these parties that she met my father, an up-and-coming interior designer named Barry Little. They eventually married and Mum opened her little dressmaking business in Five Ways, Paddington. She hadn't been running the business long when she fell pregnant with me, and with her baby bump growing daily realised how boring the choice of maternity clothes for women was. Without giving it a second thought she ran up two new outfits for herself – a white dress with big pink elephants marching across the stomach, and a green smock with a red and white target painted on the belly, which paired with a handbag that looked like a quiver of arrows.

My father wrote a weekly column for the local paper, but this particular week he was running late on his deadline and asked Mum to drop it into the publisher for him. The girls on reception saw her dress and thought it was a hoot and immediately called in one of the photographers to take her picture. She was thrilled, hoping she would get some publicity for her failing business. As fate would have it a guest dropped out of *The Mike Walsh Show* a couple of days later. The assistant producer saw the photo and had his secretary put Mum in a taxi and rush her over to Channel 9 to show off her maternity dresses. She wrote 'Back at 2 pm' and stuck it to the door of her shop and the rest, as they say, is history.

'So that's how it happened Dahling! For some reason the audience kept laughing at everything I said and I thought to myself "Gosh, Mike Walsh is very camp isn't he?"'

Unbeknown to Mum, who had never watched the show, Mike was away on holidays. The fill-in host, John-Michael Howson, later said he thought the staff of the show were playing a practical joke on him – sending on a drag queen with a pillow stuffed up her dress.

'They asked me to come back after I'd had the baby, and then again and again! I couldn't believe people got paid to do this sort of thing for a living, it was just so much fun!'

She didn't keep the dress shop going too long after I was born. Half the time she had the 'Back at 2 pm' sign stuck up on the door and the rest of the time the place was busy with people dropping in to see the baby. She got along with everyone and was never too busy for a chat, even the postman would stop in to give me a bottle along his route, and not long after traded in his uniform for a leather jacket and an earring.

Even before they were in the spotlight my parents must have made an amazing couple. Dad was one of Sydney's most inventive interior designers, importing oriental treasures, using fabulous wallpapers by his friend, the then unknown Florence Broadhurst, whose studio was also located in the bohemian suburb of Paddington. Back then pants were tight and lapels were large. Dad was handsome and confident with thick, jet-black hair and moustache to match his olive complexion, with oversized square-framed sunglasses and Mum was tall and thin and gorgeously exotic, always wearing tonnes of heavy eye make-up like her movie star heroines.

BORN TO BE WILD

When I was growing up the Sydney suburb of Paddington was certainly not the prestigious location it is today. In fact, girls at school would look down their noses when I told them where we lived. In the late seventies 'Paddo' had a pub on every corner and in the evening the streets were full of noisy drunks and stray cats in heat. I used to walk barefoot a lot and learnt early to look out for broken glass and dog poo.

Up until I turned three we lived in a small terrace on the shady side of Paddington Street. Downstairs was Dad's boutique interior design studio and up a white spiral staircase was the tiny living space. It was a nice little house except that next door was derelict and inhabited by a gang of Hells Angels.

I remember once being in the back of the car with Mum and Dad, driving on the freeway, when the unmistakable sound of Harley-Davidson bikes rumbled up behind us. I put my nose to the window but my parents were terrified. 'Don't look! Katie, sit down!' Mum said urgently. I was confused. I'd glimpsed forty or fifty bikes roaring up the freeway behind us, chrome glinting in the sunlight; it looked like the pack of winged men in Flash Gordon. I wanted to look again, but the minute I turned my head Dad snapped, 'Do what your mother says!' He'd been watching me in the rear-view mirror. Obediently I sat and looked straight ahead.

It sounded like thunder and got louder and louder. I wanted to put my hands over my ears but I dared not move. My parents were obviously scared stiff. Dad kept glancing nervously in the rear view-mirror. 'Ooh Barry, what are we going to do?' It felt like the whole car was reverberating, even Mum's voice was being drowned against the deafening noise.

'Just keep facing the front!' Dad said. 'Don't look, whatever you do.' He'd directed this last comment at me with a final glance in the mirror, a look of panic in his eyes. The first two bikes roared past either side of the car making my skull rattle. VVVVVVVRRRRROOOOOM!!!! VVVVVVVRRRRROOOOOM!!!! Mum and Dad sat still as mannequins, too terrified to blink.

I caught glimpses of the bikies in my peripheral vision, dressed from head to toe in black leather with long, flowing beards, some with girls perched on the back, others with sidecars. I'd never seen anything like it, and had they looked in our direction they would have been thinking the same thing. We were en route to a party in a tiny vehicle the size of Mr Bean's car, Dad with his big, seventies moustache and sunglasses, Mum wearing a completely over-the-top headpiece inspired by Carmen Miranda, an enormous bowl overflowing with plastic fruit strapped on her head poking up out of the sunroof.

The gang of Hells Angels eventually passed but for the rest of the journey Mum and Dad were too nervous to even look around. God knows how they survived living next to a gang for years but it probably explains why the council took so long to take action on the squatters that were such a handful, as Mum and Dad were too terrified to lodge even a single complaint. When they were finally evicted the council took away several truckloads of junk and filthy mattresses; apparently their toilet hadn't worked for a long time either.

I always found this surprising, as I remembered how shiny and beautiful the bikes on the highway had been. Obviously the Hells Angels didn't have time to clean their house because they spent every minute polishing chrome and leather. Funnily enough, Mum and Maria Venuti later dressed up together as bikers to sing 'Born to Be Wild' on *The Mike Walsh Show*. Mum had a cassette tape in the car that she played to learn the lyrics. At six years old I would sit in the passenger seat beside her, my finger at the ready on the rewind button as we sang the song over and over, singing together *voce piena* with the windows wound down – her alto and my soprano, belting out the song with the wind in our hair as we zipped along New South Head Road through Rose Bay to my all girls private school.

By then my mother had been a weekly regular on *The Mike Walsh Show* for a number of years and had become very famous – absolutely everyone wanted to talk to her! I learnt patience early on as strangers approached her everywhere we went. Mum was never too busy to talk and this used to drive my dad and me to distraction. Even walking up to Oxford Street to get some lunch became a dangerous pastime; it would take longer to get there than it did to eat the sandwich. Shop owners waved from their windows and came out from behind their counters. It was like living in Postman Pat's neighbourhood where it took all day to deliver one letter because Pat had to chat with everyone along the way. Dad's attempt to solve this problem was to keep his hand on the small of Mum's back, propelling and manoeuvring her through the busy street towards the coffee shop, even as she turned to reply to all the people who called out to her.

'Sorry Dahling, Barry must be hungry I think!' she'd shout back to them, laughing.

Our favourite place to eat was the New Edition Bookshop & Café where the three of us would sit up at the bar to enjoy our smorgasbord plates of ham sliced off the bone, hunks of fresh baguette and butter and delicious salad dressed with mustardy vinegar that I can still taste if I close my eyes. Then, while Mum and Dad ordered espresso coffees, I would slip away into the bookshop to read on an old beanbag. Dad was one of their best customers. He was always reading the latest novels – writing was his passion – and ordering in obscure books on medieval history, the setting for his novel, which had been under construction since his early twenties.

Finally, Dad would pop his head round and tell me it was time to go, I'd grab my book, the latest *Choose Your Own Adventure*, and we'd start the dreaded walk home. Dad had achieved his mission of getting Mum to the coffee shop – she often forgot to eat when she was working – but getting home was a different story. Fired up on caffeine, he needed to get back to the office and Mum might have to pop into the supermarket. Without Dad's protective arm Mum was now at the mercy of anyone who recognised her.

Strangers would stop her, amazed that this larger than life personality who they had come to know intimately in their homes via the television was the same madcap person in real life. Something about her made everyone genuinely feel she knew them like a long-lost friend. Maybe it was the magic of television, but strangely, even people who'd never seen her on TV would be captivated, stopped in their tracks like bees confronted with the most exquisite flower.

Mum appealed to everyone, but most of all to queens and housewives, with whom she struck a chord deep down – proof that anyone could make it, even a 'plain Jane' like her. She was a real life Cinderella, making outfits from the most unlikely things and showing you how to look like a movie star with nothing more than make-up, a few tricks and false eyelashes.

It wasn't only on Oxford Street they spotted her, we could be anywhere: having dinner out, in the supermarket, putting coins into a parking meter, and someone would spot her. At first it was hardly noticeable, their eyes would linger momentarily, or maybe they would hear her distinctive voice before they saw her. Whatever alerted them, it was as if their brain had temporarily malfunctioned, like they'd seen an extra-terrestrial or pink flamingo in their midst and had to pause and process the information their brain was receiving.

They would do a double-take and forget completely the first rule of etiquette their mothers taught them – not to stare. Everything would stop, people would leave what they were doing, breaking off conversations mid sentence, a lady walking would clutch her friend's arm and say 'There's Jeanne Little!', her head swivelling around as her legs kept walking.

I've seen famous people randomly in the street so I kind of know the backflip their brain is doing. It's that pause of 'Oh, that face looks familiar …' then the puzzle where you try to work it out, like when you see a friend who used to be really fat who's been drinking nothing but protein shakes and has suddenly lost tons of weight, then the penny drops and before you know it you've been staring a bit too long and a little too hard. Trust me I get it now, but as a kid I didn't and I trained myself to spot 'fans' and could pick them a mile away. That flicker of a head turn was always a dead giveaway. I could spot them and so could Dad. Sometimes we'd make Mum put on sunglasses, we'd stick a hat on her head and warn her to keep her voice down as we hurried her along the street. If we really wanted to get to a destination and someone spotted her, sometimes we'd have to just grab her and pull her off somewhere, anywhere – into a shop or around a corner – but if they were really keen it wouldn't matter, they'd come after us and hunt her down. That's when Dad would bail and I'd roll my eyes and think, 'Oh God, here we go again.'

Mum, on the other hand, was always completely oblivious until the person was on top of us. They would gently rest their hand on her arm and say 'Jeanne. You won't remember me, but …'

Mum's face would light up in surprise and she would let out an audible gasp as they said something she had no hope of remembering, and then, unbelievably, Mum would say. 'Oh yes, of course Dahling!' and they would be completely charmed and continue on and on and on and on. Mum would laugh and say 'Oh Dahling!' every now and then and finally they'd realise Mum was holding six bags of groceries, the sun had set and cicadas were singing and sometimes they'd even eventually look down and notice me standing there.

'Oh Jeanne!' they'd say, 'Is this your daughter!' Then they'd bend down and say, 'What's your name sweetheart?' I had a dreadful lisp as a child that only got worse when I started loosing teeth. 'Katie,' I'd say, my mouth full of tongue, saliva squirting through the toothless gaps.

'Casey!' they'd say brightly.

'No, Katie. Kay-tee. KAY-TEEEEE.' The harder I tried the worse it got until finally Mum intervened and made the excuse that I was probably tired and it was about time she took me home. Dad would have been home for hours by the time we got there.

In 1978 we moved across the road into an enormous terrace, four stories high, at 64 Paddington Street. It was a dump but soon looked like a palace after Dad decorated it. There were two entrances – a staircase leading down to Dad's office, another leading up to the front door of our home, where a lavish lounge opened onto a dining room with a long, gold leaf table, but these rooms were only used on formal occasions.

The kitchen and tiny sunroom where we ate our meals were at the back of the house – we were only a small family, after all. The room was always much warmer and had a little television on a stool in the corner. A small, round table was draped with a tablecloth that fell to the floor and if I had a friend for dinner I would have to warn them not to lean on the table as they ate. They would look at me strangely until I lifted the tablecloth and showed them that it wasn't really a table at all, just a pretend one, a base with a circle of plywood propped on top – perfect for an interior design showroom but not so practical for a dinner table. If my friends hadn't been taught not to place their elbows on the table, they would be compelled by necessity to learn etiquette at my house.

There were four chairs around the table, one of which was always piled high with papers, invitations to all kinds of balls and opening nights and charity events printed on fancy paper and mountains of letters and cards from people who adored my mother – fan mail. Once in a while, when the pile had become so obscenely large that my father was complaining about it, Mum would sit with a pot of tea replying to all the letters in her large, loopy handwriting, finishing each letter with a big 'OOaaaah Dahling! Love, Jeanne! XXX' She would colour two black dots in each 'O' and draw big eyelashes on them, then seal the envelope with a rubber stamp – a pair of lips puckered up like a kiss with bright red ink. She replied to every single letter by hand, often writing letters many pages long.

Upstairs on the next floor was Mum and Dad's apricot-pink bedroom, the large bed draped in a mosquito net with French doors to a verandah overlooking the street, but the doors were never open. Mum was always terrified of cockroaches flying in, and the dreaded scraggly pigeons that nested in the rafters. Rather than get the pigeons out and fix the problem my father just locked the door and pulled down the blinds, but upstairs in her sewing room Mum took matters into her own hands. She made a gigantic black bird out of wire and fabric and hung it on the balcony to frighten the pigeons away. It didn't work. The pigeons just kept cooing away contentedly, breeding more pigeons. Every now and then when my parents were farewelling a journalist or a guest and everyone was standing out the front of the house, the black shape three floors up would catch their eye.

'What's that, Jeanne?' they'd ask, squinting up through the branches of the plane tree, and Dad would just shake his head as Mum explained, 'It's to keep the rotten birds away Dahling.'

'But it doesn't work,' Dad would say.

'Well I had to try something Dahling! Every time I came out of my house the damn things would dive bomb and peck at my head!'

'Oh rubbish! They're just harmless birds!'

'They do! You don't know! They probably thought this hair of mine was a bit of straw they could build their nest with!' Mum would say, theatrically tugging at the roots of her bleached blonde hair.

'Does it work Jeanne?' the guest would ask.

'Well ... no, not really Dahling, they still make their nests up there.'

Mum and the guest would be laughing by now but Dad would be ranting. 'Well of course! They wouldn't be afraid of *that* would they! It looks more like a *bat* for heaven's sake! What am I going to do with you Jean?'

The giant plane trees along Paddington Street produced balls of seeds that attracted flocks of white cockatoos and the filaments would float down to the street. Mum hated these little bits of seeds that got stuck in her throat so she would tie a large tea towel around her face and put on an enormous straw hat to sweep the pavement, looking like some kind of strange beekeeper.

Every now and then she'd stop and wave her broom up at the trees, trying to scare off the cockatoos. They kept eating, of course, knowing they were safe from this mad woman three floors below and when they were finished eating sometimes would take their revenge by biting off pieces of the mortar from the old chimney, which would get Dad into a lather. 'Damn birds!' he would shout. 'Look what they're doing to the roof! GET OFF! *GET OFF THERE!*' and he would stand waving his arms trying to shoo them off while little bits of stone and mortar rained down, lodging pieces of sand painfully into his eyes.

One spring a family of starlings made a nest in the bathroom ceiling. They had found a little hole under the eave that allowed them access into the roof cavity and you could hear the young ones squawking and flapping right above your head. Dad was not a handyman and Mum pestered him to get someone in to fix the problem.

'Oooh Barry, I can hear them up there!' she'd say as she dressed in the wardrobe area that adjoined the bathroom.

'They're only birds!' he'd say 'Hurry up, I need to use the shower!'

If there had been another shower in the house Mum would have used it, but there wasn't, so she was stuck using the ensuite, all the while terrified of the flapping and squawking.

'What are you doing in there Jean? Hurry up!'

'I can't! They're flapping right over my head Barry! I'm going to look in the local paper and get a tradesman.'

'What? No! Don't you go getting some person in here making a mess of the ceiling!'

'They won't make a mess, they'll just get the birds out!'

'And how do you think they're going to do that! They'll rip open the whole ceiling!'

'Well we have to get them *out* Barry!' Suddenly there would be flapping and a loud thud as a bird fell out of the nest directly onto the ceiling. 'OOOAH BARRY!' Mum would scream and Dad would procrastinate at fixing the problem until it could be avoided no longer, which in this case was when a featherless baby bird with bulging blue eyes fell down the hole next to the window onto the vanity, like something out of a David Lynch movie, sending them both screaming from the bathroom.

Poor Mum was terrified of cockroaches too but Dad wouldn't hear of getting an exterminator. 'I don't want all that poison in my house!' he'd roar. 'No way Jean!' Paddington in summer was a haven for enormous cockroaches (Mum always described them being as big as rats) and even though she kept the kitchen spotless she'd still come across the odd one lurking. There was no mistaking when she saw a cockroach – her scream was so loud it sent shockwaves through the whole of Paddington Street. She would throw herself backwards in terror like she'd been zapped with electricity and would be pinned up against the wall like a heroine in a sci-fi movie, shrieking and gasping until someone rescued her.

'What's all that racket?!' my father would roar from his downstairs office.

'Ooooah Barry! It's a cockroach! ARRRRGHGHGHGHGH!!!' she'd scream as it sat staring at her, menacingly twirling its antennae. 'BARRY! OOOOOAH! *BARRY!*' Mum would be paralysed, gasping for breath in between screams. Reluctantly compelled to rescue his wife, Dad would stomp his way up the stairs. 'Ooooah Barry! ARRRRRGHGHGH!'

'ALL RIGHT JEAN! Stop making all that noise! I'm coming!' he'd huff, entering the kitchen, pausing to unlace one Italian leather shoe. 'Where is it?'

The 'beast' might be sitting on the bench top. Mum would point in its direction, hardly daring to look, and with shoe in hand Dad would sneak forward, raising his weapon to take aim. WHAM! More often than not he'd miss and the cockroach would run towards him. 'ARRRRRGHGHGHHHH!!' he'd shriek, stumbling backwards into my mother. 'Ooooah Barry! KILL IT! KILL IT! KILL IT!' Mum would scream and push him forward into the line of fire, sending the cockroach scuttling in every crazy direction while Dad slammed his shoe down all over the place. SLAM! SLAM! WHAM!

If they were really unlucky and it was the height of summer the huge cockroach would pause for one terrifying moment and open its wings. In horror they'd watch it lift off slowly before gaining enough height to begin dive-bombing them. 'ARRRRRGHGHGHGHG!!!' they'd scream, as it swerved erratically through the air, attacking from unpredictable angles. My father's high-pitched shriek and mother's gasping roar would echo through the house, and neighbours four doors down would slam their windows in irritation.

But even with these outbursts Dad still wouldn't hear of Mum getting an exterminator. Mum listened to ABC radio at all hours while she sewed and sometimes they would have programs where people phoned in with home remedies. This was probably where Mum got the idea to make the bird to scare the pigeons away but knowing Mum, who always thought bigger was better, she made a giant thing that more closely resembled a bat. One day a caller described how to make a cockroach trap by filling a jar half way with honey and smearing the top with Vaseline.

'Don't tell your father,' she'd whisper when I caught her silently setting another of her booby traps. She'd been leaving the strange little jars in corners all around the house, dozens were still lined up along the wall behind their bed when the removalists took it away thirty years later.

Although the kitchen was always spotless, the rest of the house could get a little 'out of mind, out of sight'. Mum's cleaning was always done as quickly as possible, which Dad couldn't stand, and, finally, in an effort to put things right he'd reluctantly take over, to demonstrate how it should be done.

Dad was a perfectionist; things had to be done properly, or not at all. If Dad cleaned the lounge room he'd move every piece of furniture and vacuum the light shades with the special brush attachment. Every light would be switched on, glass cleaned twice, every antique meticulously dusted and arranged 'just so'. Mum, who had quickly 'gone over' everything, leaving drifts of dust around the pretty ashtrays and antiques, would be called in to acknowledge her shortcomings.

'Jean! Did you dust this mantle? My God, look at the dust on this frame! Jean!'

Mum would roll her eyes at me and leave him to it. We both knew Mum did the majority of the cleaning, Dad just liked to make a fuss when he had to do a bit.

Living in a very tall house such as we did, Mum was forever making piles on the stairs, random collections that soon spread to take over the whole staircase leaving only a narrow pathway beside the banister. My father, the decorator, *hated* clutter.

'What are all these *things* here on the stair Jean?' he would ask loudly. He would waste no time pointing out any mess my mother or I made yet was always seemingly oblivious to his own. Mum, who was possibly at that moment three flights up bearing a load of washing on her back the size of an elephant, like a Tibetan Sherpa, would be summoned immediately. 'Jean, it's *dangerous* to leave all these things on the stairs!' he'd say, which was funny, because there were all sorts of dangerous things in our house – the piles on the stairs were the least to be concerned about.

STAYIN' ALIVE

Besides the tables that weren't really tables, and birds that pegged mortar on your head or threatened to fall on you in the shower, there were dangers all through our house. Take for instance the cupboard above the oven where the cookbooks were kept. It was no wonder Mum guessed the ingredients and quantities in many of the recipes she cooked, often with interesting results – she was too scared to open the cupboard. Mum had invented the 'flourless' chocolate cake by accident years before anyone had heard of it.

To reach the cupboard you had to stand on tiptoes on a precarious little stool, then heave at the door to get it open. Inside was an enormous collection of books, all jumbled in together, many of them big and heavy with sharp corners, waiting to slide out, knock you off the stool and pummel you to death. Somehow you had to hold back this avalanche while you got the book you wanted and when you'd finished, the book would have to be thrown back in with lightning speed before slamming the door closed with all your weight.

'One day I must clean that cupboard out,' Dad would say after another near miss with death, but he never did.

Then there was the second drawer in the kitchen that was very deep and full of sharp things. Weaving your hand through dozens of metal skewers, past razor sharp knives, blades and slicers was like playing a souped-up version of pick-up sticks. It took courage and skill not to sever a nerve or lose a finger, but in the end it wasn't the contents that got me but the simple act of pulling the drawer out too far; there was no catch to stop it and the whole enormous thing fell out and broke all the toes on my right foot.

You dared not stick your head out a window that wasn't propped up with a ruler either. The ropes that threaded the ancient window frames could lure you into thinking they were secure, but a window could come down so swiftly your head would be taken off clean at the neck like a guillotine.

The stairs were also deadly. The ones leading up to the front door were the colour of dark moss and when it rained they could take your feet out from under you so fast you would be knocked unconscious before you realised you'd slipped. Then there were areas of the house that were perilous just because no-one ever changed a light bulb. The staircase near the kitchen that led down to my father's basement office was one of these areas; the small, steep, uneven stairs and dark carpet forced you to feel your way down with mounting terror, sliding your hands along the walls through pitch dark until you reached the bottom where you then had to let go and walk with blind faith towards the wall where the light switches were.

It was a very old house, and beneath the new carpet and paint it was still the same ancient creature, one I became intimately acquainted with. The solid walls closed us off from all outside sounds, but within it, if you stood still and listened quietly you could tell where everyone in the house was. As my father entered the bedroom upstairs the chandelier in the dining room would tremble and make a pretty tinkling sound. When my mother was getting ready in the morning the kitchen ceiling would creak accommodatingly, following her footsteps on the floor above. I came to learn the areas of carpet that hid softened, decaying floorboards, the steps to avoid when I didn't want to be heard.

It was dark and cool in the house, like you were inside a great cave, but you could always tell what the weather was like outside by the whisper of wind funnelling through the disused chimneys, and if it rained in the night I'd be woken by a heavy 'pat … pat … pat …' as water started dripping onto the carpet in my bedroom, an ancient leak that turned one whole wall into a waterfall and mysteriously could never be fixed, even after the whole roof was replaced.

When we moved to the house all these things were unfamiliar to me and there was a sharp learning curve. One of my first memories was coming down the stairs when I was four years old, just after my parents had bought the house. The wood on the stairs was grey and dirty, a battlefield of old scars and repairs. My hands were dry with dust, my fingers sticky with cobwebs. My parents were downstairs in the hallway talking with their friends, Colin Brees and Colin Johnston. 'Hold on to the banister Katie!' Mum called out. But at this awkward turn in the stairs there was no banister and the stairs sliced off into ever smaller wedges. Cautiously I descended until I reached the apparent safety of the wider stairs and looked to Mum for approval. I didn't see the old raised nail until it was too late, it caught the front of my shoe and sent me down headfirst, tumbling all the way to the bottom. This was my first lesson: to always pay attention.

I overheard Mum telling people the roof space above my little bathroom on the top floor had been an alcoholic's stash and opening the manhole had revealed hundreds of empty bottles which had rained down and smashed on the tiled floor, like an apocalyptic hailstorm. Then a dog died of lead poisoning and tins of lead paint were discovered under the garage. I was warned to keep out from under there but I was worried because that was a secret place I had liked to hang out, fascinated by an old cement staircase that rose mysteriously out of the ground and stopped under the floor of the garage – a staircase that led nowhere.

I started to dig up parts of the backyard, curious as to what else I might find. Slowly I amassed a collection of clay pots and glass marbles, one with a pretty white swirl inside that Mum said was called a birdcage. She washed the pots in the kitchen sink and told me they were used for ink, to write with a pen and nib before biros were invented. When she came down to hang out the washing I showed her the bones I'd found in the dirt too, and she laughed and said they were knucklebones and that children had played games with them. She bought some lamb for dinner and saved the bones and I started a bit of a trend playing Jacks at school. Others brought in imitation plastic pieces but mine were always the most popular and grisly, made of real bone.

Not a fan of the outdoors, Mum usually only went as far as the washing line; the rest of the garden was mine. An overgrown tangle of ivy and camellia bushes led to a courtyard with doors to the office. The tiles made a clickety-clack sound as I raced across them on my red tricycle, the plastic wheels slipping and spinning when I pushed the pedals too hard. Around and around I tore, tipping the weight onto the outer back wheel as I turned the corner and thundered across the concrete driveway, skidding to a stop against the chain link fence, sending stray cats in the laneway running.

There were two enormous old trees in the garden – a gigantic lemon and a mulberry – that had far outgrown their corner. The lemon was full of sharply inhospitable spikes and stink bugs but the mulberry was easy to climb. The bark on the trunk was rough and blistered with big round swellings that made perfect hand and footholds. Pushing my way into the moist, shadowy corner of the garden I could wedge my back against the wall to slowly haul myself up, ancient pieces of bark crumbling away to reveal pockets of grey slaters that scurried for safety. Once I reached the fork in the trunk the going got easier and I could climb one of the fat branches, engulfed by a canopy of green leaves that glowed with sunlight from above. I could sit up there for hours, snacking on mulberries until it got dark and I was called inside for dinner, my hands stained a deep purple.

While the basement was devoted to Dad's office, strictly off limits to Mum and me, the top floor was ours, not because we locked doors or shouted at anyone to keep out as my father did, but because of the simple fact we were so far up. The only people who could be bothered to go up all those stairs were Mum, who always took the stairs three at a time, plus me and the little friends I invited over.

Kids loved to visit my room because of the 'rainbow staircase' that led up the last flight of stairs. Dad had put his carpet sample books to good use and it was like walking up a giant tin of Derwent pencils. All the pretty, bright colours were at the bottom leading off from my parents' bedroom floor, but where the stairs turned the corner, the inky blues, violets and indigos blended together into a pit of darkness that usually only my mother and I had the nerve or necessity to navigate.

But this was probably not a bad thing, because at the top of this final flight of stairs the world ran according to my mother's priorities – creative freedom and artistic expression ruled, things were used for whatever practical purpose was required and 'organised chaos' reigned, only on the fourth floor were my mother and I safe from my father's critical eye. Pages Mum tore out of fashion magazines were pinned straight onto his expensive wallpaper, orange garbage bags full of materials and outfits were piled high (all the wardrobes and drawers were already full and thanks to the Glad promotion, Mum always had plenty of garbage bags on hand).

Spread across the floor were outfits under construction, fabric pinned with tissue paper patterns. The carpet was a minefield of pins; no wonder I'd taken to walking early. There were half-made creations, sewn and discarded ideas that hadn't quite worked, experiments with fabrics and feathers and all kinds of materials. My mother never wasted anything and often reused the outfits she'd made, ripping them apart without hesitation to turn them into something new.

My mother's sewing machine sat on the end of a long table, the top hidden beneath a tumbled multitude of jars and giant bobbins of coloured cotton, rolls of elastic, bottles and bowls filled with sequins, and buttons and beads of every shape and colour imaginable. In the drawers were zippers and packets of needles, shoulder pads and fake flowers, ribbons and laces and knitting needles – Mum experimented with everything.

The biggest piece of furniture in the room was a four-poster bed that Mum had adapted into a makeshift clothing rack. Made to my father's specifications to match the wallpaper and curtains, the bed had an oversized frill of stiffened pink gingham attached to the top with a staple gun, and a puffed valance of still more fabric that could have made several outfits for the von Trapp family children. My bedroom, when it was first decorated, looked like a Beatrix Potter illustration. Unfortunately for Dad, I turned out to be a tomboy and loathed the colour pink. I hated the room and I hated the bed, and as it turned out, the bed hated me.

The problem was the frame of the bed, which had been made too narrow making the single mattress arch rebelliously. Mum tucked me into bed tightly each night by necessity, pushing the sheets hard in under the mattress to hold me in place. Then, asleep with my pink teddy in my fairytale bedroom, Mum would get a few hours peace before I rolled over and kept rolling. It was a long drop; every night I came down hard onto the floor above their bedroom with a loud thump and a howl.

It didn't take long for me to grow scared of the bed, which I knew would throw me out at midnight as sure as Cinderella's carriage became a pumpkin, and eventually Mum gave up on the hideously impractical four-poster bed and put me in the room next door, which had a nice, simple bed for when my grandmother stayed over. But I was now terrified of going to sleep. I would hold onto my mother's hand while she sat and whispered stories to me in the darkness, desperate not to fall asleep and let her go. Mum told lots of stories, but her favourite was always Chicken Little, which also became her nickname for me and suited me well, as I was a sensitive child whose imagination often ran wild.

I much preferred the other room decorated in sunny yellow, which had been intended as my mother's sewing room and Mum, always accommodating, happily swapped rooms with me into the pink bedroom on the shady side of the house. The thin, tough brown carpet Dad had decorated my bedroom with was more suitable for Mum to cut her patterns on anyway, and the four-poster bed made a wonderful clothes rack – wire coathangers hooked straight onto the loops of stapled fabric as if it was made for the job.

Once in a blue moon my father would be forced to come up to our level, usually searching for an item of clothing that hadn't re-emerged from the washing. We would hear him huffing his way up the stairs, the old wood under the carpet creaking under his weight. In a panic Mum would start raking through the ginormous pile of clean clothes that took up the floor of her sewing room beside the ironing board. 'Is this the shirt you're looking for?' she'd ask, holding one up at the top of the stairs, hoping to stop him coming all the way up.

'No, no Jean! My *new* shirt, the good one!'

'Don't worry, I'll find it! You don't have to come all the way up here!'

But having come this far Dad wasn't going to be dissuaded. Mum and I would burrow our way into our respective rooms and busy ourselves with whatever we were doing, knowing what was coming. Dad was always utterly appalled at what he saw. He would pause on the landing, taking in the piles of overstuffed garbage bags, the fabric and patterns spread out across the floor, the minefield of pins and scissors left lying open, he would look at the four poster bed dangling with coathangers and clothes like an industrial railing at the dry cleaners with utter distaste, his eyebrows popping up in horror.

'Dear God ...' he would mutter, nervous to let his eyes wander further. 'Jean, how do you stand living in this ... this ... filth!'

'Filth!? It's not filthy!' Mum would counter, highly offended.

'Bah!' my father would gasp sarcastically.

'It's not! I know where everything is! It's not dirty!'

'What about all those garbage bags at the top of the stairs? It's like a hoarders nightmare! No wonder we've got cockroaches downstairs!'

'What?! They're all just full of *fabric!*'

'Fabric! Not your good fabrics I hope! What about the sequins we brought back from New York?'

'No! Of course not! They're put away in the drawers, but I've only got *three drawers* for heavens sake!'

'What about that whole wall of wardrobes!'

'They're full!' Mum's clothes took up half of the wardrobes in my room too, plus all the wardrobes in their bedroom downstairs and several more in their ensuite bathroom.

Dad would look disapprovingly at the great mountain of rumpled washing on the floor, then his eye would catch sight of the carpet under the ironing board. Being a sewer Mum was always ironing as she sewed and the starch collected on the carpet below like an enormous patch of sticky white fairy floss. 'Jean! What is *that!*'

'What? It's nothing! Oh, don't look at that, it's only Fabulon!'

'Urgh ...' Dad would roll his eyes, cringing at the sight of his immaculately decorated room being laid to waste, then he'd see the magazine clippings pinned to the wall and his temper would erupt. 'JEAN! Oh my god, that beautiful wallpaper!' And next he'd see his good shirt knotted up with a pair of Mum's stockings and find that a shredded tissue had gotten into the wash and stuck to his new shirt like bad dandruff. 'JEAN! My new shirt! Oh it's ruined – *RUINED!*' he would fume. Unlike Mum, who was one of seven, my father being an only child would behave like a toddler if one of his possessions was even slightly damaged.

'It's alright, it's alright! I can fix it, don't worry!' Mum would grab the shirt and shake it roughly, belting at the fabric, sending white specks raining down onto the dark carpet. Shaking his head in disbelief at the disorganisation and mess Dad would stagger backwards, desperate to retreat back downstairs where order and sanity prevailed.

And then he'd catch sight of my room and the shock was almost heart stopping, the carpet invisible apart from small cleared areas that I used like stepping stones to get from one side to the other. My treasured doll's house surrounded by Dad's old sample books, squares of wallpapers and carpets, a roll of tinfoil I had been turning into solar panels. My desk, piled with mounds of half finished artworks, scattered with pencils and shavings, textas, glues and paints. The bed unmade, books lying open amongst the covers, blinds higgledy-piggledy, neither up nor down.

Dad would make a choking noise, and for once it wasn't my mother stuttering, 'Jean! Jean! This room! Katie's room! Don't you? Doesn't she? … Doesn't *anyone* ever *clean* it?'

EVERYBODY WANTS TO RULE THE WORLD

My father hired a cleaner; her name was Mrs Cairo. One of his wealthy clients had recommended her. She was expensive, they warned him, but she was a force to be reckoned with and could tackle anything. She had to be if she was to take on our house. Several cleaners had already turned him down.

Mrs Cairo was Spanish and didn't speak much English, she had a very stern demeanour and Mum was scared of her. After her first visit to the house she dictated a very long list of highly toxic cleaning products. Mum was amazed at the trolley full she bought at the supermarket and even more amazed at the speed Mrs Cairo went through them. Every week Mrs Cairo went through the house like a tornado, and soon I too became afraid of her.

The first time I came home from school and ran up the stairs to my room was the biggest shock. Suspiciously, as I neared the top of the stairs I saw my door was wide open, then as I turned the corner I saw carpet, then more carpet, then the shock of seeing the *entire floor of my bedroom*. The bed had been made with clean, unfriendly sheets, and all the blinds were up – sunlight blaring into every corner of the immaculate room. 'My … my … stuff!' I stammered.

Part 1

My room may have looked like a bombsite but as a true pack rat I had known the location of every single thing: all my projects in various stages of completion, toys left in suspended animation. I circled the room in a daze, taking in the blankness like Munch's silent scream. It wasn't until I saw the enormous box in the corner, piled high with a confused tumble of junk – *my* junk – that the scream erupted from my throat.

Horrified, I peered into the box, lumps of stuff joined together by milky white globs of PVA, matchsticks that had once been a doll's house table, my Han Solo figurine, Castle Grayskull's drawbridge, broken Lego constructions, a bent View-Master reel, and through the lot a strange ribbon of shiny black tape. I probed the surface of broken belongings, tracing the path of the strange black tape. A coil of twisted metal Slinky appeared and I gasped, knowing even one small kink would have destroyed its equilibrium forever. Fury ripped through me as I tipped the box on its side, sending the contents spilling out. An Etch A Sketch dripped with fluorescent green slime, a plastic dog poo and vampire teeth from a show bag. Amongst the mess my skeleton moneybox started working, sending its bony hand reaching up to claw at the air mechanically, as a strangely familiar, sickly smell hit me.

Suddenly the source of the black ribbon became apparent: in disbelief I stared at my favourite cassette of top-forty hits I'd recorded off the radio. 'NO!' I shouted. I plunged my finger into one of the cassette's holes in an effort to begin winding the tape back in but it was stretched, the music would sound like warbling drunks accompanied by sitar.

And that was when I saw the uncapped bottle of Tinkerbell perfume that I never really liked anyway and the large wet stain on the carpet that would forever fill my bedroom with this nauseating reek. I grabbed the empty bottle and threw it as hard as I could, the cheap glass vial bounced off the wall and landed on my desk that was now devoid of anything except a horrid pink vase – *pink*!!! I hated that vase and seeing it filled me with a vile fury that could no longer be contained. Outraged, I stormed across the room and snatched up the vase. Trembling, I knew what I had to do. I took the stairs down two and three at a time. '*WHO DID THIS?!*' I screamed, 'WHO DID THIS TO MY ROOM?' My voice cracked and became a shriek, my eyes were wild, my face distorted with rage as I sought out my mother. 'HOW COULD YOU DO THIS?' I screamed at her 'EVERYTHING IS *RUINED!*'

Mum looked pained, she shook her head and started stuttering horribly which only made me more furious because I loved her and I was making her so upset she couldn't talk. Like an evil pantomime villain my father materialised behind me. When he spoke his voice was thick with patronising smugness.

'Katie, your room was a pigsty. It had to be done. *I told* Mrs Cairo to do it.' His matter-of-fact tone only enraged me more.

'I *HATE* YOU!' I screamed. The fury boiled up and singed my hair, turning me into Drew Barrymore from *Firestarter;* any minute things were going to start exploding into flames around me. Suddenly my vision became blurry, snot started streaming from my nose. Mum stepped forward to put her hand on my shoulder, but I brushed her hand away. She knew about this, she had betrayed me! She was always supposed to be on *my side*! This was even more hurtful than all my stuff being ruined. She was just as much to blame as him. She was a traitor! I hated them. It always came down to this – them against me.

I stormed out of the room, ran up the stairs, stumbled and scrabbled up the last of them, fighting like a crazed animal to get to the safety of my room. Once inside I threw the door shut, the air cracked with the finality of the slam. 'I'll show them!' the slam said; it always had the final word. But then, on seeing my room again a new wave of emotion hit me. It felt like my chest was being crushed. I gulped air, my chest heaving, my head dizzy. I felt sick. I wanted to tear this feeling from my body, or spit it out. I felt like I was choking on some horrible, rancid sharpness that I didn't know how to dislodge. How could I endure the agonising torture of this unbearable emotion passing through me?

I staggered forward and collapsed onto the bed, bawling into the pillow until it was hot and soaked with tears and finally I heard the door to my room opening and Mum crept over to console me. 'Don't worry,' she would whisper sadly. I could never remain angry with her for long because she was always so irritatingly *nice*. Dad and I frequently fought. Mum was the mediator, patiently listening to each of us until our tempers simmered down, convincing us over and over again to sullenly lay down our weapons, or in the case when I was about five years old, to unpack my small brown suitcase and rethink my idea of running away, at least until the morning when she said she could give me a lift.

I stuck a big 'KEEP OUT' sign on my door and on the day of the week when Mrs Cairo was expected also tried to barricade the door to my room with furniture, but even with these measures Mrs Cairo continued to blast her way through my room. I was like a volcano, primed to erupt each time I found my room in the same hideous state of cleanliness and order. My door was slammed so many times a crack ran up the side of the timber doorframe. My father became ever more impatient at my tantrums, 'Stop being hysterical!' he'd shout, 'What's wrong with that girl Jeanne? She needs a damn good smack! I'm sending her to boarding school!'

Like a general taking control of a foreign territory Mrs Cairo claimed one room of our house at a time. The kitchen, bathrooms, bedrooms, living and dining rooms, the television room where Mum's Logies were displayed alongside framed photographs of her with Burt Lancaster, Bob Hawke, Burt Reynolds, Phyllis Diller and Princess Diana of Wales. With methodical precision Mrs Cairo scoured each room from top to bottom, leaving not one mote of dust.

Luckily for Dad, his office in the basement was guarded by his secretary Ruth, and his writing room, located in a small annex had a proper lock with a key that Dad would hide when Mrs Cairo was coming.

Opening the door to Dad's writing room was like gaining access to a crypt. Dad always kept the blinds down to protect his books from the sun and you'd have to wait, blinking while your eyes adjusted, soft beams of light filtering through clouds of swirling dust particles. Shelves covered the walls of the room entirely, filled with tomes on every imaginable facet of medieval life. A desk piled high with dictionaries several inches thick and his pride and joy, an enormous electric typewriter that he proudly called his 'word processor'. He spent more time reading the manual on how to operate it than actually using it and the sole reason I ever entered this room was to salvage the enormous spent cartridges from his overflowing wastepaper basket that looked like spaceships beside my Millennium Falcon. I'd spend the next week sneezing from the dust, but under lock and key Dad's room was safe.

Eventually there was only one other room left. Mum's final instruction as she raced out of the house was always, 'Just leave my sewing room up the top!', to which Mrs Cairo would nod and say something in Spanish. Whether Mrs Cairo didn't understand my mother, or chose to ignore her instruction, will never be determined.

Unlike my hot-headed father and I, it took a lot for Mum to get really upset and there are only a handful of times that I can ever recall my mum 'losing it'. The day that Mrs Cairo cleaned up her sewing room was one of those times. Mrs Cairo, assuming the stuffed plastic bags were garbage, hauled the lot away, cleaned up the mess of fabric and tissue paper patterns from the floor, threw all the containers of sequins, beads and buttons into one big bucket. All Mum's experiments were cleaned away: the papier-mâché flowers and fake feather boars made from shredded chiffon, the outfits ripped apart to be remade into something else. The ironing board had been folded down, the carpet slightly damp and strangely bereft of it's starchy fur, no more minefield of pins and needles. The sewing machine was hidden under a cover I didn't even know had existed and the radio stripped of Mum's wire coathanger antenna. Worst of all, the patchwork wall of ideas with its dozens of fashion magazine clippings was gone, leaving an uninterrupted expanse of pink and white gingham wallpaper.

Finally, even Dad was forced to agree that Mrs Cairo had gone too far. Dad had the unenviable task of letting her go and Mum and I were allowed to go back to living in our exquisitely creative, wonderfully uninterrupted, mess.

WAKE ME UP BEFORE YOU GO-GO

'What's it like to have Jeanne Little as your mother?'

I've been asked that question a million and one times by journalists, school friends, colleagues, even people on the street, and it's next to impossible to answer. I can tell them about Mum – 'Yes, she's like that all the time, from the minute she wakes up till the moment she goes to bed,' and people would always find that amazing and start smiling at me, like they'd discovered the Easter bunny existed.

'No-one could be like that *all the time!*' they'd wonder aloud.

'Yes,' I'd say, 'I'm afraid so, that's what she's like – *all* the time,' and I'd be thinking to myself '*You* get woken up by Jeanne Little at 7 am for school every morning and see how you like it!'

I could tell them little bits: how Mum was incredibly creative and as a child I was never, never, *never* allowed to say I was bored. That was the most terrible thing I could say and I'd be sent off with an empty ice-cream container, some wool and beads with instructions on how to make a macramé plant holder. She was always doing amazing things; one day spray painting a hat made of ice-cream cones, the next knitting a top with enormous oversized needles. More often than not the laundry tub was full of blue dye and ostrich feathers. One time Dad and I spent weeks squashing thousands of milk bottle caps while we watched TV in the evening, which Mum sewed onto a dress that looked like exquisite fish scales. Mum had a magical way of transforming the ordinary into the extraordinary.

It's impossible to sum her up in few words because she was such a contradictory mix: so incredibly intelligent yet would say the most ridiculously daft things; so well known for her self-depreciating humour, yet was the most confident person on the planet. It wasn't that Mum didn't doubt herself at times, just that her Scottish mother had brought her up to believe that hard work and determination were the keys to success – yet here she was, the most popular television personality, without even trying to get into showbiz.

Mum adored glamour and was quite vain, yet was the most down-to-earth person you'd ever meet, and was incredibly conservative and rather prudish, yet open minded enough to take me to a family planning clinic when I was fourteen. Mum would always buy the biggest box of cereal because it was the best value, but there was no way we could eat it all and so she'd have to throw half of it out, and she would never spend money on herself yet was unbelievably generous. She would always give every make-up and wardrobe girl 'something little' for Christmas, would tip every single person working in the hairdressing salon, and thought nothing of staying up till midnight to 'whip up' an outfit for my friend Danielle when she heard she didn't have a special dress to wear. And once Mum had an idea in her head nothing could talk her out of it – she was the most stubborn person on the planet.

Mum was a 'free range' parent. She let me do whatever I wanted for hours on end, not bothering to hassle me about cleaning my room or getting me to stop what I was doing to eat lunch. And when it came to brushing my teeth or bathing, that was pretty much my business too. There was no daily routine to stick to. When I got a bit whiffy Mum would say ominously that I might be starting to turn into one of those people on *Dr Who* that got covered in green slime. I would imagine the green fungus starting around my fingernails then creeping up my hands and arms, taking over me while I slept. The Barbies and I would go into the bath along with an entire bottle of bubble bath and it would only be three hours or so later that Mum would remember to get me out. The water would be stone cold and she'd rub at me furiously with the towel trying to encourage the circulation back into my blue skin while the water screamed down the plughole and giant snakes of white bubbles foamed up out of the floor drain.

Once in a blue moon my parents would tackle washing my hair. It was an extremely stressful event that we all dreaded. My ears were the cause of it. I was so deafened by glue ear as a child that I'd learnt to lip-read. I'd had grommets several times and suffered with interminable earaches that woke me screaming in the night. The doctor had warned my parents not to let a drop of water get in my ears.

My father would be forced to kneel awkwardly on the hard tile floor holding towels over my ears while Mum poured buckets of water over my head. Dad was never a very 'hands on' father and the whole exercise aggravated him enormously.

'Hurry up Jean!' he'd shout.

My mother, in a panic, would scrub at my head furiously, muscling the shampoo into my scalp like a corrugated washboard.

Water would begin trickling under the towels. 'It's getting in my ears!' I'd scream.

'Barry! Ooooah!! Hold the towels, harder Bar!'

'For god's sake hurry up Jean, these tiles are torture, I'll be crippled at the knees!'

'It's getting in my EARS!' I'd scream again.

'It's NOT getting in your ears! STOP SCREAMING!'

'It is! It IS!'

'Oh Barry it is!'

'JUST THROW THE WATER OVER HER HEAD!' my father would shout, and in near hysteria, thinking I was being drowned, with my mother throwing bucket after bucket of water over me with the urgency of someone trying to save a sinking boat, I'd scream and hiss like a cat trying to claw my way out of the tub. There was no dignity in these moments. Relations strained, each of us would retreat to our corners of the house for several hours before we could face each other again.

Perhaps because of the stress involved with hair washing, my mother, although lax about other routines, was pedantic when it came to plaiting my hair. She always marvelled at my very long, dead-straight hair, which was nothing like hers that 'snapped off'. I always wore two very long plaits, except on school photo days when Mum got more adventurous, spinning the plaits into snail buns or loops, like Princess Leia, filling my head with so many bobby pins I felt like Pinhead from *Hellraiser*, with oversized ribbons so large I looked like a Christmas cracker next to the other little girls in the school photo.

Mum would always buy my uniforms a few sizes bigger too, convinced I was about to have an enormous growth spurt, but no matter how fast I grew, I could never fill the giant tunics that came down to my ankles. Along with oversized ribbons and uniforms

Mum also went overboard preparing my school lunches. She had read somewhere that you could make a month's sandwiches in advance and freeze them to save time, so that's what she did, except that instead of dull, perfectly average fillings she bought tins of smoked oysters because she thought it sounded exotic. That was until my parents' friend Colin Johnston, who was a pharmacist and often the voice of reason in our house, chuckled and told her that shellfish left to defrost in a warm lunchbox might kill me. It was just another innocent brush with death, like enlisting me in the kitchen to fry pappadams in boiling oil wearing flannelette pyjamas. I was a fatal accident waiting to happen.

My father took over the job of making my lunches after that. He always knew my mother was impractical but never thought her farcical ideas had the potential to kill me. But try as I might to swap them with other children no-one would touch my sandwiches with a barge pole when I told them what the filling was – tinned tongue!

Growing up, Mum educated me in the things she thought were of utmost importance, like how to put on false eyelashes or fix a pre-dinner drink. Recently a friend lent me some false eyelashes to wear to The Logies and asked if I needed her to show me how to put them on. 'Are you kidding?' I said, 'I could attach eyelashes in kindergarten!'

Early on at school a trend was set for dress-up birthday parties. Seeing what my mother would dress me up as was a source of continual amusement for the other parents, who would delay leaving their children at the party until Mum arrived. The other little children would stand around picking at bowls of chips, nervously hopeful of winning the prize for Best Dressed until we got there, then they'd roll their eyes and stalk off sending looks of murderous hate in my direction. I *always* won.

Likewise, I learnt to mix drinks when I could barely see above the trolley they used as a bar. Mum held three fingers horizontally next to the glass. 'Three fingers of Scotch,' she said pouring a generous amount of amber-coloured liquid over the ice cubes. 'Then two fingers of soda,' she explained, informing me that the guests would tell me what combination to make when I asked them what they were having. I loved mixing drinks. Loved the beautiful decorative bowl of big ice cubes, the little pair of silver tongs I used to pick them out and the tinkling sound they made as I dropped them into the glass. I loved the tiny chopping board to slice the lemon and the way certain spirits went with different mixers and garnishes. It was so exciting being at the bar, like I had my very own chemistry set – corks popping, soda fizzing, tiny explosions hissing in each glass.

'Should Katie be doing that?' my father asked emerging from the kitchen.

As usual my mum looked perplexed and stuttered a bit. 'What? Katie knows how to do it, don't you?'

I nodded and squeezed a wedge of lime into Dad's drink before dropping it in.

'No Jean, don't you think she's a bit *young* to be playing with alcohol?'

'She's not playing with it Dahling, she's fixing drinks.'

I carefully carried over the drink I'd made him in a heavy crystal glass, trying my best not to let any of it spill on the carpet in case he got cross. Mum and I watched keenly as he took a sip and raised his eyebrows. His frown changed to a look of genuine surprise. 'Hmmm, not bad.'

It didn't seem to matter that I had trouble pouring the heavy bottles of spirits at times; if I poured too much into the glass by accident no-one seemed to notice, at least not until they had to stand up to move to the dining table. Quite a few fell over or lurched onto furniture to prop themselves up on the way, and occasionally someone wouldn't even make it up off the couch, but would just sink deeper into the Thai silk cushions and be left there when the party moved on. But it was a different era back then, there was no breath testing and no blood alcohol limit. No-one counted their drinks. In fact, in the 80s everyone *loved* to get totally plastered; it was kind of expected and even disappointing for the dinner party host if you didn't.

Mum and Dad's dinner parties were amazing productions, a true feast for the senses. Weeks of planning would go into the really important parties, the ones where they had guests to impress like Dad's wealthiest clients, who were regulars in the social papers, or television media tycoons. Both Mum and Dad were great cooks and made incredibly memorable dishes. They would spend days in the kitchen amidst cookbooks and piles of ingredients preparing a multi-course dinner from scratch in between cleaning the lounge and dining rooms. Our house reflected the stylish reputation of Dad's interior design business and I grew up thinking everyone lived in houses lavishly furnished like ours with real tortoiseshell tables, hand painted Japanese screens and antiques.

The long gold leaf dining table would be set with ornate placemats, layers of china, carved shell bowls of salt and pepper, crystal glassware, silver cutlery. Once, at the Oriental Hotel in Bangkok a waiter taught me how to fold napkins like bird of paradise flowers, which was to start an obsession with napkin folding in our house. Finally, Dad would arrange a centrepiece for the table, which would look like something from a Caravaggio painting with candles and fresh flowers picked from the garden, white camellias the size of small dinner plates, jasmine and gardenias. The smell of the flowers mixed with sandalwood incense that Dad burned beside his exotic Buddhist figures and the lights would be dimmed. Music would play softly and the scene would be set for an incredibly memorable evening.

In the kitchen, however, it would be a different story, like finding yourself in a tiny French galley on the busiest night of the week, every stove top red hot, bubbling with soups and sauces, pans of food waiting to be finished, mains in the oven, griller primed with hors d'oeuvres such as 'angels on horseback', or appetisers like scallops mornay served on mother of pearl plates.

Mum's famous dessert, her Thousand Layer Cake took over the whole kitchen with squares of foil piled up and spread out everywhere, the wafer-like layers of cake which she'd baked in the oven earlier ready to be assembled at the last minute with freshly whipped cream and pie apples. A gastronomic climax that would silence even the rowdiest table in gluttonous excess. All incredible food, but with just minutes to go before the guests arrived they would both be totally stressed out, desperately trying to finish whatever they were making, constantly getting in each other's way.

'JEAN!' Dad would roar. 'What are you *doing*? I need that pot!'

It usually fell to Mum to clean up afterwards and she would be trying to get ahead of the mammoth task, which would keep her up for hours after the guests had left. She'd have the sink full of water, rubber gloves on, frantically washing everything in sight.

'Oh *all right*! You don't have to be *rude*!' she'd fire back as he reached for the pot she'd just put in the sink. He'd then turn around to find she'd 'cleaned up' his chopping board.

'Just get out of the kitchen and go and get ready!' he'd say, slamming things around and shooing her out. Dad would be dressed first and would sigh with relief when Mum was out of the kitchen, finally left alone to work his magic and attend to the minutiae of details. When the doorbell went Dad would take off his apron before answering the door. 'Jeanne darling, our guests are here!' he would call up, and Mum would make a grand Hollywood entrance coming down the stairs in one of her spectacularly glamorous creations and the guests would gasp theatrically.

Everyone thought my mother was incredible, a larger than life personality, but to me she was just Mum. My lovely, brown-haired, energetic, always enthusiastic, fun Mum. That is until the day when I was about six when she picked me up from school and I came to the car to discover she'd chopped off all her hair and bleached it white blonde. I was so upset I burst into tears. Mum hadn't foreseen this reaction. She had expected me to be surprised of course, it was such a dramatic change, but I was *really* upset. My beloved Mum with her shoulder-length brown hair was gone.

'I'm still the same person!' Mum said with a laugh. 'It's still me! It's just my hair that's different – see?' She pulled the hair back from her face, covering it with her hands. 'See? It's still me under here, silly!'

But this hair change, it wasn't like the false eyelashes that she could just pull off, or the drawn on eyebrows and make-up. It wasn't a wig that could be turned inside out like a pair of socks to be put away in her closet. The bleached hair was permanent, and I think instinctively I knew this as I threw myself awkwardly across the handbrake to bury myself into her arms. The Mum I knew – the Mum I loved! – the one that smelled like fabric starch and plain yellow soap, the one that liked simple baked potatoes and staying at home making macramé plant holders with me was going, was being taken away from me by other people, little by little. Mum was my special mum but she was *so* special I had to share her with the world.

'Your mother's a saint Katie, you know that don't you?' Dad would sometimes say. And all I would think is 'I don't want her to be a saint, I just want her to be my mum.' And in my heart I wondered why all these people wanted a piece of her. There were so many other people in the world, they could take their pick but just leave her, because she was the only mum I had, and she was *my mum* and I didn't want to share her at all.

MONEY CHANGES EVERYTHING

Mum loved nothing better than being left alone to do the thing she loved most in the world – sew – and for the most part I was tremendously happy to be left to my own devices as well. Dad was usually working down in the basement and when he wasn't working he wasn't in the mood to play with me. After working he'd cook dinner most nights before retreating to the TV room upstairs where he would fall asleep in his armchair within minutes of sitting down. Mum would come upstairs after washing up.

'Bar!' she'd shout, 'Bar!'

Dad *hated* his name being abbreviated, and hated being woken up. His eyelids would flutter for a moment, then finally snap open when Mum shouted loud enough to rouse him.

'BAR!'

'WHAT?! *WHAT?!* What Jean?!'

'You're snoring! Go to bed!'

'Oh … was I?'

Then he'd drift off again. His heavy eyelids would drop, his jaw would slacken and after a few minutes of loud breathing the snoring would start again.

Dad's snoring was so loud I could hear it like a rock grinder in my bedroom a whole floor up. Mum tried all sorts of things, bought pillows in all shapes and sizes guaranteed to stop snoring, but it was no use. One time she even sewed a golf ball into a pocket on the back of his pyjama top, another 'tip' from the radio that was supposed to wake the snorer up when he rolled onto his back, but Dad cursed the top and took it off the first night.

'I'm not sleeping with a bloody golf ball sewn into my pyjamas Jean! Don't be ridiculous!'

So Mum developed a habit of sleeping with her arms folded over her head. Dad, who never felt the cold, would throw off the covers and lie on his back snoring like an express train, while Mum buried herself further into the doona. Dad always woke before dawn and Mum slept late, and if you had to wake her you might not even realise she was in the bed. Sunk well beneath the pillow, buried deep inside a fat coil of doona that looked like a giant cocoon, you'd finally find a tuft of bleached blonde hair, and if you dug a bit deeper you'd find her, curled up with her arms wrapped around her head, her face pressed with wrinkles, flushed pink and warm.

'I don't know how she sleeps like that,' Dad would always say disparagingly. 'It's a wonder she doesn't suffocate.'

When they weren't working in some form or another my parents were often attending parties that I was dragged along to. I hated being forced to get dressed up for these parties, Mum always bought the most impractical clothes: itchy woollen jumpsuits, tight black, patent leather shoes that were so stiff the backs would pinch painfully into my heels (Mum would rub the lining with soap trying to soften them but to no avail), and thick cream stockings that I was forever yanking up, the crotch like a giant elastic nappy that was always falling down, pulling my thighs together awkwardly when I walked.

'You remember Raelene?' Mum would ask, trying to entice me to go. 'Norma and Ronan's little girl? She'll be there!'

The majority of Mum and Dad's friends were gay and childless, but occasionally there would be one other child where we were going.

'Who?' I would ask hesitantly.

'Rae-leeeeen!' Dad would sing out from the kitchen, mocking Norma's pronunciation of their child's name. 'You remember! Rae-leeeeen! Rae-leeeeeeeeeen!' he sung out.

And with a vaguely sick feeling I remembered the dinner party I'd been taken to a few months back in a large house in Woollahra. Dad had laughed afterwards and called it 'the pastel palace'. Everything in the house was pastel, every wall painted a different shade – pale mint green, soft margarine yellow, Iced VoVo pink and baby blue with thick spongy, cream carpet. Everyone had to take their shoes off at the door, grown men and women walked around in their socks and stockings, even my parents.

Raelene … now I remembered. The spoilt kid. The one with a roomful of the most amazing toys; *dozens* of Cabbage Patch Kids, a few hundred Smurfs and her very own 'art room', a child-sized desk stocked with artist's paper and a tower of crayons, waist high, spiraling up from the ground with every spectrum of colour! I had sat down at the table eagerly, drawn by the smell of waxy goodness, but the second I touched a crayon Raelene snatched it from me.

'You're not allowed to use that one!' she'd said. Then when I went to take another she'd snatched that too. 'Or that one!'

Her mother overheard. 'Rae-leeeeen! Are you sharing honey?'

Her mother Norma was a big-bosomed lady with an enormous starchy bird's nest of silver hair, who swanned around in a sequined kaftan, her large bare feet sinking into the plush carpet, with garishly bright vermilion toenails. I'd seen her sashaying around the kitchen, poking her fingers into various platters of food she was arranging.

'Shhh! Don't tell anyone!' she'd said, with a wicked gleam in her eye. 'I'm not supposed to eat this!' She took a toothpick and pierced through several olives, dolmades and a large gooey wedge of camembert. In the blink of an eye she lowered it down her gullet like a sword swallower, plucked the little stick from her mouth and daintily pressed one finger to the corner of her mouth with a wink.

She glided over to inspect what was happening at the art table, the chiffon sleeves and skirt of her kaftan drifting behind, her body moving with a slight wobble like a bug-eyed goldfish. She opened a silver foil packet with a pop and dumped a load of bright orange Cheezels into a bowl for us. 'Are you hungry, honey?' she asked me. 'You're such a little slip of a thing. Like your mother, aren't you?' Raelene plunged her hand into the bowl, scooped some into her mouth and began stacking them onto her fingers.

'Now can Katie do some drawing with you, Raelene?' she asked. The kid rolled her eyes and chomped off several Cheezels. 'Aw Mum, I just got them!' Orange crumbs flew out of her mouth while she spoke.

'I know honey, but wouldn't it be nice if you did some drawing with them together? You're always saying you want a little friend to play with!'

'I'm thirsty!'

'Okay, but while I get you a Coke you let Katie draw too, okay?' She affectionately tucked a wisp of Raelene's blonde, curly hair behind one ear and licked her thumb to wipe away a smear of orange from her cheek.

'DON'T!!!' Raelene screamed.

'Oh all right princess! Goodness!' She shrugged and gave me an exaggerated look. 'Someone's a bit cranky, aren't they?'

While her mother poured the drinks Raelene glared at me. 'You can only use the ones on the top tier,' she hissed. I went to take a crayon, 'and only the *used* ones!'

I looked at the top tier with dismay; there were only about five crayons that seemed to fit the description. 'What about that silver one?' I asked, pointing to a lovely glittery crayon, the only one of its kind.

'NO! Not that one!'

Raelene's mother reappeared, 'Raeleeeeen! You have to *share* with Katie, she's our special guest, aren't you cherry pie?'

'Oh *all RIGHT* Mum, for gawd's sake!' Raelene violently pulled half a dozen poo-coloured crayons and dumped them onto my side of the table.

'And what about the silver one, honey?'

'FINE!' Raelene threw her head back to stare at the ceiling as her mother plucked up the silver crayon with two fingers like a cigarette. The diamantés on Norma's fake nails sparkled as she awkwardly placed the crayon down with the others.

'Now don't be like that my little potato scallop, no-one likes a sour puss!' she teased, affectionately pressing Raelene's nose with her fingertip. Raelene tossed her face away dramatically and folded her arms.

Once again Norma winked at me. 'Now isn't it fun to share?'

Mum appeared briefly at my side. 'Having fun?' she asked hopefully.

I gave her a desperate look with my eyes that said '*Please can we go home?*' and she answered with a look of her own that said '*I'd rather be in here with you!*' But it was no use, the drunken friends of the hostess emerged to seek Mum out and drag her back to the party. Raelene's mother followed close behind with champagne bottles clutched under each arm like machine guns pointed at my mother's back, and with the loud explosions of corks and raucous laughter I turned miserably back to the Cheezel-flecked paper in front of me.

I would colour that silver crayon down to a stump.

I grew to loathe going anywhere with my parents; even family gatherings were hell. Forget the fact that I had two cousins only a couple of years older than me, the last time I'd been taken to their house Mum had picked out a bright red jumpsuit for me to wear – an outfit that proved irresistible to them. Like a puppy out of parental supervision it didn't take long for things to get out of hand. Within seconds they had leapt on me, pinning me to the floor by sitting on my chest. They tied knots in the arms and feet of the jumpsuit and shoved my socks in my mouth when I tried to scream.

At that moment my aunt's heels came clicking down the hallway and my cousins, thinking quickly, shoved me under the coffee table.

'Having fun kids?' I heard Aunt Cherie ask.

My cousins were beside themselves, coughing loudly to cover my muffled screams.

'Well I'm glad you're all having such a good time!' Aunt Cherie said cheerily. 'We're coming in for dinner in a minute.'

I lay there trying to keep my breathing calm, nostrils flaring, eyes darting to look at the small rectangle of vision of the connected room, the dining table and chairs – when Mum came in she'd see me!

My aunt's heels click-clacked over to stand inches from my face. Glasses clinked as she collected them from the table above my head, then I watched as she walked away and paused as an afterthought, 'I might just pull these doors closed …'

I watched in horror as she pulled out sliding doors to close off the dining room.

'Now you can be as noisy as you like and we won't hear a thing!'

I tried screaming again, a muted '*Noooooooooooooooooo!*' that was easily masked by my cousins' shrieking laughter.

Several hours later when the adults came in for coffee, they found me. My cousins kept giggling but the grown-ups weren't amused. Still, no-one really wanted to make too much of a big deal about it because everyone had been having such a good night. Dad slapped me roughly on the back a couple of times.

'You're alright then aren't you?' he said cheerily. 'No harm done, she's fine!' he said loudly. 'Fine, fine!'

I swore I would never wear a jumpsuit again as long as I lived.

***

There may not have been many other children in my life but there were plenty of fun adults, most notably my parents' best friends 'the Colins' and my beloved grandmother.

The Colins lived a few doors down the road. Colin Brees worked for my father downstairs as an interior designer and Colin Johnston was a pharmacist, an occupation that always held him in high regard with my grandmother. I loved both the Colins like uncles. When they were over the house filled with conversation! They took an interest in what I had to say too, a curiously pleasant sensation as usually people directed all their attention to my parents.

The Colins of course, like everyone else, adored my mother, but Colin Brees had a vicious sense of humour and didn't hold back when poking fun. Dad loved sharing Mum's latest dippy debacle with them – the time she painted her teeth with white nail polish, the time she exploded the oven door trying to melt plastic in it, the time she asked an Asian girl who was a daughter of 'one of the Wiggles' – which one?

'Oh Jean! What have you done now?' the Colins would both exclaim, laughing at the sheer idiocy of her latest blunder. Their jovial company thawed Dad's icy moods, and like watching an episode of *I Love Lucy* my father would play up his part as the poor, long-suffering husband while Mum pooh-poohed him and tried to save face. It wasn't hard to see why I thought of the Colins as family – three's a crowd but five always felt like a party.

Colin Brees wore massage sandals to work and had a basket under his desk for his dog. He'd often knock off early to take me and Cindy to Centennial Park and driving there the dog would stand between us, its paws on the centre console, showing a little row of crooked undershot teeth, grinning between shiny black lips. The claws were probably marking the car's upholstery, but Colin didn't seem to get angry about things like that, he just put a carpeted mat down. Likewise, when he saw that I couldn't see over the dashboard he bought a foam booster seat – what a joy to see out the window while we drove! Colin played the Bee Gees and his car always smelt like Stimorol chewing gum. And unlike my father who never went near a playground, and my mother who was always nervous of me getting hurt, Colin Brees would push me on the swings so high the seat would hang in the air before free-falling down.

When Colin dropped me home we'd be greeted by the irresistible smell of Mum's roast lamb and usually once a week Colin Johnston would come over and we'd all eat together. The lights in the formal lounge and dining would be switched on and the areas of the house that were usually dark and cold would sparkle and come to life. Mum would fix a round of her killer Scotches then go into the kitchen and turn the oven dials up as high as they would go. Even after she'd shattered the oven door Mum continued to do this and I'm convinced it was the secret to her utterly incredible baked potatoes that underwent some amazing transformation in those last few moments of intense heat – so hot they didn't burn but kind of imploded like great puffs of crunchy potato chip.

When the Colins came over our family expanded, my parents talked and laughed and Mum served up enormous portions of meat and vegetables, pushing second and third helpings onto Colin Johnson's plate who would cry, 'Oh Jean no! I couldn't possibly!' but he always would.

'Poor Colin Johnston is always *hungry*,' Mum would say afterwards, 'Colin Brees makes him work all the time and feeds him nothing but awful sausages!'

Sometimes Colin Brees would take me with him to Colin Johnston's pharmacy at Balmoral Beach to help him decorate the shop windows, which were so wonderful people stopped to stare. Where Mum was a whiz with needle and thread, Colin Brees made magic with his tool kit and staple gun. He was Dad's right-hand man, putting up curtains and pictures, wallpapering small jobs, and knocking together slapdash furniture for Dad's interior decorating displays, such as the precarious table bases in our house and my not-quite-right four-poster bed.

After dressing the pharmacy windows Colin Brees would take me with him across the road to the beach. He'd lie and sunbake, slathered in Reef Oil, smoking cigarettes and digging the butts into the sand while I swam and sat for so long in the shallows that the crotch of my swimmers filled with sand.

Finally, when the sun started to fade and the myna birds began chattering noisily in the fig trees, it would be time to pack up. Showered and dressed back at the pharmacy, my skin polished from hours on the beach, shoulders glowing red and forehead marked with circles from my goggles, Colin Johnston would call me over to help him on the register.

Ringing up the purchases for customers was good fun, but then I'd be mortally embarrassed at not knowing how much change to give. For some reason Colin Johnston thought I'd get better with practice but this was not the case, I was dead hopeless at maths. Maybe it was because, along with being deaf with glue ear, for a while I was also practically blind with short-sightedness for most of primary school until someone finally figured out I needed glasses.

Colin Brees came to my rescue. Like me, he didn't know how to add up, and he couldn't spell even a three-letter word. One day he showed me there was a button on the cash register that would display the amount of change to give the customer. Colin Johnston was outraged, 'Don't show Katie that!' he said.

'Oh! Why not?' Colin Brees said, grimacing with an apologetic smile.

'Because she needs to learn!'

But Colin Brees knew I had no hope of learning how much change to give. You either had a brain for numbers, like Colin Johnston and my mother, who could recite her times tables like a parrot, or you didn't. That's why he was the pharmacist, and we were the window decorators.

Colin Johnston was stubborn enough though to keep trying. Over and over he would put us through the torture of manually working out the change for customers, making us appear ever more stupid, until finally Colin Brees would snap at him and Colin Johnston would let us eat chocolate bars from the sweets counter.

***

Colin Brees was my favourite; he was never too busy to have fun. One day, we were in the car as he drove past an enormous toyshop called Uncle Pete's Toys. I'd seen the advert on television, it had a jingle with kids singing 'Uncle Pete's Toys are magic!' I knew that Uncle Pete had a farm next door to one of my parents' friend's properties. They had taken us to see his emus and Mum had worn a jumper with coloured feathers knitted into it. The giant grey birds with their big intelligent eyes had chased after Mum and she'd run away screaming while everyone laughed. Later, after she'd recovered, Mum said the birds probably wanted their feathers back.

Along with having a paddock of emus, Uncle Pete also had his own helicopter. I was thinking how cool it would be to fly in a helicopter instead of driving places when Colin Brees put on his indicator and did a U-turn.

'Let's see if Uncle Pete's toys really are magic,' he said.

I'd never seen a toyshop so large! While I wandered awestruck down the huge isles of bright pink Mattel boxes, bicycles and pogo balls, Colin stood talking with the shop assistant, who unlocked a glass cabinet.

'Come look at these Katie!' Colin called out. It was a little box with grey pictures moving on the screen in time with a ticking noise that got faster as the game progressed.

'What are they called again?' Colin asked.

'Nintendo.'

'Nin-what?'

'Nintendo – they're from Japan.'

'Which one should I buy?' Colin asked.

'Well I'd buy this one – Donkey Kong.'

It was Colin Brees and my mother who came up with all the *really fun* ideas: all of us flying halfway around the world together to go to Disneyland via New York; going to see Gene Simmons and KISS perform at the Sydney Showground when I was six;

driving up a mountain on the spur of the moment to see *real snow*, never mind about chains on the tyres.

It was Colin's idea to see The Village People movie *Can't Stop The Music*, and he turned up the following day with white rollerskating boots for both of us. His aim was to look like Steve Guttenberg, in tight pants skating through Taylor Square, I think, but after a couple of near brushes with death in our tiled backyard he thought better of it.

Like my mother, Colin Brees had also worked in television, except where Mum was in front of the camera Colin had been behind it building sets. In retrospect, Mum and Colin Brees had a similar talent – the art of being able to make expensive looking creations from cheap materials. In my mother's case, garments that were never made to last and often still had pins holding them together; for Colin Brees it was making lavish-looking interiors and display rooms. Both having grown up in poor households bereft of luxuries, in Colin's case raised by a foster parent, being able to make something expensive looking from nothing was a handy skill to have.

Colin left TV land without hesitation when he saw the money to be made working in my father's line of work, styling the homes of the bourgeoisie who lived in Sydney's most fashionable postcodes. Having no post-nominal letters or family connections to their names, it was therefore easy for my father to lord his authority over Colin and my mother, using his critical eye for detail and a haughty superiority inherited from my grandmother, who looked down her nose at anything that could be deemed nouveau riche. But as Imelda Marcos famously said, 'Nouveau riche is better than no riche at all.'

LIVING DOLL

Somehow my father managed to escape most parental obligations, and if it wasn't for the fact that the two of us were the early risers in the house, we may never have had much interaction at all. Dad would descend the stairs in his dressing gown to find me sitting in front of the little television set in our dining nook.

There were only four channels and remotes hadn't been invented. To switch channels I turned a clunky silver knob that had another dial in the middle for 'fine tuning'. My preferred station was the ABC but most days I was up so early the programs hadn't started broadcasting, there would just be a patchwork circle of coloured shapes that I would stare at. Dad would see me on his way through to the kitchen. 'You're sitting too close to the television again,' he would say, dragging the chair back, and I'd wait till he went into the kitchen to pull it forward again.

Within a few moments the deafening buzz of the coffee grinder started up. If I was hungry I would go into the kitchen and if it was the weekend and Dad was in a good mood he would make pancakes, showing me how to mix the batter so it was silky smooth with no lumps, mashing a banana and sprinkling it with sugar. I would watch the batter in the frypan, the rim sizzling and crisping, the delicious smell of browning butter. He'd flip the crepe, add the banana to warm through before folding it to serve with maple syrup and a quenelle of ice-cream. The pancakes my father made were sublime. By the time Mum came downstairs I would be on my third or forth helping and she would be thrilled to see me eating, convinced that I never ate enough.

My father had learnt the art of cooking from his mother Dora. When I was born my grandmother didn't want to sound old so she chose the name Dor Dor. She was my only grandparent and I absolutely adored her. She lived in a unit in Kirribilli and sometimes she would come and stay with me in our big terrace if my parents went away.

My grandmother was a very vain woman who didn't like to give up her independence or appear weak, so although she had great difficulty walking and my room was at the top of our four-storey terrace, she would decline offers of help from my parents and crawl all the way up the carpeted stairs on her hands and knees. I would shoot up the stairs with her suitcase and after ten minutes or so I'd hear my father call out, 'Has she made it up?' and I'd poke my head out the door to see her cursing and muttering as she hauled herself up the last leg.

'Yeah! She's fine!' I'd call back down.

It was exciting to have my grandmother sleep over. Usually I was alone on the top floor at night and it was a great comfort to know there was another warm body sleeping beside me. I often had the same terrifying dream that the house was falling over, the room would tilt sickeningly and in slow motion I would see the ground come rushing up as the house toppled over like a great tower, with me stuck in the top. I would wake up with a jolt as I hit the ground, my heart pounding, sure the dream was real and the house was falling over. But when Dor Dor shared my room I had no nightmares, probably because I didn't get much sleep. My grandmother had a habit of continually checking and rechecking the things she had brought over in her suitcase, all of which she wrapped individually in plastic bags. Repeatedly I'd be nudged from sleep by the vaguely irritating rustling noise. I'd lift my sleep-heavy lids in what began to feel like delirium, only to see my grandmother hunched over her suitcase again.

Quite often my parents dropped me at Dor Dor's for a few hours to visit, or sometimes to stay overnight. I loved these visits. My parents were always so busy but my grandmother never had anywhere to rush off to. Also, it was very obvious that she thought I was the most special person in the world.

My grandmother had a daunting air of superiority, and whereas I was used to grown-ups fawning over my parents, and particularly my mother, my grandmother had the effect of making people feel nervous and everybody, including my parents, really put themselves out to try and please her. But she was not easy to please.

There were certain people my grandmother adored who escaped her deprecatory nature, like Colin Johnston, whose profession as a pharmacist elevated him to a higher status in her eyes. He knew how to butter her up too, always telling her she looked wonderful for her age and affecting an air of kindly concern as she told him her ailments. He would take her hand and she would bat her eyelids behind cat's-eye glasses.

But my mother had the opposite effect; she always seemed to say or do the wrong thing. She would comment on Dora's blue rinse, and my grandmother's smile would sour – it wasn't supposed to be blue, it was silver. Or Mum would compliment her dress only to be met with a hard stare: 'It's the only nice dress I have, unlike some people.' Mum would start stuttering and Dad would roll his eyes.

Dor Dor would push her vegetables to the side of her plate – 'not cooked enough'; leave her cup of tea untouched – 'not enough sugar', 'not strong enough', 'not hot enough'; and Mum would have to work hard at any conversation. 'Did you have a good night's sleep Dora?' she would ask, 'Mmmm, not bad,' would come the terse reply.

'Oh come on, Mum,' Dad would say irritably, 'Lighten up a bit will you?'

Secretly I loved watching Dor Dor put my parents through their paces. She only had to sit a certain way, compress her lips or narrow her eyes to fill the room with a distinctly uncomfortable undercurrent. But this attitude was never directed at me. For me Dor Dor kept only smiles.

***

Driving across the Harbour Bridge with my overnight bag at my feet I felt a sense of fun and anticipation. There would be a loud clunking and whirring as the prehistoric elevator came trundling down, I would push myself against the big rubber stopper to hold the doors open, waiting impatiently for Dad to catch up. The old lift was unreliable. Slowly it would take us up, stopping with a sudden clang, pausing before opening the doors, long enough that we'd worry we were trapped. The hallway of the unit block had rough, red-brick walls and wrought-iron balustrades, there was the smell of cat biscuits left in the sun and geraniums in terracotta pots, cooking smells mingling with the smoke escaping from the rubbish chute.

Dad would rap loudly on the door with the knocker. 'What is she doing in there?' he would ask, rapping a second time, and after what seemed like an age the door would open, and with a reminder to 'be good' he would depart and I would experience a little thrill of excitement that I had been left alone, followed by a tug of nervous homesickness.

'Come in the kitchen,' Dor Dor would say. 'See what I've made for later!'

The shelves were usually bare in her big, shuddering refrigerator, apart from maybe a tired-looking cut tomato or plate of tinned beetroot slices. But there, shining like a ruby red jewel, would be a glass bowl of raspberry jelly, and beside it an earthenware dish with an egg custard, still wobbly in the centre, the surface flecked with nutmeg.

Dor Dor's unit looked straight across the harbour to the Opera House. 'Look at the big passenger ship!' she'd say taking me to the window. 'See the tugboats circling?'

In the company of my grandmother I noticed things I wouldn't usually have paid attention to. Under her direction I could sit much longer, watching the boats in the harbour performing their different jobs, observing birds flying to locate their nests. In the end there was no time to be homesick, there was always so much to do. We watered her plants on the balcony with the dregs of the teapot and took cuttings of African violets to strike. Sometimes I spread a towel over the arm of the couch to paint her nails.

'Oh!' she would cry. 'Look at my old hands!'

She would stretch the skin back, try to smooth the fat purple veins, scrutinise the misshapen knuckles and fingers bent with arthritis, the thin gold wedding band that she still wore which could no longer be taken off.

'How old do you think I am?' she would ask. 'Take a guess!'

This was a running joke between us. She was well into her eighties and would live to 102, but the answer that always made her smile was 'Twenty-one!'

A favourite game we loved to play was 'shop'. With a pile of copper one and two cent coins we took turns pretending to be the owner and the customer with lots of bargaining and role playing. When Dor Dor helped me add up it was fun, with none of the pressure of being put on the spot like at Colin Johnston's pharmacy.

'What are you going to be when you grow up?' she would ask. 'A scientist? A doctor? Don't be an actress will you? You don't want to be on the silly television, you're too smart for that I hope!' Sometimes we played cards – gin rummy – she never let me win.

Later we'd sit on her hard, overstuffed couch to watch *The World Around Us*, narrated by the soothing American voice of Doctor Spock. The smell of frying onions as Dor Dor cooked two pork chops and potatoes in her electric frying pan, which we'd eat overlooking the harbour, the Opera House reflecting the last golden rays of the sun, the choppy water now midnight blue.

Once I was tucked in bed Dor Dor removed her sapphire earrings then her clothes. Sitting on the edge of my bed near the wardrobe, she untied the flesh-coloured pantyhose knotted above the knee. ('Don't those things cut off the circulation?' Dad would say..) Her house dress, then white petticoat, would be pulled awkwardly over her head with glimpses of silver hooks and eyes, brassiere straps and laced edges.

Dor Dor's flesh, pale and crepey, sagging over bands of elastic, the remains of a once solid body deflated with age, nothing like my mother's body, tall and skinny with narrow hips and a flat chest. My mother who only ever wore singlets, having nothing to keep in place, which only made Dor Dor's large bosoms seem even more surprising when she removed her bra, hanging flatly down past her stomach, swaying pendulously as she pulled her nightdress on.

Then Dor Dor would do something amazing. In the dim light of the lamp she would ask, 'Are you ready? Now don't get a fright, will you?'

She'd drop her false teeth, top and bottom, into a glass and would suddenly look completely different, the lower half of her face shrunken like a withered apple. She'd take a peak of herself in the mirror and try to speak, 'Oh, I look awful!' but the words would come out mumbled and reflexively she would cover her mouth with her hand and we'd giggle.

Hoisting herself with a good deal of effort into the bed beside me she'd extinguish the lamp and then turn on the radio and the loud staticky voices of callers would go on talking all through the night.

The following morning we'd walk to the wharf across the road, watch the swell sucking at the great straps of leathery green seaweed, blooms of transparent jellyfish floating past. Occasionally we'd be invited to visit her neighbour, Edna. With a plate of freshly made pikelets or lamingtons Dor Dor would rap on the door, then we'd be taken in, following the old lady through the dark unit, the walls sparkling with glass display cabinets that lined the unit from floor to ceiling – Edna was a doll collector.

Crowding in from all sides were hundreds of incredibly real looking porcelain dolls, their unblinking eyes framed with delicate lashes, rosebud mouths and glossy hair set in perfect curls. Dora and Edna would take their tea in the lounge room while I sat perched on the end of the couch trying to be as still as I possibly could, trying not to blink or even move my chest when I breathed, wondering if someone walked in at that very moment whether they might mistake me for one of Edna's beautiful dolls.

DANCING QUEEN

By Sunday afternoon I was ready to go home. Dor Dor's often repeated proverbs – 'everything in moderation', 'clean as you go', 'spend some and save some' – would be starting to wear me down. Eventually I would take up a seat by the window, watching for Dad's white Mazda to turn down the street, while Dor Dor sat down to make a phone call. There was not a large choice, most of the names in her Bakelite Teledex were crossed out – they were dead. The choice was between her two younger sisters, my Auntie Vonnie and Auntie Lee, or her cousin Monica.

Dor Dor's cousin Monnie lived near us in the neighbouring suburb of Darlinghurst and my parents often used her as a clandestine babysitter. I adored Monnie, but I was never, ever to speak of her visits in front of my grandmother – if Dor Dor found out she would become violently jealous, and no-one could hold a grudge as long as Dora. If I was badly behaved and moody Mum would warn me I was taking after her; she didn't have to say any more.

But Monnie had a heart of gold, never spoke badly of anyone and was never jealous, even though she had not had an easy life. She always turned up with a tin of homemade shortbread biscuits and a craft project to share with me – a flower press perhaps or a box of seashells and glue to make into cards. By contrast, I never did anything arty with my grandmother, she preferred activities that could be used to instruct me in valuable life lessons, and whereas Dora preferred plain dresses in solid colours, like navy with a string of pearls, Monnie wore bold seventies colours and patterns – mission brown and orange, large brooches and rings studded with colourful opals. She had big tortoiseshell glasses with lenses so thick they magnified her eyes enormously, one of which was a bit lazy and tended to wander off to the side while you were talking to her, and wore shoes that were so big and clunky I was always reminded of the drawings in Mr Men books.

Driving Monnie home after babysitting me, Mum and I would be tucked in the back seat of Dad's little two-door sports car. Dad would open the door for her when we arrived and Monnie would struggle to pull herself up. Each time she strained to lift herself from the seat a loud fart would let loose and Mum and I would have to throw our hands over our mouths and seal them shut to stop ourselves from screaming with laughter. Monnie would make a dozen or so attempts to get out of the car, each time letting a string of flatulence rip that would have Mum and I crying tears of silent laughter.

It was all the more funny because we had to pretend as if we hadn't heard anything – we never wanted to offend Monnie because we loved her so dearly, and of course there was Dad too, standing outside trying to keep a straight face, watching us trapped in the back with fart gas. Our stomach muscles would cripple with laughing as we watched Dad desperately try over and over again to put on a straight face to ask Monnie if he could help her get out of the car, and it would take the whole drive home for us to finally stop breaking into fits of heaving, uncontrollable giggles.

***

For whatever reason, my grandmother didn't speak to Monnie very often but she did keep in touch with her two sisters. Auntie Lee lived down in Geelong, Victoria and came up to stay with her, usually once a year for a fortnight. Dor Dor, who lived by herself, greatly anticipated her visits, but there's a saying a friend of my parents had framed on her beach house wall: 'Houseguests are like fish, after three days they stink', and as much as my grandmother loved Auntie Lee, by the end of the visit a dark cloud would have descended over the unit. Dor Dor's mood would have turned sour and she would alternate between brooding silence and snapping at Auntie Lee like a venomous cane toad.

When Auntie Lee was staying my father would phone and speak to Dor Dor then say that Mum wanted to say hello to Auntie Lee. 'Are you all right over there?' Mum would whisper, 'Just ring me if she gets nasty and I'll come and get you!'

But Auntie Lee never needed rescuing. Somehow she managed to enjoy her trip to Sydney even after my grandmother had changed from Dr Jekyll into Mr Hyde and was so nice she just laughed it off. Everyone thought she was amazing. After Auntie Lee went home there would be a few awkward weeks where my grandmother spoke only in monosyllables, but then, like a rash, her prickly nature would subside and things would go back to normal again.

Auntie Lee had little pussycat teeth and a kind voice that always sounded like she was smiling. She loved to sew and crochet and made the most exquisite granny square blankets, but if Auntie Lee was staying there was always beer in the fridge. I once insulted her by asking if she wanted a shandy. She may have looked like a sweet old lady but when five o'clock came round she cracked open a Melbourne Bitter and drank it straight from the can.

One time when I was very young my grandmother took me down on the train with her to visit Auntie Lee. I have a hazy memory of a draughty house and dangerous-looking radiator that only warmed you when you were sitting two inches away from it, and a not-so-hazy memory of how freezing bloody cold the toilet seat was. Auntie Lee had several cats, and possibly because my grandmother hated both cats and the cold, that journey down was my first and Dor Dor's last.

My fondest memory of Auntie Lee – besides opening her pantry in Geelong to discover it was completely stocked, floor to ceiling, with beer cans and nothing else – was the time my parents dropped me over to Dor Dor's when Auntie Lee was staying. It was a very hot night, a summer heatwave had hit forty degrees and a cool change wasn't predicted until late that night. The balcony door and windows were wide open but there was no breeze and Dor Dor's small, electric fan made a whirring noise as the propeller lazily swept back and forth.

Auntie Lee and my grandmother sat beside the dining table, too hot to eat, the glasses on the table stood in puddles of condensation. My grandmother swished a little sandalwood hand fan and Auntie Lee pressed her forehead and neck with a hankie dipped in iced water. It was too hot to crochet, it was too hot to do anything. The ladies had taken off their shoes and pantyhose and sat slouched on the chairs like wilted roses, their polyester dresses clinging uncomfortably. Every now and then they would pluck at their neckline or lift the hem of their skirt and flap it about a bit to unstick the fabric from their skin.

Behind them the beautiful sparkling view, the Opera House radiant like a pearl, Circular Quay and the city skyline lit up like a galaxy of stars reflected in the shimmering expanse of black harbour. A few boats bobbed about, but other than that there was hardly any movement – the city was still with anticipation, waiting for the cool change.

'Oh, this heat Dora!' Auntie Lee lamented.

Part I

'Next time I think I'll come down to you in Geelong!' Dor Dor joked.

It was too hot to eat anything except jelly and I had nearly finished the second bowl Dor Dor had served me. I was playing with the last of it, trying to make it last, breaking the bright red jelly up into little pieces with my spoon, stirring them around with the melted ice-cream. Dor Dor was watching me eat with satisfaction.

'Aren't you hot in that?' she asked. Yes, of course I was, but it hadn't occurred to me my choice of clothes might have been contributing to how uncomfortable I felt.

I looked down at what I'd chosen to wear that morning, the same thing I chose to wear every morning, my denim overalls with a T-shirt and sneakers. And also, I was wearing a singlet. Dor Dor was fanatical about wearing singlets and would always check to see if I was wearing one by plunging her arm down the neck of my top without warning.

'You must be boiling!' Auntie Lee chimed in, 'Why don't you take some of that off! Take your shoes off at least!'

Why hadn't I thought of that? I pulled at the laces as Dor Dor sighed to Auntie Lee, 'Fancy, sending her over in all that gear … She should have a pair of sandals and a nice cool cotton dress.' I tugged off my socks and wiggled my toes. They were clammy and smelt of rubber. 'Tuck your socks away inside the shoes so they don't get lost!' my grandmother called out. 'That's a good girl.'

'Why don't you take off your overalls too?' Auntie Lee called out.

'Honestly, letting her go out in all that heavy fabric … Doesn't her mother know how to dress the girl?'

'But I've only got a T-shirt on underneath,' I said to Auntie Lee.

Quick to find fault with my mother's parenting Dor Dor jumped in, 'What? You haven't got underpants on!'

'Oh of *course* I've got underpants on!' I said, mortified.

'Well, just wear them!' Auntie Lee said.

'What? Just underpants!' I giggled. 'I'm not going to do *that*! I don't want everyone to see my *undies*!' It was embarrassing enough just talking about underpants without exposing them for everyone to see! I'd never thought much about underpants until a couple of years earlier but now that I was eight years old even the word made me squirm with laughter.

Auntie Lee laughed, 'It's just Dora and I – we won't look, will we Dora?'

'Of course not! Don't be silly. Lillius is right, take off those big heavy overalls! You're making me hot just looking at you!'

'Are you going to take them off?' Auntie Lee called out. I shook my head.

'Oh well, suit yourself!' Dor Dor said, and then to Auntie Lee. 'And all that long hair she's got. She must be boiling …'

'She does have beautiful hair, doesn't she?'

'Oh it's ridiculous! All that long hair hanging everywhere. Don't they ever take her to the hairdresser's? Or at least pin it back off her face? The girl can't see through it, hanging everywhere like that, it'll damage her eyesight!'

I sat there, shuffling a deck of cards to play gin rummy but it was even too hot for that, my hands made the cards sticky. Maybe it would be cooler without overalls, maybe if I just undid the big heavy metal clasps.

'Look, she's taking them off,' Auntie Lee whispered to Dor Dor.

'I'm not taking them *off*!' I called out, 'I'm just undoing the *top bit!*'

But as soon as I unfastened the heavy top I immediately felt lighter. My T-shirt, which was wet with perspiration, picked up the breeze from the revolving fan.

'Now doesn't that feel better?' Dor Dor asked. I had to admit it did. 'Take them right off! What are you worried about?'

Yes, what was I worried about? My grandmother had seen me in the bathtub! What did I care if she saw me in my undies? I made up my mind. I'd do it. I'd take them off. Secretly I undid the big silver buttons on the side at my waist while Dor Dor and Auntie Lee pretended to talk about the heat, then I stood up and without trying to draw attention to myself, stepped out of the jeans.

'Hurray!' Dor Dor and Auntie Lee both chimed together and I felt my cheeks flush red. I stood there, in my undies and T-shirt feeling exposed and awkward, but I did feel better … unrestrained … I walked around the unit a bit enjoying the feel of my bare skin. Music drifted in from the harbour, a boat with a party on board circled lazily in front of the Opera House, ABBA floated across the water.

I started twirling slowly; the air felt thick like liquid, it circulated and caressed me. I felt light, released from the confines of clothes, like I'd escaped from a straitjacket. Suddenly I couldn't wait to be free of the rest! I leapt and circled the room, spun around till I was dizzy – finally, no more elastic pressing lines into my body, no more seams and belts and scratchy labels tickling the back of my neck! This is how I was supposed to be!

'Oh, I wish I could do that! Don't you Dora?' Auntie Lee said. Their old bodies may have been slouched in their chairs but their minds were elsewhere.

When my parents rang to say they were on their way to pick me up Dor Dor called out to put my clothes on. It had taken so much persuading to get me to take them off, but nothing would convince me to put them back on and my parents had to carry me away wrapped in a towel.

***

My grandmother's other sister, Auntie Vonnie, lived a couple of hours away in Sydney's Northern Beaches. She had jet-black hair and in her youth had been a great beauty, charming and entertaining the war vets with a sultry voice and stunning hourglass figure reminiscent of Mae West. Auntie Vonnie had done well financially accumulating real estate and had two grown daughters from her first marriage and five grandchildren (two of whom were my cousins from the jumpsuit-under-the-coffee-table incident). Her second husband John was a little gnome of a man who ran a successful panelbeaters and he loved merriment and laughter and together they made a fine couple, always keen to invite a crowd of friends over and generous to a fault. ('More money than sense,' my grandmother said.)

Uncle John had a knack of catching people off guard and getting them very drunk, plying them with large drinks and shots of lethal Sambuca. Auntie Vonnie enjoyed having a few when she was entertaining too and liked to think she was psychic ('A lot of nonsense,' Dor Dor said). With a bit of Dutch courage Auntie Vonnie would start telling her guests all kinds of things; premonitions that were entertaining but often started fierce arguments.

'Now Jean, don't let me drink too much, will you?' Dad would say en route to one of their parties, but it was hard to resist Uncle John, who always had a mischievous twinkle in his eye and a top shelf bottle of whiskey at hand.

Being my grandmother's youngest sister Auntie Vonnie and my father were not too far apart in age. They had a very close relationship, no doubt stemming from the fact that Dad was an only child and Auntie Vonnie knew better than anyone how difficult her sister could be. Dor Dor didn't usually come to Auntie Vonnie's parties because she lived too far away, but occasionally she'd be taken to one if it was a special celebration and would torture everyone in the process. She'd turn her nose up at the champagne, take small bites from the food and push the rest to the side. Auntie Vonnie and my father would exchange looks as Dor Dor made one sniping remark after another until finally Auntie Vonnie would put her in her place by saying loudly across the room, 'Dora, lighten up!' Highly offended at being publicly reprimanded, Dor Dor would clam up and sulk for the rest of the night.

To make the family dynamics more interesting, Auntie Vonnie's eldest daughter Cherie, who was as strong-willed and spirited as her mother, had a special bond with my grandmother. Many times I heard Cherie recount the story how Dor Dor had changed the course of her life when, as a young woman, barely out of her teens, she had met a tall, dark and handsome American sailor in Sydney only for a few days. It had been love at first sight and Cherie was determined to go to America to find him.

'But *no-one* would lend me money for the airfare!' Cherie would say loudly in front of her mother. Like a fairy godmother Auntie Dor had come to the rescue with the loan and Cherie's wish to marry her Prince Charming had come true. 'Without your grandmother, Katie, I wouldn't have married the man of my dreams!'

Cherie loved telling this story just as much as my grandmother loved hearing it and there was no doubt it made both my father and Auntie Vonnie uncomfortable every time, for what I can only assume to be several reasons. Firstly, it was always left unsaid why Auntie Vonnie had refused to lend the airfare to her daughter, but it was obvious they didn't have an easy relationship.

Had Auntie Vonnie disapproved of her eldest daughter chasing after a man, a sailor no less, that she had only just met? Surely, of all people, my Auntie Vonnie who had been a free spirit herself, wouldn't have objected to her daughter following her gut instinct when it came to true love. And as for her claims of being psychic, wasn't following your intuition the point? Perhaps that's why Cherie got so riled up when her mother started making tipsy premonitions.

And as for my grandmother's part, it was easy to suspect Dor Dor had been motivated by more than just the goodness of her heart. For starters, my grandmother was notoriously stingy – she made Ebenezer Scrooge look generous. The real motivation, I suspected, had more to do with the closeness of my father to his Aunt Vonnie, who was much younger and far more fun than his straight-laced mother. What better way to have stuck it to her sister than to have undermined her authority *and* won the affections of her rebellious daughter?

Cherie retold the story often at family gatherings, using the excuse of my grandmother being hard of hearing to tell it as loudly as possible, pointing out my cousins, shouting, 'You were nearly never born!' and all the while Dor Dor would sit and bask like the cat who ate the canary. But whatever the motivations the story did have a happy ending, the American Cherie had set her heart on was a charming man and a wonderful father, and the alliance between my grandmother and my Aunt Cherie was loving and genuine.

Part 1

***

Sitting waiting at the window of Dor Dor's unit, finally Dad's car would turn down the long street. Dor Dor would fold some money into my hand. 'Don't spend it all at once!' she'd admonish, pressing her palms to my cheeks. She'd stand waving at her door, blowing kisses when we entered the lift, and again when I looked up to her balcony from the street.

'How much did she give you?' Dad would ask me in the car.

I'd look at the coin in my hand. 'Fifty cents?'

'Hah!' he'd laugh. 'Don't spend it all at once!'

The little car would roar up the hill towards the Harbour Bridge and I would sit back, thinking about all the fun things I'd done.

'What on earth does she *do* every day?' he'd say to himself. 'It's a wonder she doesn't *go mad* stuck in that unit!'

***

Although we were close with Dad's side of the family, we only caught up with Mum's relatives once a year, if that. I have a couple of vague memories of Boxing Day picnics: sweltering heatwaves in the bush, a clearing overflowing with a crowd of unfamiliar people, men in stubbies and thongs round a BBQ turning blackened sausages, women hovering over tables of Tupperware and a bunch of rowdy kids playing cricket and other outdoor games I didn't understand.

Mum's sisters all had voices similar to hers but with an even stronger nasal twang and when they were all gathered together, the older ones looking a bit hunched, they were like a flock of galahs, hair teased up like feathers, bobbing their heads together, talking in their nasal drawl. I was used to my mother's distinctive voice, but even for me it was a very strange experience to hear a chorus just like hers.

A few times we went to Mum's sister Cath's house. I can remember being sent out to a swimming pool with a bunch of kids, presumably cousins, who screamed and dive-bombed while I clung to the pebbled edge, my eyes burning with chlorine, trying not to get my ears wet. Cath's husband Doug spoke loudly and told jokes. He talked about computers and was always keen to demonstrate his own for anyone who showed an interest.

It was a huge grey box that whirred and ticked before finally lighting up a grey screen with strange letters, the floppy discs were as big as large paper napkins, pushed into a slot that locked into place with a loud clunk. Dad and the men tried to follow Doug as he explained what the machine did, but it was obvious no-one had a clue. Why type in all these strange letters and words – 'prompts' Doug called them – when you could just write what you needed on a notepad?

'Oh! But you can do all kinds of things on it!' Doug would say in his salesman's voice.

'Like what?' Dad would say.

'You can add up.'

'I can use a calculator for that!'

'You can type up a memo …'

'Then what?'

'You can print it out on this machine over here.'

'I can use a typewriter for that!'

'Ah, but you could print *two copies* if you like!'

'Hah! I could just use carbon paper.'

'Well what about if you wanted *more* than two copies!'

'Why on earth would I want more than two copies?' Dad laughed, a look of smug satisfaction playing on his lips.

Perhaps if Mum's mother Nan had been around we would have been closer to Mum's side of the family, but unfortunately she died when I was too young to remember her. Dad always made a fuss whenever he had to do anything he didn't want to do, and Mum never wanted to impose on him, so we only saw her family very rarely. And although Mum had a lot of acquaintances she didn't really have any close friends; once again it was my father's friends, the Colins and a few well-healed associates, who surrounded me as I grew up.

It turned out Dad was a lot like his mother Dora, with strong opinions about people and who to mix with – a snob as it turned out, which was countered by my mother's gregarious and overly generous nature, another facet of their uniquely dynamic nature.

OWNER OF A LONELY HEART

There was only one kid I liked to hang out with.

'Is Nicole going to be there?' I'd ask when given the unwelcome news I was being dragged along to another party with my parents.

Nicole was the adopted daughter of my parents' friends Shirley and Terry Burton. Shirley had been Dad's first serious girlfriend when he was young. There were pictures of her in an old album, glamorous, soft-focus Hollywood-style portraits.

'She was a great beauty,' my father said, 'and was quite a revered actress in London in her youth. She worked with Vivien Leigh and a number of very famous actors.' In the photos Shirley's platinum-blonde hair rolled down over her shoulders in lustrous waves, her full lips gave just the hint of a smile. 'Wasn't she beautiful?' he said.

Later Mum would whisper to me, 'Dad's lucky he didn't marry Shirley! She sleeps 'til noon every day and never lifts a finger round the house! Poor Terry does everything for Nicole. Your father and Shirley would have been a *disaster!*'

Thankfully Shirley had married an Englishman named Terry instead of my father. He was loud and very opinionated, had big rubbery ears and nose, both crammed with bristles of coarse grey hair and a mouth full of large square teeth. Terry barked orders at Nicole like a sergeant major, which I found a bit scary. I wasn't used to people telling me what to do pretty much at all; our house was so big I could just disappear into it and be left alone for hours.

An only child like me, when Nicole and I got together we'd be playing riotously within minutes, sending shockwaves through the usually quiet house.

'*Children should be seen and not heard!*' Terry would bellow as we came tumbling into the kitchen. 'Isn't that right Barry?' And my father, a little unsettled at Terry's military style method of parenting, would nevertheless agree.

'Oh look at them love!' Shirley would call out. 'Look at all that beautiful *hair!*'

'Yes I'd *kill* for that hair!' Mum would say and Shirley would erupt with a deep, elegant laugh.

Like me, Nicole had dead straight hair right down to her bum, except where mine was blonde hers was jet black, complementing her beautiful brown skin. Nicole was a baby from the Vietnam War. 'I hate my hair!' she would complain. 'When I'm older Dad says I'll be allowed to cut it all off!'

Annoyed by this, Shirley would raise her voice and say with her crisp English accent, 'Now why would you do that, Pet? You're *not* cutting it off and that's *that!*'

Unlike me, Nicole always had lots of rules. She did ballet with proper pointe shoes and had to do hours and hours of piano, running her hands up and down the keys in complicated scales, playing terrifically difficult classical pieces – all of which she hated passionately.

Most of the time Shirley and Terry came to our place, but very occasionally my parents were forced into going to theirs. More often than not a piece of meat would still be defrosting on the kitchen bench when they arrived, a very bad sign that dinner was yet hours and hours away – the guests would be lucky to eat before midnight.

'I wonder if Corney will be there?' Mum would say on the drive over, trying to jolly Dad up a bit. Cornelia Frances, another English actress, was often present at the Burtons' dinner parties. She later hosted *The Weakest Link* and played Morag Bellingham in *Home and Away*, and if Cornelia was there her son, who was a couple of years older than us, would be dragged along also. He usually wore black from head to toe and would barely make eye contact with us, preferring to sit and suffer through the evening with his head in a book.

Shirley and Terry lived on the North Shore, their house was dark and smelled like cats and Nicole always had a terrible, rattling cough. After Nicole's torturous ballet and piano practice Terry would make a big deal about giving us a Golden Rough chocolate from the freezer. Nicole would be thrilled – me, not so much. We'd sit on the lounge room floor gnawing at our frozen ration of chocolate, surrounded by a bunch of dark grey cats with pushed-in faces sitting all over the leather couches. I would wonder again why we were forced to eat chocolate in such a horrible way – surely the best thing about chocolate was how *fast* you could eat it so you could greedily gobble down some more.

Nicole didn't have many good toys. There was only one terrific thing at her house and that was an enormous doll's house down in the basement, kitted out with indescribably wonderful miniature furniture and proper electric lights. Unfortunately, however, we weren't allowed to go anywhere near it as the doll's house belonged to Shirley. I would beg Nicole to take me down to look at it but Nicole would be terrified, her eyes opening as wide as saucers as she begged me to come back upstairs with her. If we were caught down there she'd be 'grounded for sure'. I didn't know what that meant but it sounded awful, like being stoned to death.

The first time I got drunk was with Nicole. We were six years old, at a party where the host was making martinis in a silver cocktail shaker, dancing around to Peter Allen. We made ourselves useful, taking empty glasses back to the kitchen while the guests sang 'When My Baby Goes to Rio' and a small conga line formed with people laughing and kicking their legs out to the side.

'Jeanne!' someone called, and despite her protests the conga line snaked towards Mum and swept her along too, much to the party's delight.

Meanwhile, Nicole and I were amassing towering collections of glasses in the kitchen. We tipped the dregs into a jug, making our own cocktail, and went out to collect more glasses, but this time we didn't wait for them to be finished. Soon the guests stopped saying, 'You've got them well trained Jeanne – hah hah hah!' and started wondering where their glasses had gone.

Terry was the one who found us.

'Shirl! Jean!' he called out like an English detective, 'I think you both should come take a look at this!'

Mum, gratefully released from the conga line, joined a small party of people crowding the doorway to the kitchen. 'Ooah, what is it?' she asked nervously as the guests stepped back from the crime scene to let her in.

'Look what we've found here!' Terry boomed. Nicole and I were rolling around on the linoleum laughing hysterically.

'What are they doing?' Mum asked. And Shirley, in her glamorous, laissez-faire manner laughed and stated the obvious: 'They're drunk love!'

It was with a sudden climactic event that the party came to an end. The host went to do a big finale dance move, leaping off the arm of his sofa, but forgot about the ceiling fan he'd had installed recently. His head was split open like a watermelon and he had to be rushed to hospital. That was good news for Nicole and me, however, as it meant we wouldn't be put in with the pile of jackets on the host's bed when we got tired, attempting to sleep in the makeshift cloakroom until our parents were ready to go home.

Nicole was my best, and only, friend up until I started school. If it hadn't been for Nicole Christmas Day would have been another unbearably grown-up occasion. Held at our Paddington house every year it was an extravagant production buoyed by the financial bonanza of the 80s. Nicole's family was always running hours late and I'd work myself into a lather each time the doorbell went, getting more and more anxious for her to arrive. Mounds of presents would be piled up around the enormous plastic Christmas tree and my room would be overflowing with a plethora of new toys from Santa – a collection of completely impractical things such as a 5-metre-long fishing rod or a professional dart board with heavy, very deadly looking, stainless steel darts.

After lunch, when the guests were so full they could hardly breathe yet dared not refuse my grandmother's pudding, Nicole and I would finally be unleashed on the mound of presents under the tree. As we handed them out a grotesquely enormous heap would pile up on my side of the fireplace next to a paltry few for Nicole, leaving me with a confusing feeling of glutinous guilt that I didn't know how to resolve and which do doubt doomed the friendship from the outset.

LIKE A VIRGIN

The Colins bought a dilapidated terrace on the same street as our house. It was so filthy and run-down I told them it looked like a real live haunted house.

'We should have a Halloween party,' Colin Brees said. 'Isn't it your birthday soon Katie?'

So I head off to school with a bag load of invitations. Mum said it would be mean to invite some kids and not others in case we hurt someone's feelings, so I invited the whole year.

'That's going to be about fifty kids, isn't it?' Dad asks, alarmed.

'Oh, well some of them won't be able to come …' Mum says evasively, and tells me later that under no circumstances is Dad allowed to see the list of girls who are coming. There's nearly eighty on the list – nobody's missing this party for the world. They're even more excited than they were for Jordan Spence's Madonna party, where everyone dressed in lace tops and bubble skirts with big elastic cinch belts and diamanté crucifixes around their necks, hair teased up with tons of hairspray. When they played 'Like a Virgin' everyone mimed the moves from the video clip and sang at the tops of their lungs, even the straightest girls, hanging onto each other and collapsing into each other's arms at the end.

But nobody's talking about that party anymore, they're all talking about mine.

Colin Brees and Mum are making the food. Mum fills up two shopping trolleys, full to overflowing with party pies, chips and soft drink. She takes most of it straight to the Colins' house instead of taking it home, so Dad won't see. 'Jean, what have you bought?!' Colin Johnston says as he helps her with the bulging shopping bags. Colin Brees stacks the food away, eyeing her suspiciously.

'Well, I don't want anyone to be *hungry!*' she says.

On the morning of the party Mum is in a state, our kitchen is snowed under with cupcakes, an enormous pot – the one usually reserved only for boiling the Christmas pudding – is boiling away on the stove. 'What's this for?' Dad asks. Mum keeps boiling the kettle over and over again. She's throwing in dozens of packets of spaghetti and has pulled everything out of the freezer to make room for two steaming buckets of jelly.

'Oh! I should've made this earlier!' Mum says. 'I'm running out of time!'

'What are you doing?' Dad asks. He can't stand chaos. 'Get dressed for heaven's sake! We have to go!'

Mum comes back downstairs dressed as a witch with bright purple eyeshadow, fake pointy nose and shaggy black wig. 'Are you wearing the gorilla suit?' she asks Dad. 'Oh go on! Go on!'

Mum madly drains the spaghetti; it fills up the whole sink. She doesn't have time to use tongs so she pulls on her trusty rubber gloves and yells, 'Quick! Hold this garbage bag open!' She pours oil over the spaghetti then grabs great handfuls of the slippery threads and throws them in, tearing open packets of little plastic party toys to add.

'Ugh! Ugh! Ugh!' Gruff monkey noises come down the hall and Dad appears – enormous ape hands and feet and a huge hairy black gorilla head. 'Ugh! Ugh!' the giant ape says again, beating his rubber hands against his chest. Mum shrieks and jumps with laughter. The ape chases her across the kitchen and tries to kiss her.

'Oh! Stop it! Stop it Barry!' Mum laughs, then the ape turns to me and somewhere inside the little round eyeholes I see my father's eyes staring out. 'Ugh!' it says.

The ape stares at me menacingly. 'Dad? … Dad?!'

It comes towards me and I scream. Dad takes off the mask laughing, 'Phew!' he says, 'It's hot in there, like a sauna! I might loose some weight! Be careful of that witch's nose too Jean, it nearly poked my eye out!'

Up at the Colins' we join them setting up for the party. I've made a cassette of spooky sound effects and I set up my stereo behind a ghost that the Colins have hung up in the hallway, with a fan blowing behind it. Dad has gone to pick up Dor Dor and everyone else is in the kitchen madly icing the cupcakes, sticking lollies on them that look like snakes.

'Whose stupid idea was it to make these?' Colin Brees says, feigning irritation.

'Yours Colin!' Colin Johnston says, but they're both obviously enjoying themselves, eating more snakes than they're putting on the cakes.

When Dor Dor arrives they put her in a big wing chair and throw a sheet over her.

'Have a seat Katie,' they say. 'Try it out …' When I sit Dor Dor wraps her arms around me; it feels like the chair has come to life and we laugh.

'Are you alright under there?' Colin Brees asks Dora. 'Let's take this sheet off until the guests arrive.' Dor Dor sits touching her hair, making sure the sheet hasn't ruined her perm.

'What's that you're doing Colin?' she asks and Colin Johnston tells her they're making punch. A huge clear plastic punch bowl filled with bright pink liquid is lit up from behind. Colin drops in a block of dry ice and smoke starts curling up from the surface. 'See that Katie?' he asks. 'It's frozen carbon dioxide!'

Guests start arriving but they're too scared to enter; the dark old house looks nothing like the usual party houses with balloons tied to the gate. Inside, the Colins are still running around with trays of fairy bread and a platter of orange frankfurters goes past with a very realistic arm coming up out of it, oozing with tomato sauce.

I'm trying to straighten the sheet over Dor Dor while Dad struggles back into his gorilla suit, so Mum puts on an impromptu performance out the front, cackling and rubbing her hands together.

'Aaaaaah ha ha ha!' she calls out, 'Who's brave enough to enter the haunted house?!'

Nobody is. Mum looks too convincing as a witch, even to the girls who've been over to my house to play. The girls cower behind their parents.

'Come on Nicole!' Terry Burton says laughing. 'You know Jeanne? Don't be silly, it's only Katie's mother!'

Mum kneels down next to Nicole to prove that it's her under the costume. Some of the girls start crying. 'Ooah, did I make them cry?' she says, 'Ooah, sorry!' The parents laugh. Finally Mum has to take her pointy nose off and let them see it's only a wig before they believe it's really her. 'But don't tell anyone!' she whispers, putting the nose back on.

A mob of children and parents are gathered at the gate, like the entrance to Willy Wonka's chocolate factory. 'Come on then!' Mum says, trying not to be too scary anymore. 'Shall we all go in together?' All the kids go in, except for Nicole who still won't budge from the gate.

Inside the dark, spooky house the white ghost flutters in the hallway, my sound effects cassette reverberates creaking doors, a howling wind and warbling ghosts.

Suddenly Dad jumps out in his gorilla suit sending up a wail of screams, the kids grab onto Mum for dear life.

'Don't worry! Don't worry!' she says, 'It's just pretend! Quick, let's go up the stairs!' Some of the kids are really freaked out, others are just laughing with the thrill of being scared. Upstairs it looks more like a regular party; a big, albeit derelict, room with a table of food and black balloons – and one large chair covered in a sheet.

'Would you like a seat?' Colin Brees asks Angela Fletcher and everyone looks at her to see what she'll say.

'Is this some kind of trick?' she asks. Angela Fletcher is short and chubby, chews gum and has lots of attitude, like Violet Beauregarde.

Colin looks shocked, 'No! Have a seat. It's really comfortable.' Finally Angela Fletcher agrees, she walks across the room and sits down in the chair, which comes to life under her.

'*Ahhhhhhhhhh!*' she screams leaping out. 'I swallowed my gum!' and everyone laughs.

'Who would like a frankfurter?' Colin Johnston asks.

'Oh heavens, is that *real?*' Zoe Emanuel asks, her eyes going wide at the arm oozing with sauce, 'Maybe I'll just have some chips for now …'

Another group of guests with their parents have arrived at the gate downstairs and Nicole is warning them not to go in; she's heard the screams coming from within. Dad leaps out from the landing again, sending up more screams, and this time it's Angie Fletcher who encourages someone to take a seat.

Mum carries in two enormous garbage bags – it's time for the party games! The girls assemble into two lines to try their luck.

'Are you brave enough?' Mum calls out over the kids, 'One bag is full of *slime*! The other is full of *worms*!'

The only problem is that Mum was in such a rush the spaghetti worms are still scorching hot and the jelly slime has partly frozen. The kids that put their arms down into the bags scream in real pain. They can only keep their arms in the bags for a few seconds, making the search for a prize a real test of endurance and courage.

'I got one! *I got one!*' screams one girl victoriously, wrenching her slime-coated arm out of the bag and holding up a plastic toy gripped in fingers purple with cold.

The cake comes out – a giant spider with silver sparklers – and everyone sings Happy Birthday loudly. The room is packed with kids spinning around in a sugar-fuelled frenzy, sticky with jelly and icing, screaming and slipping on cold spaghetti. Some kids cry and nobody wants to leave when their parents come to collect them, not even Nicole, who is still standing by the gate listening to the terrifying noises coming from inside the haunted house.

LITTLE LIES

Since Dad decided he wants to buy a beach house every weekend is taken up driving for miles up and down the coast. This goes on for months; I feel like I spend all my spare time trapped in the back seat of the car. I take a pillow and my Speak & Spell and sometimes I build a labyrinth out of Lego and catch a big brown, furry caterpillar to put inside it.

Mum tells Dad to head north over the Harbour Bridge this time. She's in the front beside him, with the newspaper propped up on the dashboard, looking up the houses that Dad has circled in pen. She has several fingers wedged into the pages of the street directory as she goes back and forth trying to navigate us up and down the coastline.

Dad's in a good mood. He rolls the window down and turns the radio up loud; *The Goon Show* is coming on soon. 'Ooah Bah, poor Katie's getting blown away back there! Can't you put your window up?' He grumbles but concedes, putting it up halfway. I huddle in behind Mum's seat to watch the progress of my caterpillar. An hour later we're winding up into hills to look at the first house and Dad's already saying 'No, no, no! This is too far away from the beach!' long before we get there.

'But it might have a good view Dahling?' Mum says.

'I don't care about the *view* Jean!' Dad says. 'I want to *hear* the ocean!'

'Well we're here now, we might as well take a look,' Mum says. The road turns into a dirt driveway and Dad starts to get nervous about the car. 'Maybe we should turn around,' he says. But we can't turn around, firstly because Dad can't reverse a car to save himself and secondly because the owners of the house have seen us.

I instantly fall in love with the house; it has an outdoor shower with a coil of copper piping that heats water over a fire, a vegetable garden and rainwater tank. 'Oh isn't it wonderful!' Mum keeps saying as the owner shows them the composting toilet and patchwork interior constructed from salvaged materials.

'Please can we buy it Dad?' I ask. He laughs nervously and tousles my hair, 'Off you go and play!'

I head towards a kid with long, dirty blonde hair swinging an enormous machete around, chopping chunks out of a tree trunk.

'Don't get lost Katie!' Mum calls out after me.

'She won't get lost Jean!' Dad says, then adds 'But stay where we can see you!'

'And watch out for *snakes!*' Mum shouts.

'Wanna play fire engines with me?'

The kid runs around making a siren sound then stops and unzips, sending a large arc of water streaming out into the bushes. My parents are in the car with the engine running calling me to get in. I tell them about the girl who magically made a stream of water come out of her pants. My parents start laughing.

'What?' I ask them. 'What's so funny?'

'That was a *boy!*' Dad says.

'What? No ...'

'Of course it was a boy, how do you think the water came out?'

I'm confused. They keep laughing and it's obvious neither of them is going to give me a straight answer, so I change the subject, 'Are we going to buy the house?'

'No! God no!' they both say, 'Not on your life!'

'Oh please can't we buy it!'

'And take lukewarm showers outside in the bush?!' Dad shudders and Mum screams, 'Yikes! Imagine the *spiders!*'

Dad pulls up out the front of a takeaway shop. 'Just get some fish and chips or something, Jean,' he says, but nothing is ever easy or straightforward when Mum's involved.

'I thought that was you Jeanne!' the owner says and a crowd of locals start lining up to get autographs.

'Come on Jean ...' Dad's grumbling, 'the fish and chips will be cold.' Finally, he toots the horn. The owner is kissing her on both cheeks, following her out to the car. Dad's forced into putting on a smile as she gets in and the owner leans into the car to keep talking. Dad has his hand on the gearstick; he could put it in drive if the man would just take his head out of the car.

'Wait! Wait Jeanne!' he's saying, as his wife brings over a styrofoam plate. 'These are on the house, they're local Sydney rocks!' They stand waving as the car roars off shouting, 'We love you Jeanneeee!'

'Can I try one?' I ask when we're on the freeway again.

'Of course!' Mum says, just as Dad says, 'No! Let your mother eat her lunch.'

'Of course she can try one!' Mum says. She seems quite excited by the idea.

'She won't like it,' Dad says.

'Yes she will,' Mum says. 'She might. She likes smoked salmon and capers, she has very sophisticated taste!'

I like the sound of having 'sophisticated taste'. Mum squeezes lemon onto two of the oysters, gives me one and picks up the other. 'Now, you just tip your head back and let it slide in, like this!'

My oyster sits plump in its silvery shell reminding me a bit of the creature dissected in *Alien*. I hope it doesn't have acid for blood. 'Do I chew it?' I ask.

'No! You just swallow it,' Dad says. 'Let it slither down your throat, like phlegm!'

'Oh stop it Barry! That's awful!' Mum laughs. 'Don't listen to him. Yes, you can chew it if you want to.' Dad's glancing back at me now in the rear-vision mirror, curious.

'Go on!' Mum says. 'Throw your head back, it tastes like the ocean!'

The oyster is cold and slimy, it tastes like water from a rock pool. I chew it once and the creamy insides split open. The taste is too strong and I grimace and swallow it.

'Did you like it?' Mum asks.

I swish my tongue around the inside of my mouth, 'I don't know … kind of.'

Dad laughs. 'It's an acquired taste,' he says.

Fifteen minutes later we're driving down a particularly curvy stretch of road that leads to a secluded little beach.

'I think I'm going to be sick,' I say.

'Ooah!' Mum says 'Really? Quick! Put the windows down!' The wind blasts into the back like a tornado and my hair whips against my face.

'I told you not to give her that oyster!' Dad says.

'Pull over Bah! Pull over!' Mum holds out a plastic bag, which rustles noisily in front of me. 'Pull over Barry! She does look green!'

'I can't pull over now!' Dad says. 'We're almost there!'

'You have to pull over!' Mum's saying.

'There's nowhere to pull over Jean! It's an unbroken white line!'

'There! There! Pull over in that ditch!'

Part I

'What? I can't pull over there! We'd go over the edge of a cliff! Thank God *you're* not driving! Remind me never to let you drive …'

They're still shouting at each other as I throw up into the bag.

***

'It's perfect Barry, buy it,' Mum says after the real estate agent leaves.

'There's a lot to think about …' Dad starts. He gazes wistfully at the old cottage. A wattlebird jumps through the branches of a paperbark tree; it calls, a loud, raucous noise and once it stops there's only the sound of the ocean again, a muted swirling noise like a shell against your ear. 'It's only fibro of course,' Dad says, 'but we only want a little place, nothing flash … I want it to look like one of those Balinese houses. I could put shutters around the verandah that prop open …'

Mum, who has a nose for property, like her mother, cuts to the chase. 'It's a steal,' she says, 'we'd be fools not to buy it!'

'Yes, but I want to *think* about it Jean, let's not *rush* into anything.'

I run ahead of my parents down a yellow dirt track that leads to the beach, my sneakers slip over big eroded cracks as the path leads through the bush, finally disintegrating into sand. I run up the soft embankment and see the ocean, wild and tumultuous, like an untamed creature. The water is swelling into enormous troughs that roll up and over, breaking into a spectacular curl that comes down with the force of cannons being set off down the beach. The ground shudders and froth explodes up into the sky.

Brown, slimy ropes of seaweed have been tossed up on the high tide mark and hundreds of the long, twisted plants lie scattered along the shore in a line that runs the crescent of the beach, like the ring left in a bath after the water is let out. I pull off my shoes and run across the hot sand, which squeaks loudly with each stride. The wind is so heavy with salt spray it feels like rain. The sand becomes coarser and wet, my feet sinking down deliciously into cold pebbles.

The swell of the last wave rides up the bank swiftly and ice-cold water surges over my feet, suddenly swirling up and soaking the legs of my jeans. I squeal and run back up the beach, the noise insignificant beside the roar of the ocean.

My parents are walking along the beach further up. Mum waves to me when she sees me looking, signalling with both arms like a technician directing a plane. I run up to them. 'Be careful of the water!' Mum is saying.

'Oh leave the child alone Jean! She knows to be careful, don't you Katie?'

'There's a strong rip!' Mum continues.

'Yes, yes Jean, she knows! What's the water like?' Dad asks.

'I bet it's freeeeezing!' Mum says. 'Look, it goes straight out to the ocean! That water would be full of *sharks!*' She shudders.

***

Back at Paddington, Dad comes up to eat dinner excited to tell us that one of his clients also has a house at Pearl Beach. 'Oh how wonderful!' Mum says. If it was up to her she'd have made an offer on the house already, but she's waiting for Dad to come around in his own time.

'She knows the house we're looking at,' he says. 'Mike Willesee has a house across the road. She says it will be a great investment.'

'Of course it will!' Mum says.

'Yes, and she said that beach is very dangerous, that people get taken out to sea, last year someone had to be rescued by helicopter! So you be very careful Katie.'

'Yes! Yes! I told you!' Mum says.

'Shhh Jean, stop interrupting! She said you have to go swimming down the other end of the beach, where it's calm. There's a tidal pool down that end.'

'Oh I hate those pools,' Mum says. 'Full of *sea lice!*' She screws up her face.

'Stop being so *dramatic* Jean!' Dad says. He tells us that his client has a son, 'He's about your age Katie!'

'Oooooh! I hope he's good looking!' Mum says making me shrink with embarrassment.

'They go up nearly every weekend,' Dad says, 'so you'll have someone to play with!'

I can feel my cheeks flushing.

'So are we buying it?' Mum asks, 'I think we should! We've been looking for *months* Barry.'

'Oh I know, I know!' he says, annoyed. He takes a large mouthful of cauliflower cheese then says finally, 'I'll call the real estate agent in the morning.'

'Why don't you just ring them *now!*' Mum says.

'They won't be open now!'

'But you could leave a message! Someone else might make an offer! What if *I* phone them and leave a message saying I'm your secretary and can they please call first thing in the morning?'

'Don't be ridiculous!' Dad says laughing with the absurdity of Mum's suggestion, '*You* ring? They'd know your voice!'

'No they won't! I'll whisper!' Mum makes a very sensible looking face and puts on a phoney voice, which is impossibly low and husky, saying 'Hello. This is Barry Little's secretary speaking …'

Dad laughs. 'You sound like The Freak in *Prisoner! I'll* call them in the morning, and that's that!'

'Goodie!' Mum says. 'How exciting!'

'Alright Jean, now settle down and eat some dinner,' Dad says.

LOVE IS A STRANGER

Dad is digging a hole in the yard at Pearl Beach, the dirt is curiously fine and grey, nothing like Paddington's soil. I watch my father with interest as he pokes the tip of the spade into the ground and puts his weight onto it. It slides easily into the ground; he pulls the handle, tearing grass and roots as a large wedge of earth is lifted. He dumps each load of soil onto a heaped pile beside the hole, where an earthworm wriggles furiously.

I've never seen my father in the garden, yet since they bought the house at Pearl Beach he's planted several hibiscus and this morning stopped to buy a Tahitian lime. He wedged it in the front passenger seat of his small sports car, between Mum's legs, and for the rest of the drive she sat holding the trunk at arm's length to keep the thorny branches from spiking her. Still, it was better than the hibiscus, whose enormous flowers were crawling with ants.

Mum struggles up the side of the house, carrying a gigantic sack of potting mix awkwardly on her back. 'Jean! What are you doing? I told you to leave that in the car!' But Mum can never wait; Dad should know that by now, it's not in her nature. He instructs Mum to turn on the hose for him and the water blasts out. Dad screams, 'Not that much!'

After the plant is in Dad stands back to admire his handiwork and I picture the little tree growing up into a great big one, like the massive old grapefruit further up the yard, its enormous branches weighed down with fruit the size of soccer balls. Dad's not interested in picking the fruit though, he's only glad of the thick foliage blocking the neighbour's yard and he's not interested in what's beyond. Mum and I, however, have been keen to explore every corner.

A rambling choko vine covers the fence; they look like spiky green pears. Mum steams some for me and serves them with butter and seasoning – they're delicious! I ask for seconds, which makes Dad laugh; he doesn't like them. We serve some when the Colins come round for dinner at Paddington and they laugh but have mixed reactions eating them. They all start talking about something called the depression. 'A time when people were very, very poor,' Mum says. 'You don't know what that's like Katie, we're all very lucky now you know.'

Mum and I push our way through the undergrowth of scrubby tea-trees as the yard morphs into bush. She is snapping off some of the thin, brittle branches, when a young girl, about my age, with fair blonde hair pops up over the fence. A smaller brown boy climbs up to look over beside her.

'You shouldn't be under there,' the girl says. 'My father says those trees have ticks!'

Ticks are tiny insects that drop out of the branches and burrow into your head, the girl says, and I run my fingers over my scalp.

'You should be wearing hats!' the girl says. A woman's voice calls out in a thick, rasping language. 'We have to go, it's dinner!' she says, and as suddenly as they appeared the two children are gone, followed by the sharp slamming of a wire door.

I wonder who eats dinner at this time in the afternoon; it's not even dark yet.

Colin and Colin build a barbecue up the back of the yard out of old bricks; I love watching them build something new out of something old. I collect twigs and Colin Brees arranges them under the cast-iron grill, he adds some balled up pieces of newspaper and lights them with a match. It catches immediately and arcs of orange flame eat into the paper, briefly illuminating the type before it turns black and the fire catches onto the kindling.

They leave me to watch the fire while they go inside and I feel very responsible, the guardian in charge of a dragon, licking up trying to escape through the iron bars of the grill, tame for now inside its tower of old grey bricks. The barbecue stands beside an overgrown bramble of lantana, 'egg and bacon' Mum called it, saying she was going to buy a saw and cut it out.

'You'll do no such thing!' Dad said, overhearing her. 'You're not chopping anything out!'

'But it's a dreadful *weed* Barry!' Mum said, and left it at that, and I knew she was already secretly plotting to do it one day when he was dozing on the lounge.

Dad has fun decorating their tropical hideaway. Hawaiian prints of ladies in colourful sarongs adorn the walls, a papier-mâché toucan hangs in the verandah and a giant bamboo banana palm stands beside the dining table. 'Be careful!' Mum says to guests when they go to sit down. 'It's so spiky I'm terrified someone will poke their eye out!'

Dad tries a new recipe from a South American cookbook – bananas wrapped in ham in white sauce baked in the oven – which is surprisingly delicious. Mum tries her hand at making mango ice cream and watermelon sorbet, taking tins out of the freezer every hour to beat them over and over.

***

One afternoon Dad's client pops around with her son Josh.

'Oh Katie's been *dying* to meet you! Haven't you Katie?' Mum says. I'm mortally embarrassed.

'Shush Jean,' Dad says. 'Why don't you go and put the coffee on?'

'Teach Katie to play Spite and Malice,' Josh's mother says. She rummages around in her handbag and pulls out a large stack of playing cards.

'Have you ever played Patience?' Josh asks me.

I shake my head, 'But I know how to play Gin Rummy.' The grown-ups laugh at this. Dad suggests I sit with Josh on the verandah while they have coffee in the lounge room.

We sit opposite each other at a little round table and Josh shuffles the cards and deals them into piles. Spite and Malice is much more complicated than the card game my grandmother has taught me. There are several piles of cards on the table and Josh is constantly telling me what to do, pointing at cards in front of me and pulling cards out of my hand. I have to concentrate really hard and even then I keep making mistakes. Sometimes too, he doesn't tell me what I should be doing and takes great enjoyment when I don't do something important. I get upset and pout.

'Awwwww …' he says, 'sooky wooky!' He pretends to trace tear marks down his cheeks and looks right at me as he does it too, hoping I'll start to cry or storm off or something. Seething with anger I narrow my eyes, vowing to concentrate harder so I can beat him.

Dad walks by, sees my scowl and says, 'Remind me to give you *Gone With The Wind* to read. I should have called you Scarlett!' and the next weekend when the weather is cold and rainy he knocks on my bedroom door with the big, heavy book. 'Now look after it,' he says, 'You might still be too young to read it.' I don't want to be young so I delve into the book, determined to read it if only to prove a point.

I read *Gone With The Wind* from cover to cover and when I'm finished I open it up and read the start all over again. I *love* Scarlett O'Hara. I want to be just like her; fiery and determined with cunning green eyes!

The next weekend the phone rings. It hardly ever rings at Pearl Beach, my parents are cautious about giving out the number. I'm surprised when I hear my name called. The phone is mounted to the wall in the kitchen and Dad's left the phone lying horizontally across the top for me. I put it to my ear and turn my back to my father who's buttering toast.

'Hello?' I say into the receiver.

'Hi. It's Josh. I was wondering if you want to come for a bike ride.'

I wind my free hand round and round, looping the telephone's coiled plastic cord up my arm. The blood in my hand pools and when it starts to feel a bit numb and tingly I unwind it, leaving coil marks circling up the white flesh.

'Okay, sure,' I say.

I follow the directions Josh has given me to get to his house, cycling up a hill to the point. I'm nearly at the top when a magpie swoops me. I hear its beak snap closed just as I duck my head. 'Ow!' I yell, and pedal harder. By the time I reach the house I'm breathless with exertion. Josh is standing in his driveway beside his bike, laughing.

'They won't swoop you if they think you're looking at them,' he says. 'You put a pair of sunglasses on backwards and then they won't attack.'

I wonder why I agreed to go for a bike ride with this know-it-all; I'm sure he knew the bird was there and was waiting to watch me get attacked.

'Well I don't have sunglasses,' I say incensed.

He picks up a long stick and gets on his bike. 'You ride first and I'll protect you,' he says to mollify me, but I don't want to be protected.

I pick up my own long stick. 'After you,' I say.

'Suit yourself then,' he says and pushes off down the hill waving the stick above his head.

We chuck the sticks once we're past the broody magpie and I follow him along a road that leads back into the bush. I pedal up beside him. 'Where are we going?' I call out.

'The arboretum!' he says, 'It's like Noah's ark for plants ... C'mon!'

He pedals harder and gets back in the lead again. The houses grow fewer and fewer and the road becomes gravelly and dotted with potholes. We ride past a sign showing a bicycle with a cross through it, a dirt track leads into the arboretum winding around giant trees through clumps of tangled thicket. Birds call loudly from the treetops, creatures scuttle away through the undergrowth and a chorus of frogs gets louder the deeper we ride into the reserve.

The track forks and Josh turns left in the direction of an old sign pointing to 'Bracken Swamp'. The frog chorus amps in volume and the dirt track becomes wet and muddy, a black slash of mud spatters up the back of my shirt. The undergrowth grows thicker, giant ferns line the sides of the track. Josh rides past a frond that slaps back into me, his laughter grating my nerves, then suddenly the track opens to reveal a metal walkway and the wheels make a ticking noise as we pedal easily along it. My legs feel warm and rubbery.

About halfway along is a viewing platform. Josh stops, his face blotched with colour, his dark brown hair clumped with sweat. Tiny black spots of mud are flecked across his face and when he pulls his forearm across his brow a few of them smear into dark lines that look like claw marks. I laugh and he finds this amusing, his mouth twists into a smile. He leans back confidently against the railing. 'Good ride,' he says, 'I didn't think you'd be able to keep up.'

'Hah!' I say. 'What's that supposed to mean?'

I lean over the railing and look down into the swampy water below. Several fat black tadpoles are wriggling in the shallow water, their shiny bodies bulging from the surface.

'Well ...' he says, 'most girls can't.' He has that smirky smile on his face.

'Was that supposed to be a compliment or an insult?' I say, then to my surprise he reaches out and touches my hair. I flinch.

'Sorry,' he says. 'There's something in your hair.' He pulls and gingerly I turn my head a bit for him while he untangles a piece of bracken. 'There,' he says, 'Better now.' He pats my head awkwardly and tucks a piece of hair back; my ear starts burning where he's touched it. We ride on a bit further, dump our bikes on the ground next to a fence with a large metal sign that reads: 'PRIVATE PROPERTY – KEEP OUT'.

Josh climbs through the wires first and I follow, entering into a very different landscape, a pine plantation with rows and rows of enormous trees, trunks several feet wide, bark rough and scaly, oozing in places with large globs of glistening red sap. Giant branches stretch out from the trunks above our heads, the trunks disappearing into a canopy, thick with needles. Below this ceiling the light is dim and the forest floor is springy, mulched so thickly with fallen brown needles that it feels like I'm walking on marshmallows.

A fallen branch leans up against one of the trunks. We drag over a couple more and make the skeleton of a teepee, positioning smaller branches of green needles over it to fill in the walls. The largest branch has a few stumpy arms that make a ladder to climb up into the arms of the tree but it's nicer on the forest floor, soft and cosy like a tent. I lie back, interlacing my hands behind my head. Josh is still carrying branches over to add to the cubbyhouse. 'Hey, no slacking on the job!' he calls out. I laugh. I like this feeling of being deep in the wilderness, cocooned in nature. I close my eyes and breathe in the sharp, piney smell, feel my heart singing in harmony with the insects and creatures, feathered and furred, all around me.

Josh plonks himself down. 'We should have brought the playing cards,' he says.

'And something to eat!' I add.

'Hey yeah,' he says, 'you're right, I'm starving. I wonder how long we've been here for …'

There's no way of knowing because the light never changes. Suddenly I feel anxious. 'We'd better go,' I say, 'Mum and Dad will wonder where I am.'

'They know you're with me,' Josh says. 'I'll keep you safe.'

'I think I can keep myself safe actually!' I say sitting up and dusting the pine needles off my clothing.

'Oh yeah?' he says. I glance up to find him looking at me with an air of patronising superiority. I go back to plucking the pine needles off my clothes.

'What if I tried to grab you?' he says after a time. He props himself up on his elbows.

'Grab me?' I laugh. 'I could outrun you easily!' The challenge is there, hanging in the air as we size each other up.

Suddenly he launches and I spring to my feet and take flight. I run back the way we came, the pine needles slipping beneath my feet, knowing he's close behind. I take a quick look back over my shoulder and scream and laugh when I see how close he is. He throws himself forward to grab my ankle but he only gets close enough to clutch at my shoe, which I wrench free easily. He yelps and when I stop and turn he's hunched over holding his wrist.

'Are you alright?' I say running back to help him, but it's a trick. As soon as I'm close enough he pounces. He tackles me to the ground and pushes my head onto the pine needle floor. I scream in pain as he sinks his knee into my back.

'I got you!' he says. '*I got you!*'

'I can't breathe!' I yell. He holds me for a few more painful seconds before releasing me, but not before he digs his knee into my back one last time.

I'm furious. 'That wasn't fair!' I shout.

'Oh what? And you think someone who wanted to kidnap you wouldn't play dirty?' he shouts back. 'You're easy prey!'

I turn and start walking for the fence, tears are welling in my eyes and I don't want to let him see them. I'm hungry and tired and my back feels bruised where his knee was. I want to go home. My legs are shaking. He runs up to me and tries to take my hand.

'Don't *touch* me!' I shout.

'Fine! Fine!' he says and I can hear him following me, then he says finally, 'Look I'm *sorry* alright? I'm sorry!' I stop and turn to look at him and for once he's not wearing that self-satisfied smirk, he genuinely looks sorry. 'Apology accepted?' he says, and puts out a hand. I look at it for a moment then look back at his face.

'Really …' he says, 'I'm sorry, I didn't mean to hurt you.'

I take his hand, lock my foot behind his ankle and push him back hard onto his arse. 'Now we're even!' I say triumphantly. His face turns dark like a storm cloud, he doesn't like being laughed at.

'Awwwww … sooky wooky!' I say, copying his annoying taunt.

His mouth twists into a sneer and I bolt because this time if he catches me I don't know what will happen. I run to the fence, my heart beating like a trapped bird, scramble through the wires and grab my bike, start pedalling – *hard*.

My tyres slide on the metal boardwalk until finally they get traction, I surge forward and my bike leaps off onto the wet track. I focus hard to steer clear of the puddles that threaten to bog my tyres. There's a fork in the track which looks vaguely familiar, I take the turn but the path looks different than I remember. I steel glimpses behind me, sure I can hear a bike behind me but there's none, and I have to stay focused, looking ahead for tree roots and boulders that might send me flying. It feels like I've been on the track too long, and it's only when I'm on the verge of panic that a final twist signals the end of the track and I'm suddenly catapulted out onto the gravelly road. Within minutes

I'm out of the bush and pedalling the beachside roads again where the sky is blue and people are out walking with dogs and children.

My hands are trembling when I get off my bike at my house. I can hear laughter and talking coming from within my parents' beach house and when I take off my shoes and open the back door the smell of coffee and food and sandalwood incense envelops me. The table of guests turn to look, 'Katie!' Mum says jumping up out of her seat. 'You must be *starving*! Come and sit down!' And for once I'm grateful when she tells me to take her seat and rushes to the kitchen to fetch the plate of food she's kept warm in the oven. Maria Venuti is at the table. 'Tell us what you've been up to Darling!' she says. 'Look at those pink cheeks!'

The phone rings in the kitchen while I'm bolting down the meal and Mum, who's closest, picks it up. 'It's Josh for you Katie!' she calls out.

'Ooooooah! Is that *a boy* Darling!' Maria shrieks and thankfully my mouth is full of food so I can't answer. I just kind of shrug and keep chewing and Dad says, 'I think he likes you Katie!'

I swallow hard and get up to go to the phone.

'Who's Josh, Barry? Tell us!' I hear a guest ask, and there's laughter as I take the phone and stretch the cord as far as it will go, wishing I could go somewhere they weren't all watching me.

'Hello?' I say.

'Hi,' he says. 'I just wanted to make sure you got home alright. I didn't know where you went to … I was worried.'

Mum's at the sink rinsing some plates a few feet away. I look down at my feet and mumble, 'Yeah, uh-huh.'

'Your parents are there?' he asks.

'Uh-huh,' I say again.

'Well, anyway, I had fun today before things, kind of, got a bit … well, you know …' he says.

'Yep,' I say, then after a pause, 'Me too.'

'Hey, you wanna meet tomorrow?' he says.

I don't know if I want to meet him so I tell him I'm not sure what time we're leaving to drive back to Sydney.

'Oh we're not leaving 'til late in the afternoon!' Mum says loudly. I turn to stare at her incredulously as Josh cheerily says, 'Great I'll meet you at the swings at ten!' before he hangs up.

'Mum!' I say, flabbergasted and when I turn around Maria calls out 'Oh! Tell us, are you meeting him?' and one of the other guests makes a whooping noise.

'Oh, sorry,' Mum says pushing a huge bowl of mango ice cream towards me, 'Wasn't I supposed to say that?'

THE KILLING MOON

The next morning I ride my bike down to the swings. Josh is waiting, sitting on one of the swings, his bike propped against the metal struts.

'Hi,' he says as I pull up. He's wearing a dark green shirt and has a pair of Ray-Ban sunglasses up on his head. 'For the magpies,' he says, pointing at them, and I can't help but laugh. I guess he does look at bit like Tom Cruise in *Top Gear*. I'm sure some of the girls at school would think he's good looking. I sit on the other swing, my sneakers sliding over the dirt while we talk.

'You want me to teach you how to shake hands with someone?' he says. I give him a look.

'No, really,' he says, 'my dad taught me this. When you shake someone's hand you should always have your hand on top, it's like a subliminal message saying you're the boss! C'mon I'll try it with you.' I look at him, nervous that this might be some kind of trick to get revenge for yesterday, but there are people about, a lady with her dog is close enough to hear me scream.

'Okay,' I say.

For the next few minutes we practise shaking hands so Josh can demonstrate his concept of subliminal superiority. 'You know what my dad said too?' he says. 'He said if you want to kill someone in a fight all you have to do is punch them once really hard in the windpipe. They'll suffocate on their own blood!'

'Oh,' I say.

'Yeah,' he says. 'It's important to know.'

I sit on one of the swings again and start turning. The heavy chain pulls together almost magnetically as I complete the first turn, I turn a couple more times then lift my feet up and spin as the chains unwind, finally jerking me back as the chains come apart. I start turning again and then Josh says suddenly 'Here, let me help you!' He grabs the swing and twists it round and round and I laugh saying 'Stop! Stop!' and then hang on because when he lets go the force is much greater than last time, I spin back and the swing does its best to almost throw me at the end and I feel dizzy and so I laugh and hang on, but let my head dangle over down to the ground, my hair brushing the dirt.

When I stop laughing I sit back up. Josh has taken the other swing and before I know what's happening he's launched himself towards me to kiss me on the mouth. He pushes his tongue inside and moves his head from side to side a bit.

'So this is what a kiss feels like!' I think to myself. It's not very pleasant but I like the idea that I'm actually kissing someone, so I kind of turn my head a bit too and open my mouth a bit more just to see what it's like. Josh's tongue darts around, slimy like a fish, and he opens his mouth more too, and then it all gets a bit much and I feel like I'm kind of being swallowed alive and so I pull away a bit, and he does too, and I wipe my mouth with the back of my hand.

'Want to get an ice cream?' he says then, and I say, 'Sure.'

I get on my bike and ride behind him down to the shop thinking about the kiss, thrilled about this big new secret I've got but also feeling a bit weird at the same time, like there's something not quite right.

STREETS OF YOUR TOWN

The next weekend I ride past Josh's house and am both relieved and disappointed to find it closed up. I ride my bike home again, not sure what to do with myself, loud red wattlebirds like truncated roosters calling from the trees.

'You weren't gone long,' Dad says as I come in the back door. I plonk myself down in front of the TV, a map of Russia and the USA is on the screen, with nuclear symbols popping up on them like radioactive chicken pox.

'Well, you're not sitting about watching television!' Dad says, switching it off.

'Ugh,' I sigh, 'but there's nothing to *do*.'

'Rubbish!' he says. 'It's a beautiful day! Go to the beach!'

I grab one of Mum's hats and cut through Mike Willesee's house, my thongs slapping down the side of the empty house. It's always empty so everyone uses it as a shortcut to the beach. Mum's said she'll meet me down at the pool in an hour. The grassy dune in front of the Willesee house gives way to sand, the sun already surprisingly hot, cicadas rhythmically grinding with the heat. I abandon my thongs beside a tussock of grass and walk to the water's edge, enjoying the cold, foamy ocean as it runs up over my feet.

The next enormous wave is gathering, slurping the water back to expose a final steep few metres before suddenly the wall of water curls and slams back down. The ground shudders and a load of salt spray is hurled into the air. I start walking towards the calm end where the pool is, the tide is coming in and waves rolling in from the point explode against the end of the pool.

The beach is almost empty apart from a few people sitting on towels. As I walk past them I feel their gaze on me and wish I had sunglasses so I could look at them without them seeing my eyes. I wonder if they see me as an adult or a child. I lift my chin and look out to the ocean, keep walking to the calm end. When I turn my gaze back to the beach I spot two boys. One of them is looking in my direction. He ruffles his hand through his hair then goes back to talking to the other boy. Was he looking at me, or out to the water?

A gust of wind takes my hat off; the water takes it and starts sucking it away. I run after it, finally catching it, and flick it a couple of times before putting it on my head; the cold water is pleasant dripping down my back. When I start walking again the boys are looking but they turn away quickly and laugh.

I walk past, not daring to look. I can feel their eyes on my legs, my bum, my back. I wonder if they noticed how flat-chested I am, like my mother. Some of the girls at school are getting bras already; I'll never get one at the rate I'm going.

There are people swimming in the pool. I recognise the silvery blonde hair of the girl from the house next to ours. Her little brother has blow-up floaties on his arms. The pool is a long rectangle of concrete, a silver handrail disappears down into the dark water. I take the first step and a torrent of rasping chatter erupts behind me.

'Mum said to hold on. She said it's very slippery,' the girl with the silvery hair smiles. 'I'm Eve, this is my brother Paul,' she says, before disappearing underwater, swimming away like a mermaid.

I take the handrail and Eve's mother, who is sitting on a silver bench, smiles and nods.

I take the next step down, sucking in my breath as the water reaches my stomach. The walls of the pool are dark green and soft, like velvet. The water is full of tiny green specs, I can hardly see my feet already, and when I step down the last step I can feel sand on the bottom of the pool.

Eve pops up beside me. 'You want to come sit on the edge?' she asks.

'Sure,' I say. I follow her out of the pool past her mother, who starts up another rapid exchange of language. 'Mum doesn't like me sitting on the edge, she thinks it's dangerous. Don't worry Mumma, alright?' Eve's little brother calls something in a whiny voice and we run off to the deep end before he can follow. At the deep end Eve stops and looks out to the ocean, then scoots down onto the edge and crawls on her hands and knees along the edge.

'C'mon!' she says to me and I slide myself down like she did.

The edge of the pool is about a foot wide, covered in the thick green weed that feels slippery at first but is squishy enough that if I spread my fingers out I can kind of hold on. I half-crawl, half-slide my way along the ledge to Eve, who sits with her legs dangling in the pool.

'C'mon!' she says again. 'Hurry!'

She glances out to the ocean and when I follow her gaze I see a large set of waves off the point. Adrenaline trickles through me. I try to hurry but it's not so easy and I'm scared if I rush I'll slip off. On my right the pool drops down to the natural rock that runs out to the point. It's only a little drop but with the waves coming in it would be disastrous …

'C'mon! C'mon!' Eve says stretching her hand to me. I reach out my hand and she pulls me to sit beside her just as the first wave breaks on the point. A churning tumble of white foam is charging towards us across the rock ledge, getting closer and closer. My body stiffens and a wall of foamy water slams into my back. With a scream, I'm lifted off the edge and thrown into the pool! Millions of tiny bubbles effervesce around me as I swim up and when I break the surface Eve's smile is as bright as mine, water running from her silvery hair as she blinks away the sea water and turns to swim back to the wall for the next wave.

More kids arrive at the pool; soon there are half a dozen sitting along the edge. Eve's mother waddles over with Paul, blue and shivering, wrapped in a towel. It's time to go she's saying, tapping the watch on her wrist and pointing up to the sun. The two boys from the beach walk past and one of the kids on the ledge calls out to them.

'Come and sit with us!' the kid says, but the bigger boys shake their heads – they're too old for that, they've been swimming already at the beach. And then it's my mother I see walking across the sand to the pool. She's wearing a hot pink pantsuit and a pink straw hat the size of a satellite dish.

'You're Jeanne Little!' the boy sitting beside me says.

'Ooooh yes! How do you know that?' Mum says laughing. 'You're too young to watch daytime television! Aren't you all brave sitting out there on that edge! Aren't you all terrified?'

And then a big wave starts rolling in and Mum screams 'Oooah! Oooah! Oooah!' and the kids sitting beside me laugh thinking this is hilarious. The wave throws us into the water and when I bob up to the surface Mum is standing at the edge of the pool looking scared. 'I thought you'd all drowned!' she says putting her hand to her throat, and all the kids laugh again.

'It's okay Mum,' I say, 'we're just having fun!'

***

I can't wait to go back to the tidal pool, but when I ride my bike down the next morning the water is flat and the pool is empty. The beach is littered with hundreds of strange brown curls that look like seaweed and when I pick one up a lady who's out walking her dog stops to talk to me.

'You know what that is?' she asks. 'It's a shark egg!'

I must look like I don't believe her but she insists, showing me the opening at the end and the hollow inside.

I keep walking up the beach thinking about the hundreds of baby sharks that must be in the ocean now, swimming around out of sight. The two boys from the day before are sitting on towels further up. 'Hey,' one calls out as I get closer. 'Hey!' and when I walk over he says, 'Didn't we see you yesterday? Isn't your mum Jeanne Little?'

'Ah-huh,' I say.

'Ha! I told you so!' he says to his friend.

The boy who's called me over is stockier, and now the tall boy talks, he's tanned with a few angry looking blemishes on his cheeks. 'I'm Don,' he says, 'and this is my brother Martin. What's your name?'

'Katie,' I say. I only give each of them a cursory glance; I don't want them to think I'm checking them out.

'How old are you?' Don asks.

'Guess,' I say, and they laugh. They look at me critically and then Martin whispers something to Don.

'Fourteen?' he says and I nod, even though I'm two years short of that.

'So what are you doing?' I realise he's talking about the shark eggs I've been collecting to take home. 'No way!' Don says when I tell him what they are and Martin says, 'Well, I'm sure as hell not going swimming in there today!'

'Oh come on! They're only *baby* sharks!' Don says, 'What are you scared of?'

'The mother!'

Don laughs, 'Well then you'll have to go in the kiddie pool Martin, I'm going swimming in the ocean! You coming Katie?'

Is he serious? He's asking *me* if I want to go swimming with *him*? Mum and Dad are always telling me never to go in unless an adult is there, that it's far too dangerous … but the ocean doesn't look as wild as it usually does. And Don and Martin are sort of adults …

'Sure,' I say, 'I guess.'

Don pulls his shirt up over his head in that way hot guys do to show off their back. He sprints down the sand, runs through the water and dives straight under a wave. Coming up he flicks the water from his hair and calls, 'C'mon Martin! Don't be a girl's blouse!'

Martin rolls his eyes and says to me, 'Might as well get eaten by a shark, eh?'

I follow him to the water. Martin dives under a wave, staying under for a long time before surfacing just behind Don to push him under. They stay out past the breakers, squirting water at each other as I edge further out. The water is choppy, a strong rip swirling around my thighs. I jump over the waves, which are too small to break, but then a bigger wave starts building, the crest already foaming as it comes in.

Don calls, waving me over. I can still touch the bottom but only just, ridges of sand fall away under my feet as the undertow pulls me towards the gathering wave. Fear begins to shoot through me. Don puts his head down and swims over with a few powerful strokes. He offers me his hand and I take it. I must be crazy to follow him into deeper water, but as soon as I stop fighting the rip it gets easier.

'Take a breath!' he yells. 'Dive!'

An enormous mountain of water rises up in front of us. Don disappears through the wall first and I have no choice but to follow. The raging noise of the ocean stops, I open my eyes and blink in the turquoise light, following Don swimming in front of me. The sand stirs on the ocean floor, particles and bubbles floating before me, disappearing off into blackness.

When I pop up I'm out beyond the breakers with the boys. We laugh, float easily up and down over the waves as they move through to break on the shore. Out here it is so peaceful, the sky open and blue with a half-moon, white and powdery in the sky, like a single cloud.

'What was that?' Don says, 'A *shark!*' He suddenly dives down and I feel him grab at my legs. I shriek and he pops up again laughing.

'Shut up Don!' Martin says.

The surf gets bigger and other kids join us, bobbing about waiting for waves to catch. I wait for a big one to come in, paddle in front of it and the wave rises up behind me and slides me down, like going headfirst down a waterslide!

***

'Gee Katie, you're sunburned,' Dad says when I get home. The Colins are sitting with him on the balcony and Mum is pouring coffee.

'Turn around!' Colin Brees calls out and they all shriek, 'Look at your back! Look at your shoulders!' They laugh. I bend my head to try and see, press my finger onto my shoulder a few times like I'm testing the doneness of a piece of steak and shrug.

'Have you had fun? Tell us what you've been doing!' Mum says. I show them the shark eggs and tell them about swimming in the ocean. Dad looks alarmed.

'Don't worry, there were grown-ups there,' I add quickly, but I don't tell them about Don and Martin's address in my bag. One shock is enough.

THERE IS A LIGHT THAT NEVER GOES OUT

The last time Nicole came for a sleepover at Paddington I woke her up in the middle of the night and told her I had a surprise. Dor Dor was asleep, snoring in the next room with the bedside light on. Leaving Nicole giggling by the door, I crept stealthily across the room towards her bed.

'What are you doing?' Nicole whispered. 'Are you crazy?'

Dor Dor lay on her back propped up with pillows, her mouth agape, jaw strangely sunken without her false teeth. On her chin a couple of stray whiskers that she'd missed with the tweezers quivered. I leaned over silently to steal her walking stick from beside the bed. Nicole shook her head as I ran triumphantly back with the stick.

'Are you mad?' she whispered.

I took her hand and led her towards the dark stairs. Using the banister as a guide we snuck down into the pitch-blackness, past my parents' bedroom, where my father snored like a truck going past, then further down.

'Are we having a midnight feast?' Nicole whispered.

'No!' I said, 'This is way more fun!'

I passed Dor Dor's walking stick to her in the darkness and she giggled again. Nicole giggled more when she was nervous.

I crept to the front door and took Mum's umbrella. A car drove down the laneway opposite our house and a sliver of light slid eerily across the room. I pointed out the big rubber stopper on the end of Dor Dor's walking stick to Nicole, then, as a soldier checks his weapon, I looked at the end of Mum's umbrella. It had a long, pointy metal tip. It would require much greater accuracy than Dor Dor's stick but I figured I had enough experience now to warrant such a challenge.

'This way,' I said to Nicole and took her hand again. My bare feet felt across the carpeted hallway towards the kitchen, the floor changed to linoleum and I walked blindly across to where I knew the light switch was. This was always the scariest part, creeping through the blackness, knowing what was coming. Nicole clung to me, giggling in trepidation.

'Now, when I turn the light on,' I whispered, 'don't scream.'

I flicked the switch and the lights came on with a blinding flash. Dozens of black roaches ran crazily in every direction across the white laminate, the benches, and the floor towards our bare feet. Nicole opened her mouth wide to scream and I clamped my hand over it, her panicked eyes darted around and her nostrils flared in terror.

'Shhh! Just kill them – like this!'

I swivelled with my umbrella and stabbed three roaches running towards us. Crunch! Crunch! Crunch!

'Your turn!' I whispered, and with her eyes bulging in fear, she raised the walking stick with both hands and aimed the rubber stopper at a roach on the floor coming towards us. It came down with a satisfying squish.

'Bullseye!' I whispered and Nicole let out a kind of stifled, hysterical laugh.

A huge cockroach careened towards us across the bench top, I brought the metal tip of the umbrella down. Crunch!

On the wall behind us, three more roaches, zigzagging across the cupboards. Crunch! Crunch! Crunch!

Nicole and I were back to back now; I could feel her jolting backwards in repulsion, as she stabbed furiously with the walking stick. One jab and another jab and then another, and then I could feel her hopping around from foot to foot, the sounds of a strangled scream erupting from her throat.

I spun around to save her, smashing the fat bodies of the roaches clamouring to climb up her legs. It was revolting! It was thrilling! It was like being in the movie *Alien*, roaches even dropping from the ceiling!

When the massacre was over we climbed trembling back up the stairs. When we closed our eyes we could still see the roaches and slept with our backs pressed against each other.

***

I ask my parents if Nicole can come up to Pearl Beach. I decide the first thing I'm going to do is take her swimming in the surf, which is about the most fun thing I've ever done in my life. We walk about half way down the beach with Mum, who has come to watch. The waves here are still pretty big and there's a group of kids swimming and catching waves.

'Now you know at school when you play skip rope? You have to pick your moment to run into the middle and start jumping, it's just like that … you run in when the waves are small and when you get right out past where they break you're safe!'

Nicole looks hesitant. 'Trust me!' I say. 'I'll be right next to you!'

We walk down to the surf and the water comes up and spills over our feet. Nicole giggles nervously. She starts running on the spot 'No! No! No! I don't think I can do it!' she says.

'Of course you can!' I say. 'Come on!'

I hold her hand to steady her nerves. We watch the waves roll in together. The group of kids in the surf bob over the small ones and dive under the big ones, shrieking and laughing. I can't wait to get in. I'm so excited my whole body feels like a can of jumping beans.

'I can't do it!' Nicole says again and turns, but I tug her hand and pull her back.

'Come on, you'll love it! You just have to get in, that's the hard part. And remember what I told you – never turn back!'

'Okay! Never turn back!' she says.

A set of waves roars and crashes in, the shallow water is foamy and white, swirling around our legs like whipped egg whites. This is the moment. We run together into the surf, still holding hands. The water quickly rises up to our thighs, then our waists. Nicole squeals. The water sucks and swirls around us. I run as hard as I can, pulling her with me. The sand is moving below my feet and we're barely making any progress as the current continues to push us to shore with the end of the last wave.

And then the water turns and starts sucking us out. The next wave looks big from where we are. The kids in the surf excitedly whoop and start swimming out to it.

'C'mon!' I yell. 'We have to get out there before it breaks!'

Nicole screams and starts to panic, she wrenches her hand free of mine and turns to run.

'No! No!' I scream, 'NEVER TURN BACK!'

The water is strong now, pulling and sucking both of us towards the mouth of the wave. It begins to crest and if I swim towards it now I might just get there in time – I have to save myself. I kick and pull my arms through the water with all my strength, the wave draws me up and up and up, taking me away from Nicole whose screams get louder and louder before the wave breaks over her.

It's a long time before she resurfaces. The monster wave had pounded down and pushed her face-first into the sand; it threw her about like a rag doll in a washing machine. Her lungs had burned and her brain had screamed for oxygen, and finally when the water released her Nicole had come gasping up for air like a person breaking out of a grave.

I watched as she tried to stand up in the shallow water. Her knees wobbling and head dizzy, sea water streaming like acid from her nose and eyes. She stood there in shock, hair tangled and so heavy that it made her lean to the side like a zombie. I start laughing.

Mum is running down with a towel. 'Oooooooh!' she's screaming. 'Did you get dumped? Oooah look out! LOOK OUT!'

Nicole turns and opens her mouth to scream when the second wall of water slams into her face.

Nicole wants to go home. Mum has been sitting with her on the beach rubbing her back like crazy, something Mum does that drives me nuts, but Nicole is a wreck and is tolerating it. Mum tells Nicole the story of how she nearly drowned when her older brother decided she should learn to swim.

'He threw me in a swimming pool and held the straps on the back of my swimming costume! It was awful! All that water! I couldn't *breathe* for heaven's sake! I thought I was going to *die!*'

'I nearly drowned once too,' I say.

'*What?* When?!' Mum says.

'That time you took me to lunch at your friend's when I was really little, remember?' Mum looks worried, like she's forgotten something important.

'Remember? I was sitting on the edge of the pool and decided I'd clean the tiles around the edge. I wasn't really cleaning them, of course, they just changed to a darker colour when I put water on them. I got a bit carried away and the next thing I toppled head first into the water.'

'Oh heavens! Really?' Mum says.

'Yeah, you don't remember? I was bobbing up and down in the water. I felt like I was stuck under the water looking up. Someone must have jumped in to rescue me I guess, because I'm still here.'

'Ooooh, that's terrible!' Mum says. 'I must ask Barry!'

'Hey what about that time I almost fell out of the car while you were driving through the Kings Cross tunnel?' I say.

'Oh! Yes! I do remember that!' Mum says, happy to at least remember that incident, and for Nicole's benefit she tells the story, even though we're not sure if she's really even listening. 'You were in the front seat and somehow you undid your seat belt and *opened* the car door! Oh! I nearly died!'

'I'm the one that nearly died!' I butt in.

'Lucky you had those overalls on that day!' Mum says. 'I reached across and grabbed you while I was still driving!'

'It was actually pretty cool,' I say. 'I remember hanging onto the car door handle, seeing the road whizzing underneath me. I felt like I was flying!'

Mum shakes her head at the horror of the thought then suddenly gets teary and wraps her big strong arms around both Nicole and me. 'Oh! You two precious things! Oh! Oh!'

'It's alright Jeanne,' Nicole says, finally awakening from her comatose state to comfort Mum. Nobody can ever bear to see Mum cry because she's so nice.

We walk back along the beach. I'm starting to giggle again about the sight of Nicole emerging from the ocean. I throw my hair over my face and put my hands out to stagger around, like I'm in Michael Jackson's 'Thriller', but Nicole doesn't find it funny. She gives me a filthy look and picks up the pace.

Mum shakes her head and gives me one of those looks that says to be quiet.

'Oh c'mon! She did! She looked like a zombie!' I can't help it; I can't stop laughing. Just because this is only the first time she's nearly died, it doesn't mean *everyone* has to be so boring and serious!

***

Nicole spends a long time in the shower when we get back to the house, combing conditioner through her hair.

'She wants to go home so I'll drive her,' Mum is saying quietly. Dad has been cooking, he's set the table and delicious aromas waft through the house.

'What?' he says. 'She wants to go *home?* Don't be ridiculous!'

'Where are the keys, I'll take her,' Mum says.

'You're not driving her *home* for heaven's sake! We're about to eat!'

'Just save me some, I won't be long …'

Dad scoffs. 'Don't be *absurd* Jean! It's an hour and a half drive back to Sydney – *three hours* at least! It'll be midnight by the time you get back!'

'Well that's alright …'

Dad takes charge; it's time to put a stop to this nonsense. 'Just go and sit at the table Jean! I'll have a talk with her.' He huffs and puffs as he takes the piece of roast meat from the oven. 'Drive her home …' he mutters, 'at this hour … ridiculous …'

My father knows how to be persuasive and by the time Nicole comes out, carrying her bag, with her long hair untangled and combed straight down to her waist, we're sitting at the table waiting to eat dinner and my father has his plan worked out.

'I'm ready, Jeanne,' Nicole says timidly.

Mum goes to answer but Dad cuts her off, 'Shush Jean, start eating! Now, what's all this about wanting to go home then?' he says to Nicole. 'Come and tell us now. Put your bag on the sofa for a bit, no-one's leaving until after we eat anyway.'

'You must be starving!' Mum blurts out.

'Shush Jean!' Dad reprimands, and he pulls the chair out beside him and pats the seat. 'Look! I've made lovely roast beef!' and Nicole has to admit she's starving. He heaps roast potatoes onto Nicole's plate, peas and gravy, a fresh bread roll warmed in the oven with a block of cold butter. Food never tastes so good as when you've just nearly died.

'Did I ever tell you about the time I was a little boy and the polar bear nearly ate me?' Dad says.

Nicole has her mouth full, she looks at Dad with wide eyes and shakes her head. Mum has scurried off to get a towel to put over Nicole's wet shoulders and she brings back a huge feather pillow as well to push in awkwardly behind Nicole's back. She's always doing things like this, trying to make people feel more comfortable in the most cumbersome way, or putting enormous doonas around people's shoulders on the balcony when they're not even cold.

'Jean! Sit down and eat! Stop fussing over the girl! You're alright aren't you?' Nicole gives a small nod. 'Of course you are! You've just had a bit of a fright that's all! Now let me tell you about the time Dora took me to the zoo when I was a little boy … I was only five or six you see, an only child, like you and Katie. Mum had this idea that my ears stuck out so she used to dress me with a beret to keep my ears pinned back.' He laughs wryly. 'Well, this one day, she took me to the zoo and when we got to the polar bear exhibit I couldn't see, so she lifted me up onto the railing. There was a crowd gathered around and there was this big white polar bear roaming around down in this pit.'

'The poor thing …'

'Shush Jean! I'm talking! Anyway, the bear liked the look of me and each time it went round it would stop to look up at me … it probably wanted to eat me of course, but everyone was stupid back in those days, so my mother Dora, she lifted me out further over the railing so the polar bear could see me better and I was waving to the bear and everyone thought it was adorable, but then suddenly I slipped! Luckily Dora managed to grab me by the ankle! And so there I was hanging, just dangling into the pit, and the polar bear came right over and leapt up and took the beret off my head!'

'Ooooh! Did it really?'

'Yes! Isn't that an amazing story!'

'What happened then?' I ask spellbound.

'Oh, I think some men ran over to help. Knowing Dora she would've put on a show for them. She probably pretended to faint or something after they pulled me back up!'

'What about the beret, Dad?'

'The polar bear ate it! But Dora bought me a new one of course, so my ears wouldn't stick out. Do they stick out? I don't think my ears stick out?'

'No Barry, you have lovely ears!' Mum says.

'Yes I do, don't I, but I've always been self-conscious of them because of that!'

'Were you upset?' Nicole asks.

'Well, apparently I only cried *after* they pulled me out. I loved the polar bear and I didn't want to say goodbye! But I didn't cry long, Dora bought me an ice cream and ice cream *always* fixes everything! Now, let's not worry about driving home tonight, let's eat ice cream, shall we?'

Nicole claps her hands and I laugh, thrilled at the story and the promise of ice cream, but most of all because my friend has decided to stay.

BLUE MONDAY

We'd been having dinner at the little round table in Paddington when Dad said Josh would be up at Pearl Beach on the weekend. 'They didn't go last week,' Dad said, 'because Josh had a fencing tournament on. Did you know Josh does fencing?'

'That's incredible!' Mum had said.

'Yes, isn't it! Apparently he's very talented at it.'

I'm looking forward to going swimming in the surf; I've already got my swimmers on under my shorts when Josh knocks on the back door at Pearl Beach.

'Oh, hi Dahling!' Mum says. 'Would you like a cup of coffee or anything?' Josh sniggers and shakes his head.

'He's *too young* for coffee Jean!' Dad says. 'Your mother tells me you're a fencer! How wonderful!' Josh looks pleased.

'I placed fourth in the state,' he says.

'Wow!' Dad says. 'That's impressive! You hear that Katie? Now you be careful of that surf!'

'Don't worry Mister Little, I'll look after her,' Josh says.

I roll my eyes and say, 'C'mon, let's go already.' But when we get down to the beach it's deserted, the shoreline littered with electric-blue jellyfish.

'Bluebottles!' Josh says. 'No swimming today.'

He takes a stick and stabs one of the little air sacks. 'Argh!' he yells jumping back, 'Damn thing exploded and nearly got me!'

'They're like bees,' I tell him, 'even after they're dead they can still sting.' But Josh is too busy stabbing more bluebottles, some of them make little popping noises.

He lifts the stick up. 'Hey! This would make an awesome poison-tipped spear!' he says.

I've read that bluebottles have floats that face one way or the other, so that when one colony is blown into shore, another blows further out to sea.

We go back to the house and play Spite and Malice on the balcony. It's an animated game; Josh gloats each time he has a run and takes more pleasure than he should from blocking me any time he gets an opportunity. But then towards the end of the game I suddenly get a run of good cards, I can see the end of the game and it's mine! I put down two wild cards and Josh suddenly shouts, 'No! No! You can't do that! You're not allowed to put down two wild cards!' Josh always seems to be adding new rules when I'm winning.

'You never said that!' I shout back. 'That's not fair! I was going to win!'

As soon as I've lost my temper Josh knows he's won more than just the card game.

'I'm not playing with you anymore!' I shout. I throw the cards down onto the table and sit back with my arms crossed.

'Awwwww, sooky wooky,' he says, doing that thing with his fingers tracing tear marks down his cheeks. We stare at each other, my lip curling like a dog about to attack, Josh's eyes twinkle with sadistic mischief. 'Alright, I guess I'll let you have that game,' he says. 'Best out of three?'

'Why don't you two go for a bike ride?' Dad has come out to see what all the fuss is about. 'Josh, weren't you going to take Katie up to the creek and show her how to catch yabbies? I've got some meat in the fridge you can take.'

I know Dad wants us out of the house so he can go back to bed; their bedroom is next to the verandah where we're playing cards. Mum and Dad's bed is framed with a giant mosquito net Mum sewed out of tulle. It's stiff, unlike a regular net, but it looks good, like you'd imagine a photoshoot of Joan Collins' bedroom would look. A ceiling fan over the bed turns lazily. Dad has declared after lunch at Pearl Beach is siesta.

'Come and lie down with me Jean,' he'll say. 'Come and have a rest.'

Dad loves sleeping, but Mum loves action.

'Heavens no!' she'll say. 'There's too much to do!'

Mum is always busy, madly working her way through a never-ending list of things requiring urgent attention, shaking her head and muttering 'How can he *sleep* in the daytime?'

'Suit yourself,' Dad will say with a twinge of hurt in his voice, and then moments later his snores will rumble in time with the sound of the waves.

***

Later that night, as Josh's parents sit having drinks with the Colins, Josh and I stand up the back of the moonlit yard barbecuing chicken. Josh pokes the coals with a stick, releasing little showers of sparks. The chicken sizzles as it cooks, garlic and soy mingling with Aerogard and the smells of the bush. The birds are quiet now, leaves rustle with possums and small marsupials, and far away the sound of the waves crashing down on the blackened beach.

'Are you cold?' Josh asks.

The air here is always chilly at night but my shoulders are glowing with the residual heat of sunburn. Josh puts his arm around my shoulder, it's heavy and a bit uncomfortable. Slowly I feel his hand creeping down over my shoulder like one of those big orange and brown tarantulas in *Raiders of the Lost Ark*. I have the impulse to brush it away, but for some reason I freeze. The hand fumbles its way inside my top and I stand there barely daring to breathe, until Dad's voice suddenly calls out from the back porch, he has a plate to put the chicken on.

BARRACUDA

Summer has nearly finished. Mum has been working on the weekends a lot so we haven't been to Pearl Beach in ages. Dad is annoyed and keeps threatening to put the house up for sale.

I come home from school to find an envelope waiting for me on the kitchen table. Don and Martin have written to me! I race up to my bedroom and carefully open it, scan the small, cramped writing. Don says he misses the beach, school is boring, he can't wait to go swimming with sharks again. Ha, ha, ha. At the bottom is an XO, and my heart skips a beat. Mum winks at me at dinner.

'Katie got a letter from the two boys she met on the beach!' Mum says.

Dad doesn't look pleased; there are a lot of 'undesirable elements' up there he says. Where do these boys live he wants to know.

'Oh, they're nice boys Barry, they were up staying with their grandparents.'

They live in Penrith I tell Dad. He changes the subject, tells me tomorrow he's taking Josh's mother to look at tiles and samples for her renovation. Would I like to come too?

Dad used to take me along to jobs with him when I was small. I loved the smell of fresh timber and wet concrete on the building sites, loved watching the bricklayers mix piles of mortar on squares of cladding, the scrape and slop of the trowel, like a giant mud pie.

'Watch my thumb!' the old Italian tiler would say, pretending to detach it. His large thumb, the giant cuticle and the whorls of skin over his large, mortar-flecked hands. He'd watch my reaction as the thumb unjoined and rejoined. 'She's a smart one!' he'd say to my father, tapping his temple. 'You'll have to watch out!'

I'm ready early the next morning. I sit in the front seat with Dad as he drives to Josh's house. He pulls up out the front of a large residence surrounded by a tall security fence, tells me to go and ring the bell. 'But I thought we were going to a building site ...' I say to him.

No, Dad laughs, Josh's mother is just redecorating.

'Aren't you coming in too?' I ask him. No he says, there's been a change of plans, Josh's mother is meeting him at the showroom, he'll be back later to pick me up. But I would have rather stayed home with Mum, I say.

'Your mother's working!' Dad says. 'She's got a dress to finish ... Go on,' he says, 'you'll have fun. They have a swimming pool and everything. It's an amazing house.'

Hesitantly I get out of the car. I press the buzzer on the gate and it clicks open, Dad waves at me before driving off.

Josh opens the front door. 'Hi,' he says, 'c'mon in!' he leads me through to the kitchen and opens the pantry door, takes out a packet of chips and loudly pops it open. 'You want a drink or something?' I shake my head. We walk through the house past windows overlooking a large swimming pool. 'Oh, Dad said you had a pool,' I say.

'Yeah, but it's too cold for swimming, the heating's not on. You want to play on the Atari?'

'Sure,' I say.

I follow him upstairs to a room that smells like musty socks. I look through the collection of cartridges. 'Pac Man,' he says. 'Good choice!'

I push the knob of the controller from side to side, the little yellow circle glides around the maze. A ghost turns the corner and catches me.

'Here, let me show you,' Josh says. He takes the controller from me and I watch him play for a while. When it's my turn he puts his arm around my shoulder.

'Josh, I can't play if you do that,' I say.

I shrug it off and try to concentrate on the game, but the arm comes back and his hand goes down my shirt.

'Josh ...' I say, but he won't stop. Finally I ask him where the bathroom is. I go in and lock the door. I look at my watch; Dad dropped me here only half an hour ago. I want to go home. After a few minutes I flush the toilet and turn the tap on for a bit. Look at myself in the mirror and straighten my top.

When I go back out Josh is waiting for me. 'It's your turn,' he says, smiling, patting the floor beside him. I pick up the controller and play the game, I start to relax, but then his hand is back. I try to ignore it, wishing it would go away, and very slowly it creeps down and feels my small breast, his fingers probing like he's checking the ripeness of a piece of fruit.

Suddenly his tongue is in my ear. He pushes himself onto me, and starts pushing his tongue in my mouth. His hands are pulling at the button on my jeans and I freeze, just like I did at the barbecue. He turns me over and yanks my jeans down and spits on me, rubbing his penis up and down furiously between my buttocks. He cums with a sighing sound, jerking a bit before he lifts himself off.

When I hear him walk out of the room I sit up and pull up my pants. My hands are shaking, I can't do up the button. Awkwardly, I pull my shirt down and stand up. I hear the toilet flush and Josh comes back into the room. 'You want to play a different game?' he asks.

'I'm just going … I'm just going to the loo,' I say.

I close the bathroom door and slide the silver lock across with trembling fingers. I stay there until Dad arrives some hours later.

'How was it?' Dad asks when I'm in the car.

My bottom lip trembles. 'What's wrong?' he asks. 'Katie, what is it? Tell me.'

I don't know how to say it. 'He … he … forced himself on me.'

'He *what?* What did he do?' He sounds angry.

'You know … he … put his hands all over me … he wouldn't stop …'

'Oh, is that all!' Dad says. 'Well, boys are like that! He just likes you, that's all!'

But I'm not alright. I want Dad to *do* something. 'You have to phone his mother,' I say. 'You have to tell her …'

'What?' he says again. He lets out a guffaw. 'I can't do *that!* She's a good client of mine! That's preposterous!'

But you're my father I want to say. You're meant to *fix* this somehow. 'He hurt me,' I say in a small voice, but when he asks me to clarify I have to say that no, I'm not physically harmed.

'Stop being so dramatic!' he says.

'Some boys are like that,' Mum says when I come downstairs for dinner. 'I'll tell him off next time I see him!'

'Jean, you stay out of this! You'll do no such thing! Josh's mother owes me a lot of money for heaven's sake!' Dad says.

'I had a boyfriend who tried to race me off once too,' Mum says.

'Who?' Dad says.

'You know … D'arcy.'

'Did he?' Dad says. 'When was that?'

'When I went travelling overseas. I was twenty mind you, not as young as Katie is.'

'Yes,' Dad says looking at me, 'you're all a bit young for this.' I feel confused.

'It's not Katie's fault!' Mum says.

'Yes I know *that!*' Dad says. 'I'm just saying ... there's plenty of time for all this nonsense! That Josh should know better ... It's a bit cheeky of him behaving like that.'

I can't get that day out of my head. I size myself up in the mirror, wondering why I didn't do something to stop what happened and I see something in my eyes that I've never seen before.

'You shouldn't ever hate someone,' Mum has said, 'It's like poison.'

I feel guilty, but there it is, this dark cold feeling inside me like a lump of coal being compressed into a diamond of pure hatred. The next time I see him at Pearl Beach I'll spit in his face I think, or throw sand in his eyes! I'll punch him hard in the throat and laugh at his surprised look when he starts suffocating on his own blood!

But I never get to say any of these things because one afternoon Dad comes up from the office and tells us he has some awful news. Josh is dead. 'He went on a school camp,' Dad says, 'He drowned ... hit his head on a rock diving into a river. He never came home.' He looks shocked.

'Oh heavens, poor Josh's mother!' Mum starts sobbing and Dad hugs her.

Mum cries every time she thinks about it for the next week, but I don't cry; I'm too angry. I ride around the streets of Pearl Beach thinking about him. I ride past his house, which is closed up. 'They're going to sell it,' Dad has said. 'His mother will never recover from this.'

It's my hatred that has done this, I know it, I can feel the guilt in my bones. I ride hard up the street that leads back into the bush, along the track to the creek where Josh took me yabby fishing. I throw my bike against a tree and scramble up the red dirt fire break.

'Fuck you Josh!' I scream. 'Why did you die? You chickenshit asshole!'

The noise of cicadas swells hypnotically around me as I head deeper into the bush. Tea-trees scratch me as I push past. I glimpse someone running behind me and a panicky feeling tears through my chest. I break into a run, glance behind and stumble over a tree root straight into a huge spider web. I claw it off and fall forwards over a rock, badly grazing my knee, but there's no time to look, I just run and keep running, finally getting to the path that leads up to the waterfall. There's a secret cave under the fall, I'll be safe there. My sneakers skid and slide across the wet rocks and then finally I'm in, hidden away, safe in my rock cave.

I'm breathing too hard, I can't seem to catch my breath, I wipe the blood that's running from my knee.

'Get a hold of yourself,' I whisper, 'there's no-one following you …'

But I know that's a lie. Josh is following me, I can't get away from him. I put my head between my knees to try and stop the nausea, then catch some water from the cascade to splash over my face, grateful for the shock it gives me. It's ice cold, not burning hot like my tears.

***

I try to sound as casual as possible when I ask my parents when Josh's funeral is.

'It was last Monday,' Dad says.

'But I wanted to go …'

'You're too young,' he says, cutting me off.

'Oh, we couldn't have gone,' Mum says, choking, 'it would have been too sad.' She starts crying again. The sound of Mum crying is awful, like someone with a chicken bone stuck in their throat.

'I can't believe you didn't tell me.'

'That's enough Katie,' Dad says sharply. 'Children don't go to funerals. You've upset your mother again.'

'You are so *fucked!*' I scream, and the slap takes both of us by surprise.

In my room I inspect the red handprint which has risen on my cheek. I'm so angry I feel I might tear apart. I start smashing things, I wipe a load of stuff straight off my desk and it comes down to the floor with a satisfying crash. I kick the chair over and intend to hurl everything off the bookshelf too when the sight of my wooden spirit house stops me. It's so delicate, the hand-carved wood painted gold, its sloping roof studded with coloured squares of glass that reflect sunlight around the room.

I think back to the overseas trip where Dad told me I could choose one thing to bring home. I said I wanted a spirit house, like the ones we saw everywhere we went, around which were offerings of fruit, flowers and incense.

'Why would you want that?' Dad said. 'Don't you want some kind of toy or something? It's not supposed to be a dolls house you know.'

'Oh, let her buy one if she wants Barry!' Mum had said.

'Yeah Dad, you said I could choose!'

'How on earth will we take it back?' he'd said, and Mum had answered, 'I'll carry it on the plane!'

When it was wrapped up in newspaper and put in a box it was much larger than any of us had expected. Mum had apologised as she took it to the plane but the Qantas stewards had just laughed and asked if she was kidnapping a baby elephant. The Qantas stewards love Mum, especially since she judged one of their drag shows, and the guys at customs seemed happy enough to open the box to inspect it even though Dad was sighing and looking at his watch.

I wipe the dust off the spirit house and light some incense, then decide to build something bigger in my room. I stack several boxes on top of each other and drape black fabric over them then raid a cupboard in the dining room that's full of interesting-looking things. I find some coloured resin prisms, a small vase and candles. If I can't go to a church or something for Josh's funeral then I'll make my own. I don't believe in god the way they talk about him in churches anyway; god wouldn't be a man for starters.

'She's been acting weird,' Dad says. 'Are teenage girls always like this? She's not even a teenager yet.'

'She's upset,' Mum says. 'It's understandable after what happened.' That's as close as Mum can get to talking about Josh's death.

I'm sitting on the step outside my bedroom, eavesdropping as they get ready for bed. That's the way I usually found out what's going on.

'Maybe we shouldn't go to Melbourne for the Logies …'

'Don't be ridiculous Jean, we have to go. It'll be good for her, get her out of this bloody house for a while. What's she doing up there anyhow? She's not going to burn the house down with candles and things is she? I hope you're keeping an eye on her …'

PART 2

EVERY LITTLE THING SHE DOES IS MAGIC

I'm twelve years old when something really remarkable happens. Mum gets asked to audition for Jerry Herman, an American director who's coming over from New York to cast the Australian production of his hit musical *Jerry's Girls*. Mum and Dad are excited but nervous. Mum has lots of experience with television but none in the theatre; it's a completely different ball game. Mum and Dad share the news with Colin and Colin, eager to hear their reaction.

'Truly?' Colin Brees gasps.

'Oh Jean! That's wonderful!' Colin Johnston says.

'But I'll have to *dance* Colin! They're all proper singers, not like me! They're all trained for this sort of thing! They're big *stars*!'

Dad shushes her, 'Oh Jean! Have some *confidence* in yourself for heavens sake!' But I can tell even Dad thinks it's a long shot. Mum is going into an audition beside big names like Marcia Hines and Judi Connelli – women with proper musical training and chests like barrels, who break glass on a high note without even raising a sweat.

Mum is going for the part Carol Channing has played on Broadway, a humorous role which needs someone with character to play it. No-one really expects her to get the part, including Mum herself, but she puts her heart into preparing for the audition anyway, determined to give it everything she's got. It's a job offer after all, and since *The Mike Walsh Show* ended it's been slim pickings. The last thing her agent offered her was a cameo roll in a movie called *Crocodile Dundee*, which Dad turned down saying the script sounded atrocious – and who wanted to be in a movie with Paul Hogan?

Mum stands and prays next to the telephone sometimes. 'Please God,' she says, putting her hands together under her chin, looking heavenward like a little girl, 'Please God let me get some work!'

Her agent gives her the number of a dance teacher and a professional vocal coach. She practises the time step while she's washing up and waiting in line at the supermarket. She sings crazy-sounding vocal exercises morning, noon and night.

'*Mee mar mee mar mee mar mee mar mee mar mee mar mee mar maaaaaaaaay,*' she sings, warbling up and down the scales. The noise echoes from the shower and her sewing room, reverberates in the car over an echoey backing tape of piano arpeggios.

And then the most *unthinkable* thing happens: Mum gets the part! The American director loves her, says unequivocally she is perfect for the role, and now the really hard work begins.

Rehearsals every day for only six weeks before the opening night at the Footbridge Theatre in Sydney. It will be a packed house, a red carpet extravaganza – showbiz critics from every newspaper sitting beside socialites and moneyed producers. The pressure is intense, Mum's name is billed alongside the other leading ladies and more than a few noses are put out of joint. One performer refuses even to talk to her, but she often turns up late to rehearsals and sometimes not at all. Gossip is rampant.

It turns out life in the theatre is hard in more ways than one; there's no room for error or weakness of any kind. Rehearsals are long and relentless, and Mum comes home physically and mentally exhausted.

The big stars have big egos to match; they have to, it's what sets them apart from the chorus girls who are all younger and perkier, stunningly beautiful and determined to make it. As well as learning their own parts they're also understudies to the main roles. When Debra Byrne falls off the stage and breaks her ankle, the girl who steps into her place tries not to look pleased, but this could be it, the moment a critic is in the audience, her name thrust into the spotlight!

The leading ladies throw their weight around and come to blows over an endless succession of entitlements. They fight over who gets which show-stopping songs or who has been given the best seats on opening night, then seemingly inconsequential things: who gets which change room, the choreography, whose costume is more flamboyant. The costume designer Roger Kirk is forced to alter dresses, add sequins or extra frills, he complains he has to keep making alterations – one star's hips keep getting wider, one of the chorus girls will eat nothing but celery.

'The poor thing has anorexia,' Mum says.

If there's a chink in your armour the pressure of working in theatre will test it – someone's taking too many pills, someone else is hitting the bottle, some eat too much, some too little. Even love is a weakness. Scandal soon spreads; the young, married stage manager is having a big affair backstage with one of the chorus girls.

Mum keeps her head down in rehearsals and works hard, but the stress gets to her too – she comes home in tears, says she doesn't think she'll ever be good enough, hasn't a hope of remembering all the dance steps, the lyrics and harmonies, the cues! This is not learning one song for *The Mike Walsh Show*, this is a Broadway production with songs from some of the biggest shows ever written for the stage – *Hello, Dolly!*, *Mame*, *La Cage aux Folles*.

Dad consoles her the only way he knows how, by shouting and telling her to snap out of it. After he's stormed off I put on my tap shoes and ask Mum if she feels like practising her steps with me in the kitchen; after all, I've been learning tap and ballet for a few years now.

'Shuffle ball change … and hop, step, and shuffle ball change … Good one Mum! Let's try it again, now try doing this with your arms …'

Dad hears the tapping and comes in to watch. 'Yes, you're right Katie,' he says. 'That looks much better! Jean, copy what Katie's doing with her arms, stop being so *stiff*! Loosen up a bit … Much better!'

I go over her sheet music too, explain how to count the bars of the intro, draw pencil marks on the paper just like my singing teacher does at school – where to take a breath, where to hold a note. Mum's never had to read music before either. I put my hands on her ribs and tell her to breathe down deep into her diaphragm. By opening night I know all the words and every step; I could be her understudy, albeit a small one.

Comps on opening night are in short supply and Mum is only given three. Colin Brees parks the car nervously and Dad complains his bow tie is too tight. He pulls at the collar of his shirt but I know it's not the tie that's the problem; we're all so terrified for Mum we can hardly breathe. The atmosphere in the darkened theatre is electric, the house is full with not one seat to spare. 'Ladies and gentlemen!' says a booming voice over the speakers. 'Tonight's performance of *Jerry's Girls* is about to commence. Please, no flash photography! And now, direct from Broadway, the music of Jerry Herman and *Jerry's Girls!*'

A drummer breaks into a roll on a snare so tight it raises the hairs on my arms. Music fills the theatre right up to the roof – soaring, whirling music full of strings and wind and brass – then the red curtain goes up and the set is revealed, balconies studded with the beautiful chorus girls. The big stars join them one at a time, the audience applauds each enthusiastically as they make their entrance: Judi, Debbie, Marcia and then Mum. I clap madly.

'There she is!' I feel like shouting, 'That's *MY* mum!'

I breathe with her and mouth the words to the song. If I was watching her stepping out onto a tightrope strung between two skyscrapers I wouldn't be more nervous. I bite my lip throughout 'Tap Your Troubles Away', dancing each step in my head. 'She's doing it!' I think to myself, 'She's going to pull it off!' Mum's in line with the other dancers, keeping up with them, matching them tap for tap. The audience applauds thunderously at the end!

Mum does her big number 'Take It All Off'. She walks onto the stage after the young attractive chorus girls, dressed as a worn-out stripper, her costume, part made of rubber, makes her look like she has a big sagging belly with a diamanté in the naval and enormous boobs complete with pasties. Everyone knows Mum's figure is thin like Twiggy and the audience goes mad with laughter and applause just at the sight of her. The American director was right – this is the perfect part with her gravelly voice and exaggerated facial expressions. Mum earns the standing ovation alongside the big stars. She's paid her dues.

The critics are exuberant, the show is a hit! More than one column mentions Mum – 'What a surprise!' they say. 'Jeanne Little steals the show!'

But not everyone is thrilled by the attention Mum's getting. When she won the Gold Logie for most popular personality on television there were some in the industry who resented her success and refused to congratulate her. Mum knows she'll have to watch her back in the theatre too.

Huge bouquets of flowers start arriving at the house. 'Congratulations!' the cards say. 'A star is born!'. The house begins to look like a florist, with flowers piling up in the sinks. The phone rings off the hook and Dad is exuberant, taking up a breakfast tray to Mum in bed, laughing as he recounts the dozens of calls he's already taken – suddenly everyone wants her. I get in a quick good morning hug but Mum is not allowed to talk and after a moment Dad shoos me out so she can rest.

Mum's voice is now her most precious asset, requiring constant care. She wears a scarf to keep her throat warm and only nods or whispers. The kitchen smells strongly of tea-tree oil – Judi Connelli's tip is to always carry a thermos to have inhalations on the go, Marcia Hines swears by wheatgrass shots and Siberian ginseng.

This is the life of a musical theatre star. Seven gruelling shows a week and only one day off, a mainline of adrenaline before driving home at midnight. Dad tries to wait up for Mum most nights, heats her dinner and listens sleepily to how the show went. She's asleep when I leave for school and at the theatre when I get home. I miss her, but work must always take priority.

BURNING DOWN THE HOUSE

I've been catching the bus to school since I was ten. Dad didn't think I was old enough but Mum convinced him I'd be safe walking to the station with the twins my age who live around the corner, and in the end he had to agree because he wasn't offering to take over the car pool.

Danielle and Melanie are non-identical twins and we go back to their house most afternoons because their mother doesn't get home till five-thirty, so we have the house to ourself. Mum calls the Cope children 'latchkey kids' and talks about them sympathetically. We're always starving after school and we make piles of white toast with margarine and Vegemite. Sometimes there's no bread, and if we get desperately hungry Danielle will pull a frozen steak out of the freezer and blast it in the microwave.

I hate the smell of the meat defrosting. It goes round and round, the frost melting and pooling with blood, meat changing to pale grey. Danielle takes it out and prods it a few times. 'It's still frozen!' she'll say after half a dozen blasts in the microwave. Round and round the steak goes.

When it's finally done it's as tough as boot leather. Danielle hacks at it with a knife.

'Urgh Danielle, that looks disgusting,' Melanie will say.

'I'm not hungry,' their younger brother Adam calls out.

Melanie, who is taller and slimmer than her sister with pale blue eyes, is a good girl through and through; she's the kind of girl who does extra homework. She sweeps the garden and brings in the washing every afternoon, while Danielle roams the house looking for something new and preferably naughty for us to do. One day we tried removing the hair from our legs with some stinking foam stuff, today she tells me proudly she's nicked one of her mother's cigarettes.

We secretively squat in the corner of her balcony, the end of the cigarette sizzles when Danielle puts it into the flame. She inhales and offers it to me. I don't really like it, it leaves a minty feeling in my mouth, like toothpaste, but tastes like an ashtray; nevertheless, I like the gesture of doing it. I hold the cigarette between my finger and thumb like Sonny Crockett in *Miami Vice*.

Danielle is excited. 'Wait there,' she says, 'I'll get Melanie!' Shocking Melanie is even more fun than being devious ourselves.

'What are you guys up to?' Melanie says nervously. She sees the cigarette and her eyes nearly pop out. Danielle laughs.

'C'mon Melanie!' she says. 'You have to try it!'

'No, no, no, no, no, Danielle! *No way!* Mum would KILL YOU if she found out.'

'She's not going to find out,' Danielle says. 'Go on, try it.'

Cautiously, Melanie takes the cigarette and Danielle gives me a look to say, 'I can't believe she's going to do it!'. Having Melanie try smoking serves two important purposes: first, she won't be able to dob on us because she'd implicate herself, and secondly, we'll be successful in corrupting her!

Melanie explodes in violent coughing. 'Oh Danielle!' she says finally, her eyes watering. 'That's *awful!*'

Danielle laughs wickedly, takes the cigarette back and taps the ash too hard.

'Oops! I think I broke it!' She flicks the lighter – once, twice, on the third try it lights and the flame catches her fringe. *Zip!* The hair is gone, leaving a large singed bald patch where her temple is. 'Holy cow!' she laughs. 'Whoops!' The smell of burnt hair lingers strongly.

'Now you're in trouble!' Melanie says. 'Mum's going to see that!'

'Oh stop freaking out!' She looks at me and says, 'Is it really that bad?'

'Well you might need to wear a beret or something for a while ...'

It's starting to get dark. Sue will be home soon and Dad will wonder where I am. Danielle runs after me as I go to leave. 'Hang on! Hang on!' she says, blasting me with a spray of Melanie's Impulse deodorant.

'Urgh!' I shout. 'What is that stuff!'

'Well now, let me see ...' she says, 'it says it's called ... *Mischief!*'

'Hey! Give that *back* to me!' Melanie shouts, she tries to grab the canister but Danielle holds it out of reach and sprays more into the air. We've all seen the Impulse commercial on television where a man chases a woman down the street to give her a bunch of flowers.

'For when a complete stranger gives you flowers!' Danielle calls out after me down the street.

Dad is putting dinner on the table when I get home. I've eaten too much Vegemite toast but I dare not tell him I'm not hungry. We sit at the little table. It's just the two of us now that Mum's at the theatre every night, the small television keeping us company. 'Turn that off,' Dad says after the news headlines are finished. 'Now, there's something I wanted to talk to you about.' He tells me *Jerry's Girls* is touring, Mum will be living down in Melbourne for a few months, maybe I can go down with her.

'Sure,' I say, 'Sounds fun!'

'Remember, your mother will be working though, you'll have to behave yourself if you go down and not interfere with her work …'

'Of course!' I say.

He looks at me and says finally, 'Alright, well, look after her then. And make sure she eats!'

***

Mum is sharing a townhouse with Marcia Hines. Every afternoon I go to the theatre with Mum, we get home after midnight and sit up watching television with TV dinners until two in the morning before sharing a bed with pillows down the middle. Mum says it's a strange life, out of sync with the rest of the world, but I think it's cosy – and I get to have Mum all to myself.

Being part of theatre life is like being part of a big family; I've never been part of a big family before and I like it. Judi Connelli and her friend adore me and say I give the best hugs. 'They're a couple,' Mum tells me later, 'you know, like Colin and Colin are. Some women just like women, some men only men.'

Marcia with her sage-like confidence is always keen to encourage creativity and individuality. She has a daughter named Deni, about my age too, she tells me. Corinne, who looks after the wigs, wears the coolest clothes – stonewashed jeans slashed with a razor so they almost fall off. 'She's a woman,' Mum says 'born in a man's body.'

Women come to Mum's dressing room to chat and gossip, lowering their voices when they get to the scandalous bits, glancing at me before they continue. 'It's all right,' Mum says, 'Katie understands, don't you?' I feel at home in the theatre, sitting with Mum in her dressing room while people flit about in undergarments, their hair tucked under stocking caps, singing scales and doing stretches.

As show time approaches the energy intensifies, the people around me transform into larger than life beings. The stage manager runs through the rabbit warren of corridors knocking, calling out, 'Ten minutes till curtain! Places please!'

On the dark stage behind the curtain, the murmur of the audience on the other side, discordant notes of the orchestra warming up, the chorus girls stand in the wings mouthing their lines, miming dance steps, the odd gleam of a sequin the only hint of what's to come. I scurry through the hidden crevices of the old theatre, weave beside lighting rigs and disused sets, past ladders leading up to holes in the ceiling that branch off into still more hidden spaces. I've discovered a route that takes me up to the seats 'in the Gods' – the lower house is packed to standing room only but the top balcony is closed to the public. I pull down the spring seat in the centre of the front row and sit up on my knees to peer over the balcony.

I watch every show, each is subtly different. I know all the drama of life backstage – who's struggling with laryngitis, who's dancing on a sprained ankle, who had a fight with whom or came in slurring their words, but the show must always go on. I notice when a performer really nails their big number and I notice when things go awry, like the time Marcia makes her entrance to sing 'It Only Takes a Moment' – she stands on a platform that turns like a Lazy Susan to bring her onto the stage, but this time it doesn't stop turning and Marcia goes round and has to keep singing off stage until she reappears like a figure in a cuckoo clock. The audience are none the wiser but the cast and crew are set to explode with laughing.

The audience is also variable. Sometimes I think they're a little lacklustre and need some prompting so I take it upon myself to amp them up, clapping loudly and sticking my fingers in my mouth to wolf whistle. Mum laughs nervously backstage but doesn't specifically tell me not to do it, Judi Connelli ruffles my hair and Marcia pinches my cheeks.

Mum takes me with her to Chapel Street, she wants to walk the whole length of it taking in all the fashion, window shopping. 'Melburnians have so much more style than Sydneysiders!' she says. We eat pizza straight out of the box and go shopping at markets. We do all the things we're never allowed to do in Sydney under Dad's watch. One day we pass a curiously pokey little bookshop, incense wafts out to the street.

'Shall we have a look?' Mum asks conspiratorially, and I nod because I love bookshops, but this is not like bookshops I've been in before.

Mum finds several books on tea leaf reading and Edgar Cayce and one on the Bermuda Triangle that she takes to the register. 'My old boss went missing on the *Mary Celeste*,' she tells the woman behind the counter, 'he just disappeared without a trace! Imagine a whole ship floating in the ocean with not a soul on it. And the table left with all the plates and cutlery, halfway through dinner!'

'Oh yes,' says the lady, 'fascinating!'

'I think aliens took them,' Mum says. 'How else could a whole ship of people just disappear? Poor Mister Timms … he was a nice man. I wonder what they did with him …'

I buy two books, one on UFOs, with blurry looking pictures, flying saucers that look like hub caps shot with a bad camera. But there's one photo of an alien I find so creepy I can barely bring myself to look; actually, it looks like a man wrapped head to foot in tin foil, but something about it raises goosebumps all over me. The book talks about people seeing strange lights in the sky, their cars stop working on deserted roads and all the electronics heat up and go crazy. The stories creep me out so much I become scared stiff of the dark and utterly terrified of looking up at the night sky in case I see a UFO. The other book is a fat encyclopedia called *Unexplained Phenomena*.

'Listen to this!' I say to Mum. 'It says sleeping under a pyramid charges you with pyramid power!' Mum is excited – doing a show every night is totally exhausting. Marcia gets home to find us making pyramids out of drinking straws and kitchen string.

'Fabulous!' she says.

Mum thinks Marcia is teasing. 'Oh it's a bit mad sounding I know!' she says, but Marcia isn't kidding.

'Seriously!' she says. 'Can you make one for me too?'

Marcia loves alternate therapies. She's always popping open little brown glass vials of Royal Jelly.

'All bees are born the same, but only *one* is fed royal jelly and becomes the queen!' she says. 'Try one.'

The vials look too special to share, 'Oh no, no! I couldn't Marcia!' but Marcia is insistent and finally Mum takes one to share with me. We both make a face, it tastes awful! Marcia looks pleased. She tells Mum she should also try a flotation tank.

'It's *the best* relaxation! You lie floating in water …'

Mum can't bear the thought, she'd probably sink and drown. Marcia laughs, 'Jeanne, you can't drown, it's only a foot deep! And besides, it's special water with salts so you float!'

'No, no, no! I couldn't!' Mum shakes her head emphatically, 'I'd be *terrified!*' So she volunteers me instead.

The tank is a huge round thing that looks like a spaceship, inside is a shallow pool of glowing water, the surface misty with steam like a nuclear reactor. The water is the same temperature as the air and when I lie back I feel like I'm floating, being pulled up in the beam of a waiting UFO.

In Sydney Dad berates Mum, 'What did you buy all those silly books for? Fill the child's head with nonsense!'

I show Danielle and Melanie *Unexplained Phenomena* when we're driving in the car. My favourite page is 'Spontaneous Human Combustion'. There's a crime scene photo of a walking frame and a burn mark on the linoleum, next to which lies a charred stump wearing a slipper. When I read out the copy it says the person just burst into flames – spontaneously!

'And it can happen to anyone at any time!'

The Cope twins gasp along with Mum who cries, '*Ooooooah!*'

I TOUCH MYSELF

During afternoon roll call, I overhear Kate McDonald asking a friend to go to the movies. I know Kate pretty well because our surnames are close so we're often in the same classes, and also because she has a famous parent like me. Kate's father's real name is Garry McDonald but he's more well known as his iconic character Norman Gunston, a pasty-faced reporter with greasy hair and terrible comb-over.

Two older students had sought Kate out in the hallway at recess, they tapped her on the shoulder and asked, 'Is your father really like that?'

Kate scoffed, 'Don't be *ridiculous!* Norman Gunston's a made up character, my father's an actor!' Kate turned back to her circle of friends with a flick of her ponytail saying, 'How stupid can you be!'

Undeterred the two older students had turned to me, 'Hey, isn't your mum Jeanne Little?'

'Uh-huh,' I said.

'Is she really like that?'

'Ummm … Yep.'

'Say "Hello Dahling!"'

I shook my head, 'Oh, I can't, I don't say it like Mum …'

But the two girls had already started taking her off anyway, 'Hello DAAAAAHHHLING! HELLO DAAAAAHHHLING!' they screamed and ran off together down the corridor. The sound of their voices ricocheted throughout the school, '*HELLO DAAAAAAAAAAAAHHHHHHLING!!!*'

Maybe I should have lied and said Mum was an actress too, it sounded so impressive when Kate said it.

PART 2

When Kate's dad turns up to school pick-up in the afternoons he looks a little different from the other parents too. Last week Mum drove straight from television wearing purple hot pants and a yellow afro wig. Garry McDonald looks subdued next to this; his usual get-up is a sarong and bare feet, which still raises a few eyebrows with the conservative set.

'Dad has a guru,' Kate said once by way of explanation and I left it at that, not wanting to give away the fact I had no idea what she was talking about. I thought maybe it meant he was part Scottish like Mum, maybe a sarong was a bit like wearing a kilt …

I often feel stupid when I'm around Kate so I try not to talk too much. Luckily Kate has lots of opinions about all sorts of things so as long as I keep my mouth shut I'm fine. Last week she said her parents are Labor supporters because they're in 'the arts', she said anyone who supports the Liberal party must be a bloody idiot. I didn't mention my parents vote Liberal and that when Bob Hawke cried when Australia won the America's Cup Dad laughed and swore at the television.

I asked Mum what Kate meant saying her parents were in the arts, and she said that Kate's mother is also an actress and a very successful one at that, she was even in a movie with Mick Jagger. But Kate said her mother prefers to be called an actor as it's not gender specific and once again I had to keep my mouth shut because I didn't know what that meant either.

Now Kate's talking about going to see *Dirty Dancing* on the weekend with the girl next to her.

'Hey, I've heard that movie is supposed to be great!' I say to Kate. 'Can I come too?'

She looks me over critically. Like her father she's got a quick brain and razor-sharp tongue. Her personality reminds me a little of my grandmother.

'So you like Patrick Swayze?' she says.

I must look puzzled, but I say, 'Sure.'

'Oh, never mind,' she says, 'you can come. I'm meeting Tiffy at two o'clock at Double Bay cinemas on Saturday. But don't tell Danielle Cope. I know you hang out with her but I don't want her coming too.'

'Okay,' I say and look at my Swatch watch, to make it look like I'm busy, like I have stuff to do.

'Great,' she says, 'see you then, and DON'T be late!'

Tiffy Farrington lives in Woollahra, one suburb away. Her mother Angela phones to say she's happy to pick me up on the way to the movies and so at a quarter to two a red vintage Jaguar pulls up out the front.

'Oh thank you *so* much Angela!' Mum calls out, running up to the window of the car. 'Oh heavens, I shouldn't come out on the street, I look like *death* without make-up!'

Tiffy's older sister Fleur sits in the front seat beside her mother, I slide into the back seat with Tiffy and pull on my belt. 'I love your bubble skirt!' I say to Tiffy who looks pleased, she tells me it's from a shop called Cherry Lane near the cinemas.

'Can we go there afterwards Mum?' Tiffy asks. 'Oh my god, it's the *coolest* shop – you wait! If you like this skirt you're going to go *crazy*!'

'Your mother,' Angela says, eyeballing me in the rear-vision mirror, 'is the most *heavenly* person. Can I tell you, it is an absolute *delight*, to be picking you up ... she is just a *darling*.' Angie Farrington has French heritage, her daughters have dark brown hair and chestnut eyes just like her, and when she looks at me she looks very intensely, like she can read my thoughts. 'Do you know, we only moved up from Melbourne a few years ago, and I had *no idea* who she was. I've never watched daytime television. Anyway, the school sent home an invitation inviting parents to participate in a music class, and do you know, she was the only other parent who went. Not one other mother came! The music teacher ...'

'Mrs Laudon,' Tiffy interrupts.

'Yes, Mrs Laudon played the piano and all you little girls started galloping around the room pretending to be ponies! I'd come in a little late and there was your mother with her shoes off, galloping around the room in her stockings! "This old nag is ready for the glue factory!" she called out to me as she went past,' Angie laughed. 'Oh! I had *no idea* she was so famous! She's so down to earth and made me feel so welcome at the school! Oh, we had the most hilarious time!'

Tiffy, Kate and I sit transfixed in the dark watching Jennifer Grey run and swan dive into Patrick Swayze's arms. Afterwards we head to Cherry Lane and on the way pass a staircase with a poster advertising jazz dancing classes.

'Let's do it!' Kate says. 'We might meet Patrick Swayze!'

'Oh my god, do you want to?' Tiffy asks thrilled.

'Sure,' I say, 'Why not?'

After Saturday dancing I often go back with one of the girls to their house, sometimes even stay for a sleepover. Kate lives in Rose Bay in a large house with a rose garden, Garry's parents live upstairs. I think how nice it would be to have my grandmother living upstairs but Kate says her Mum's always saying Garry spends too much time up there and they fight about it.

Part 2

Kate's parents each have their own creative space, Diane's is a sewing room, Garry's is an enormous model train set. It's strictly off limits but Kate sneaks me in, I catch a glimpse of dozens of tiny rail lines crisscrossing over mountains carpeted with bright green grass, a tiny town with shops and houses – I could stand looking at it all day but Kate is nervous and pulls me out.

Inside Kate's house are a sagging couch and a coffee table cluttered with books and Frank Zappa LPs. We go into the kitchen to get a drink of water. There's never anything to eat or drink at their house, I'm always hungry when I stay there. Kate takes me into the kitchen and fills two glasses of water from the tap. Garry is making coffee, pressing grounds into a percolator, standing there in the cramped kitchen in his sarong and bare feet.

'Ah, who have you got there Kate?' he asks in a gravelly voice. He looks like he just woke up even though it's late in the afternoon.

'You *know* Dad,' she says, sounding irritated. I'm relieved I'm not the only one she uses that tone with.

He looks at me over wire-framed glasses, peering down like I'm some kind of abstract curiosity. 'Hello there,' he says. Kate's right, he's not a bit like Norman Gunston.

Kate's older brother David sits in the sunroom at a drafting table, the artworks he's working on are made up entirely of dots in black ink, close-ups of faces and hands bunched into fists. Even though art's my thing I can't imagine ever producing something even half as amazing as these by my final school year. But Kate doesn't want to linger over her brother's artworks. 'C'mon,' she says, 'let's play in my room.'

We play Barbies for a bit until Kate's mum knocks on the door to tell us they're going out, there's money on the kitchen bench to order a pizza later. Kate's grandparents are in the flat above but it feels exciting because it's like we're in the house alone. David's girlfriend turns up and they go out to the swimming pool, she screams when he picks her up and jumps in with her. When they tire of swimming they go off into David's room, only a thin wall separates them from where we sit watching television. We start giggling when we hear the noises, it seems to go on for ages and gets so loud we can't hear the television. Finally Kate shouts, 'Oh just have a bloody orgasm already!' and turns the TV up louder.

We go back to Kate's room and she pulls out the trundle bed. We play Barbies for a while, improvising a love scene, tearing the clothes off the plastic Ken doll and mashing him up against the Barbie with the longest hair. We hear David and his girlfriend in the kitchen talking. 'They're always starving after sex!' Kate says, then she says 'Hey, wanna see some of my brother's pornos?'

'Sure,' I say. She sneaks out of the room, peering around the corner first, then returns with the *Playboy* magazines shoved under her T-shirt. She closes the door as quietly as she can before we dissolve into laughter.

I flick through the pages. Flesh, skin, bodies and hair everywhere I look, boobs, enormous boobs like giant cow's udders! Is this what grown-ups really look like without clothes on?

'This one's my favourite,' Kate says, 'they're playing tennis!' She throws it to me. Two girls this time, in a series of photos posing in tiny white tennis outfits. Kate laughs, a harsh, crackling sound. She turns the next page which has an extra fold of paper. 'Wait till you see the centrefold,' she says. My mouth drops open. A woman lies on her back, the camera looks straight up between her legs. I look away and feel my cheeks burning. Kate is still laughing. 'Look at all that hair!' she's saying. 'Isn't it revolting! That's her *cunt!*' She laughs again. 'That's what David calls it. It's the most awful sounding word, still, it's better than *vagina!*' We're both laughing so hard now we can barely breathe.

I don't know if I want to look at any more pictures, they're repulsive, yet compelling and give me a weird feeling between my legs. Near the back of the magazine are pages of letters. I read part of a letter out to her, 'Signed Horny Housewife,' and we both dissolve into laughter again.

Where it all began! Appalled at the boring maternity clothes on offer Mum started designing and making her own. This photo was the start of her incredible television career. 'Look at that fat face!' Mum would have said. (Courtesy of Mirror Newspapers Ltd)

Not your average mum ... 'When you got home you screamed and screamed,' Dad often said. 'It's a wonder you survived.' (Courtesy of Bauer Media Pty Limited/ Woman's Day)

Mum was a weekly regular on The Mike Walsh Show, *the number-one daytime television show in the late 70s and early 80s. (Courtesy of Hayden Productions)*

Mum won the Gold Logie for Most Popular Personality in 1976, shown here with Don Lane and Paul Hogan. (Courtesy of Bauer Media Pty Limited/ Woman's Day)

In some ways the Glad Bag competition summed up the essence of my mother's persona – a little bit of fun and frivolity in an otherwise dull world. (Courtesy of New Idea)

Mum's extraordinary talent was sewing. With next to no budget for her television spots she had to be resourceful. This dress was a family affair – Dad and I squashed milk bottle caps in front of the telly for a week while Mum sewed them on. (Courtesy of Bernina Sewing Machines)

Little Jeanne, the youngest of seven siblings (left), with her sisters Cathie, Elsie, Charlotte and Margaret and her mother Nan, a truly remarkable woman who brought up her large family to believe 'anything you set your mind to you can achieve'.

In contrast to my mother's family, my father was an only child — shown here in the arms of my grandmother Dora, wearing his trademark beret because she thought his ears stuck out.

A photo from another era, my grandmother Dora (right), the eldest with my Great Aunties Yvonne and Lilius, or Auntie Vonnie and Auntie Lee for short.

An early photo of my father taken by the famous photographer Helmut Newton.

Dad met my mother at a party of course, where else? Here dressed casually in feathers and pasties, way ahead of her time, wearing foundation as fake tan.

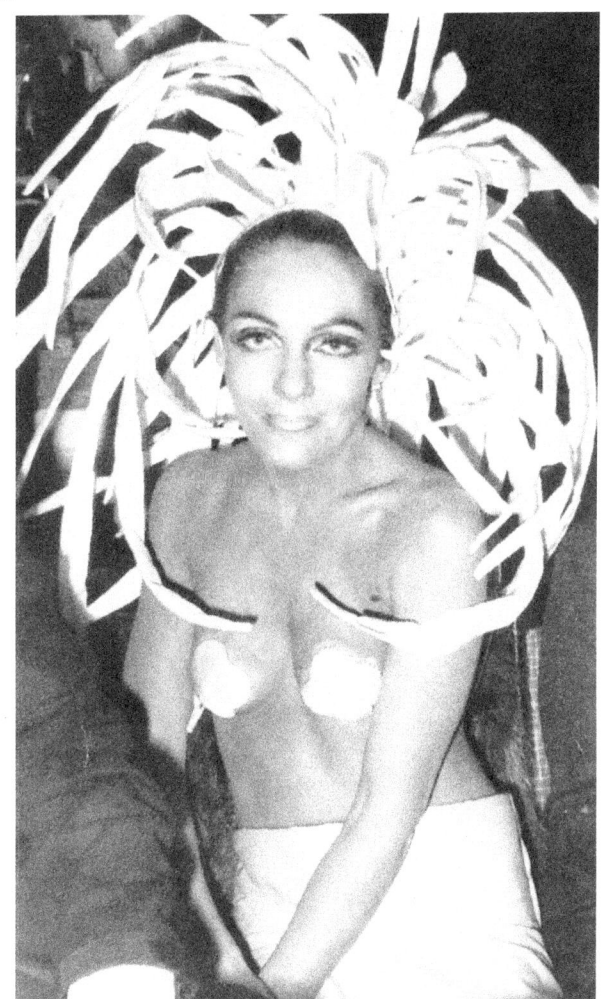

The Little family – Dad, Mum and me, complete with 70s shag rug.

The two other people I thought of as family, my 'uncles' Colin Brees and Colin Johnston.

My favourite 'uncle' Colin Brees worked with my father in the basement of our house. In a magazine article Mum described him as her best friend. 'Truly Dahling, Colin is the type of man I'd have married if Barry hadn't come along!'

There was only one kid I liked to hang out with, Nicole, the adopted daughter of my parents' friends Shirley and Terry, who was also an only child. Shown here with one of the Christmas presents from my grotesque pile, my grandmother Dor Dor in the background, for whom I could do no wrong.

On the hunt for a beach house – my lovely fun mum with brown hair.

The Cope twins – Danielle, my partner in crime, and goody-two-shoes Melanie, who we were always trying to corrupt.

Mum with Craig Bennett at his twenty-fifth birthday party.

I love this photo of Dad and me, it sums up our relationship so well. We annoy the crap out of each other and rarely show affection, but deep down I know he loves me.

Baby Tom was cut from the same mould as Mum – blue eyes and a big forehead, loud and no 'off' switch!

The last photo I have of Mum out and about with Tom and Dad.

A showbiz family. Tom Poulton doing what he loves most – filming on set!

On set for the Arnott's commercial – a dream come true for a little boy who gets to eat biscuits all day – but life was beginning to take its toll on me by this point.

There's no business like show business! A final photoshoot with New Idea *before things really went pear-shaped. (Courtesy of* New Idea*)*

A rare last photo of Mum with Craig and Craig and Helen Zerefos, who recognised the signs of Alzheimer's long before any of us knew.

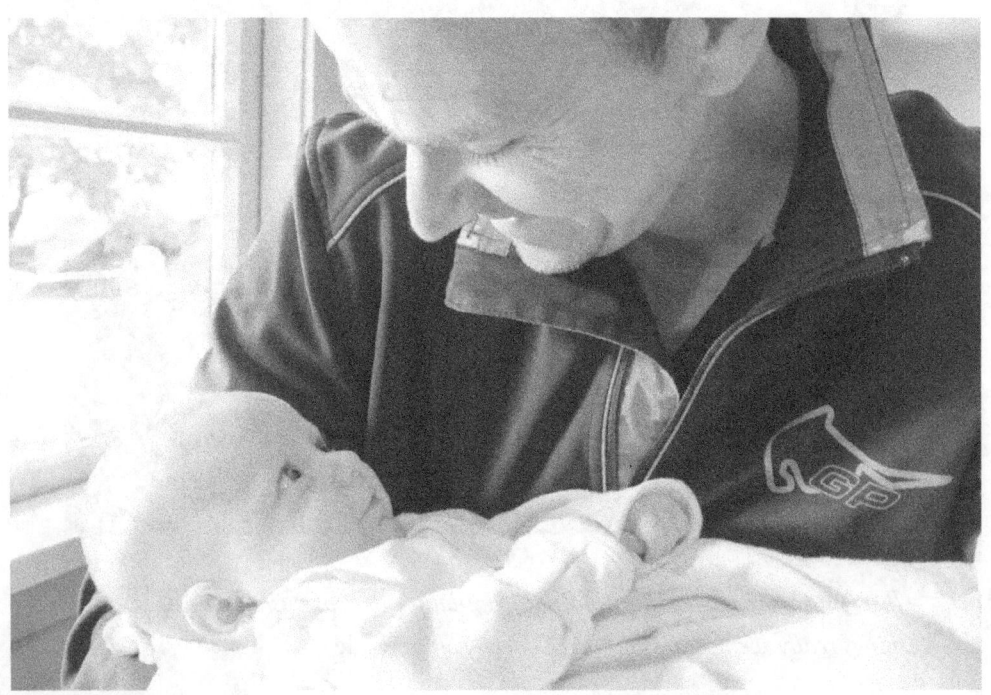

Our 'happy accident' baby Hunter was a surprise and a bundle of joy.

Marcia Hines and me at one of Craig Bennett's luncheons: 'Your mother loved you, you know.' Some of the most healing words ever spoken.

With Richard Roxburgh at The Logies. Tom played the youngest, cheeky son of Cleaver Greene's best friend in Rake.

My three gorgeous kids who make sure my life is always more entertaining than fiction.

Determined to laugh! With my beautiful, fearless, long-time friend Sally Dingle Wall.

My daughter Charlotte, otherwise known as La La gets dressed up for a photoshoot with New Idea *in some of Mum's wardrobe.*

Learning to live after Mum. Top: my father with Hunter and me, Christmas 2015. Bottom: my husband Timothy Poulton and children keeping the tradition of my grandmother Dor Dor's pudding alive.

Waiting in the green room with Tom and Mum's Gold Logie to go on The Morning Show.

Cleaning out my parents' apartment took forever – amongst the detritus, my mother's iconic eyelashes and a letter which broke my heart.

Representing the sandwich generation! Stuck between looking after ageing parents and young children, on The Daily Edition.

I SEE RED

It's Saturday, I'm supposed to be going to dance classes but finally I've got my period – *the* period. I take a shower and pull out the bag from Colin Johnston's pharmacy that's been sitting in my bathroom cupboard forever.

Mum had told Colin Johnston I'd need a belt and sanitary towels and he'd laughed and said, 'Jean, nobody uses those things anymore!'

I don't even know where to begin with a tampon so I take out one of the pads, read the instructions, peel off the backing paper and stick it in my undies. It's enormous; I feel like I'm walking around with a brick between my legs, surely everyone is going to see this. Even wearing the biggest, baggiest top I've got over my leggings I still feel like I've got a sign around my neck saying SHE JUST GOT HER PERIOD.

I tie a sloppy joe round my waist and go downstairs. Mum is making me pancakes but she's rushing them, she pours all the batter into the pan at once, squashing a couple of lumps of flour with a fork. The pancake sizzles fiercely. I feel like I should tell her even though it's awkward.

'Mum …' I say and wait for her, 'Mum! I've got some … news. I got my … you know …' She looks at me blankly. 'You know … my *period*.'

'Oooah that's wonderful!' She hugs me and I stiffen, then she shouts, 'Barry! Katie got her period!'

He's walked into the kitchen at just the wrong time. 'Oh!' he says, 'Well … congratulations.' You can tell he's as confused and as uncomfortable as I am. Is that the right word? Should he have said congratulations? 'Why can I smell smoke?' he says. 'Jean! The pancake!'

'Oh! Go and sit down Katie, I'll bring it to you!' Mum says. I waddle to the table. Oh god, this is awful, I can't wait to leave, but I have to eat the pancake first, I don't want to hurt Mum's feelings after she's gone to the trouble of making it. It's half an inch thick, tough as rubber and the bottom is burnt black, so Mum has put extra ice cream and maple syrup on it to compensate. She hugs me again after she puts it in front of me.

A few days later it's Colin Johnston's birthday so Mum is making a cake, but she's rushed it and burnt the bottom of that too. She cuts off the burnt bits, 'Oh, that looks terrible,' she says, 'doesn't it?'

I shrug. I don't mind, I'm getting to eat the bits she's cutting off.

'I know,' she says, 'I'll hide it under lots of whipped cream!' Mum is a master at fixing things that haven't gone quite right.

After dinner Mum brings the cake out piled high with cream. Colin Johnston blows out the candles and when Mum goes to fetch plates Colin Brees orders him to take the camera.

'Oh no,' Colin Johnston says, 'don't …' but it's too late, Colin Brees has a mischievous twinkle in his eye.

'Jean!' Colin Brees calls out. 'The cream's off!'

'Oooah, *what?*' she says.

'The cream – it's off!' Colin Brees says, 'Smell it!' He sniffs it and wrinkles his nose.

'Oh! But it couldn't be! That rotten shop …'

'It is, it is!' Colin Brees says. 'You smell it!' He slides the cake towards her. She looks disappointed. 'Go on, smell it,' Colin Brees says again, 'You'll see …'

Mum dutifully bends to smell the cream on the cake and Colin Brees pushes her face straight into it, Mum lifts her head up and the flash pops on the camera.

HEART OF GLASS

My parents tell me I'm staying the night at Dor Dor's on the weekend. 'Not again!' I say, putting up mild resistance. I never really mind going to Dor Dor's, everything there is still the same as when I was little, the butterfly sheets and the bowls of jelly and custard in the bare refrigerator. We watch *The World Around Us* but this time the end of the program shows the orangutan's rainforest being cut down.

I've been staying at Dor Dor's and the Colins' a lot lately and it's not until a few weeks later that I find out why.

'Your mother has to go in for a little operation,' Dad says. 'It's nothing,' he says, 'she'll be fine.' But when we visit Mum in the hospital after the operation she looks pale and groggy, like she can't wake up. 'That's just the anaesthetic,' Dad says. Mum struggles to open her eyes and a weak smile crosses her face as Dad pats her hand. 'It's good news,' Dad says to her and Mum's eyes fill with tears.

***

'So how did you feel when you found out your mother had cancer?' the journalist asks me. 'You must have been really worried …' She's nodding and smiling at me sympathetically, her pen poised eagerly above the notepad on her knee. Mum's on the lounge with that face she has when she's been told she's not allowed to speak, like it's taking all her energy to keep her mouth shut and it's going to bust open any second.

Dad's in the background hovering like he does when he's listening to Mum doing interviews, to make sure she doesn't say anything terrible, like that time she said she'd read a friend's tea cup and told her she was going to have a black baby. I don't know what the big deal about that was, after all, the daughter they adopted did turn out to have dark skin, but apparently you're not allowed to say stuff like that.

It was a surprise when the journalist asked Mum if she could ask me a few questions. 'Sure Dahling, I'm sure Katie would love that!' Mum said and I was called into the lounge room, all lit up with the crystal chandelier sparkling.

Being interviewed is like putting on a show, inviting a stranger into the house to tell them stories. I know this as well as they do, so Dad shouldn't look so worried. I've been brought up backstage – remember?

'Yes,' I say, 'I was terribly worried.' I'm a good actress, I don't give away the fact that I had no idea Mum was sick, with cancer or anything else for that matter.

'How did they break the tragic news?'

I have plenty of practice at lying to adults, the trick is to use a little bit of the truth and elaborate on it. 'Well, Dad told me that Mum had to get an operation ... and that it might be serious, that we wouldn't know until we saw her, after she woke up ... *if* she woke up that is ...' Dad gives me an alarmed look in the background and I think maybe I might have gone too far so I shut up.

'Oh good heavens!' the interviewer says. Wide-eyed, she looks to my parents for confirmation of this grizzly fate that could have been.

Mum nods and quickly adds, 'Oh! Poor Katie, we tried not to tell her too much, didn't we Barry? But children know, don't they ... they just *know*.' Mum takes the reins of the conversation back and I ask if I can go. The journalist thanks me and Dad catches my eye as I leave the room, a look equivalent to a seal keeper throwing a sardine from the bucket.

The article comes out, it's made the front cover of one of the major gossip magazines. 'JEANNE'S BRUSH WITH DEATH!' it says.

I wonder how much of the article is true and how much is fiction, how worried should I really have been? It's impossible to know, just like any good tabloid story. In any case, it doesn't matter now, the phone's been ringing off the hook with requests for interviews and Mum's running around saying, 'Oh Dahling, I'm fine! Fit as a fiddle! Healthy as a horse!' to all the people who ask her everywhere she goes – the woman working the Franklins checkout, the bank teller, the owner of the coffee shop, and the old lady who takes her arm outside the pharmacy.

***

I tell Tiffy I'm going on Bert Newton's morning show with Mum.

'Oh how exciting!' she says. 'Are you nervous?' I hadn't really thought about that, I'm more excited I'm getting to take a couple of days off school to fly down to Melbourne.

At the studio Bert meets us, his big round face lighting up when he sees my parents.

'Are you nervous?' he asks me. 'Don't be nervous!'

'Oh, she's not nervous Bert!' Mum says.

All this talking about not being nervous is starting to make me nervous. I look around the room, one side is dark and full of equipment, the other is made to look like a brightly lit-up lounge room with frosted windows lit from behind. The sound guy approaches to wire us up with microphones.

'Not me,' Dad says, 'I'm not going on,' but Bert insists.

'Yes, come on Bah!' Mum says, 'It'll be fun!'

Dad doesn't like going on television, he doesn't like being in the limelight, but Bert convinces him. The sound guy is clipping a little microphone to my neckline and dropping the wire down my top. 'Excuse me,' he says fumbling with the waistline of my skirt to attach the battery pack.

'Watch your step!' Bert says, leading us into the fake living room, which is set up on a large wooden platform. A few people rush and scurry around us and then they all disappear down into the dark area of the room and the little red light on the camera goes on. My heart beats faster.

'And now!' Bert says into the camera, 'Please welcome our next guest, star of stage and screen, the very wonderful Jeanne Little and her family!'

In the end it's like being taken out to dinner with my parents where I just sit there and Mum does all the talking and once in a while Dad interrupts her to tell a story and then Mum takes over again and he says with a comical edge of annoyance, 'Let me finish Jean!' He looks to Bert and says, 'See what I have to live with Bert?' and everybody laughs loudly. Bert asks me what it's like to have Jeanne Little as my mother and I nod and say lamely, 'Pretty good really,' and then Mum starts talking again.

They give Dad a tape of the show and when we get back to the hotel he sticks it in to watch it. 'What did you make me go on for?' he asks Mum. 'Look how fat I look!'

But I'm not looking at him, I'm looking at me, my legs are slightly apart and because the set was built on a stage the camera angle shows straight up my skirt. The blood drains from my face. Tiffy was going to tell Kate to watch too, who is going to have a field day with this when I get back to school.

'Doesn't Katie look gorgeous!' Mum says. I'm so horrified; I think I might be sick.

DAMN IT, JANET

Mum and Dad have gone to India to film a pilot for a show. I was disappointed they weren't taking me until I heard I was staying at the Farringtons'. It's like living in the Tom Hanks movie *Big*, there are piles of comics and shelves of board games, unrestricted access to TV and a wardrobe full of the coolest clothes. I'm used to living in an odd assortment of Mum's hand-me-downs and completely impractical outfits that Mum either buys or makes me.

Tiffy's father Richard is British, he wears bow ties and laughs a lot. He does card tricks and tells us silly jokes when he gets home from work. Angie is always taking photos, the walls of their house are crowded with them, there's even one of Tiffy posing with Michael Jackson. Along with the photos there are also clippings from the social papers and in the hallway taking pride of place, the article about Richard winning Black Jack and breaking the bank at the casino.

Richard Farrington doesn't drive, he gets picked up by taxi every morning, leaving the house with an umbrella and newspaper tucked under his arm. Last school holidays I worked in his office with Tiffy, mailing envelopes for the salesmen who spent all day on the phone, selling newsletters about commodities and investments.

At the end of the week I was shocked at the amount of money he gave me. I was used to collecting spare change left in public telephones.

'Thanks Daddy!' Tiffy said throwing her arms around him.

'Well done my little receptionists, what are you going to buy?' he asked.

'Clothes!' Tiffy said.

'How about you Katie?'

'Um ... I've been saving up to buy a piano,' I said finally. 'There's one in the *Trading Post* for four hundred dollars ...'

Richard laughed good-naturedly, 'Gosh, for that price it might only have one octave!' Tiffy giggled, 'Daaaad!'

'I'm just warning Katie before she gets into treble! Did you know I can play piano? I bang my head on the keys and play by ear!'

Richard's hobby is Scrabble and he often sits with another man, looking very serious, at a small table in the garden. But there's no time for Scrabble these days because he's producing a stage show of *The Rocky Horror Show* and his evenings are now taken up with meetings with the director Richard Morley, sometimes the cast come to the house too, Daniel Abineri and Steve Bastoni, who we all have mad crushes on, and a young unknown actor called Russell Crowe, who isn't bad looking either.

After school Tiffy and I sit and watch *Ferris Bueller's Day Off*; we almost know it word for word. Tiffy sits on the floor beside the VCR, her finger on the rewind button replaying a tricky bit of script. We ride our bikes to McDonald's and buy Cokes, and sit on the overpass of the multi-laned freeway talking about our favourite bits of the movie.

'I love it when his sister karate kicks Ed Rooney in the kitchen!' I say and Tiffy tells me a secret, that when they went to Egypt last holidays a man who worked in the hotel crept into Fleur and Tiffy's room and got into bed with Fleur.

'That's awful!' I say. 'What did you do?'

The man was only in their room a few minutes, Tiffy says, before Fleur screamed so nothing much happened.

'You must have been terrified!' I say to her.

Tiffy shrugs and takes another sip of her Coke, 'Not really,' she says, 'I actually slept through the whole thing. I feel a bit bad about that.'

After dinner when it's dark we play a game we've made up called Psychic Guess Who inspired by the page on telepathy in the *Unexplained Phenomena* book. When one of us concentrates on the card we're holding the other can guess it almost straight off every time; it's so creepy we get shivers up our spines and have to sleep with the light on.

On Friday nights the Farringtons go out to the movies and Tiffy and I are the last to come downstairs.

'Oh my god, you're not actually going out looking like that, are you?' Fleur says.

Tiffy and I love Bros, the English boy band, we're both wearing cut-off denim shorts that we've decorated with marker pen. My back pocket has a Union Jack and the words

'I LOVE MATT' on one leg with a heart. Tiffy's shorts are the same as mine, but hers reads 'I LOVE LUKE'. We're both wearing Doc Martins and belt buckles like Bros do in their video clip, with our hair up in matching side ponytails.

'Oh look Richard,' Angie says, 'look at the girls!' Richard gives a lovely toffee-nosed chuckle and Angie runs off to fetch the camera.

I've never been in the city at night before, the lights are big and bright and there are masses of people. At the cinemas Tiffy's parents go off to see one movie while we go with Fleur to see a different one. 'I can't believe you're making me babysit,' Fleur says. 'If someone actually sees me with you two looking like this, I'll die. I'll seriously die.'

The one and only time I've ever been to see a movie with my parents was when they took me to an art house cinema. It was a Japanese movie with subtitles that someone had told them they must see. It turned out to be full of kinky sex scenes and the three of us sat in the dark theatre awkwardly, me in the middle, none of us able to turn away from the huge screen where a woman was ecstatically screaming in a scene that involved live prawns.

'Well, that was ... unusual,' Dad had finally said on the walk back to the car and Mum just kind of tittered and said, 'Yes, aren't the Japanese mad!' That was the time I thought I'd die.

After the movie we head to an enormous food court in Chinatown and Tiffy and I load our all-you-can-eat plates with hot sticky noodles and bright pink sweet and sour pork. It's the most fun night I think I've ever had and when we pile into Angie's Jaguar the vehicle purrs out of the car park sitting so low to the ground it feels like we're gliding just over the tarmac. Simply Red fills the car with saxophones, Tiffy giggles and whispers in my ear, 'Wait till you hear the lyrics!'

'Oooh it's getting harder now,' Mick Hucknall croons, 'I'm going deeper, deeper'.

Fleur and Tiffy sing along, laughing, Richard and Angie join in. 'Oooooh deeper now! It's getting deeper now!' My embarrassment is excruciating. All four of the Farringtons are singing along at the tops of their voices, laughing together at the end.

Mum and Dad get back from India and I'm eager to see them but sad to leave the Farringtons. 'Who would you rather live with,' Dad asks, 'if you could choose?'

'You and Mum, of course,' I say, but I've taken too long to answer and Dad looks offended.

On opening night of *The Rocky Horror Show* I go through Mum's wardrobe with her. 'What are these?' I ask, holding up a dangly thing, all purple silk and black lace.

'Oh they're called suspenders!' Mum says. 'You clip stockings onto them, like this …' She pulls out fishnets and garter belts.

'You'll have to wear a big overcoat!' Mum says, not because I'm dressed up like a twelve-year-old hooker, but because she doesn't want me getting cold.

'Good heavens Jean,' Dad says when I come downstairs. 'Is she really going out like that?'

Mum drives me to Kate McDonald's house and Tiffy and Kate answer the door looking like twelve-year-old hookers as well. The grown-ups scream with laughter.

'Well at least someone's getting some use out of all this lingerie!' Mum says. Kate's mum Diane puts make-up on us and Garry gets a camera.

'A man could go to jail for fifty years for taking a photo like this!' he says.

The front of the theatre is lit up with spotlights that shine up into the sky like Batman's signal and the red carpet is crowded on either side with onlookers and press. We walk in beside Richard Farrington, thrilled to bits, and sneak looks to see who's checking us out when we get inside. The show is nothing like *Jerry's Girls;* the audience does all sorts of crazy things throughout the show, they throw rice at the stage and jump out of their seats to do the Time Warp.

At the afterparty we scurry around with our programmes getting them signed by all the actors. I'm particularly thrilled to get the autograph of Richard O'Brien, the creator, who's come out from England to play the part of Riff Raff for the first few weeks.

'What is this, kindergarten?' Russell Crowe says scornfully when we approach him.

'C'mon,' I say to the girls, 'we don't need his autograph, it's not like he's famous or anything.'

KISS ME, KISS ME, KISS ME

My parents are furious. I told them I smoked pot for the first time last weekend. They've always said, 'You can tell us anything!' so I took them at their word – and now they want to KILL me.

The room went all quiet and both of them pretended they were really focused on what they were doing. They didn't look at each other, just kept peeling vegetables and washing plates in the sink. Then Dad asked a few questions trying to keep his tone light. Who was there? Where did we do this? Where were the parents?

Stupidly, I answered all the questions honestly. Danielle and her boyfriend Michael, at his house when his mother was out.

Michael's father is famous too. He's often on the television but not like my mum who's an entertainer. His dad is in politics, rubbing shoulders with Bob Hawke and Paul Keating. Danielle and Michael's mothers have a lot in common; both are going through an ugly divorce and are single mothers of three children. The papers print photos of Michael's father getting around town with his new girlfriend in a red sports car.

Dad chopped the potatoes a bit too hard with the knife, 'Did you know about this Jean?'

'No! Of course not!' she stuttered.

Dad threw the potatoes into a dish, vigorously turned the pepper grinder. 'They're fourteen … Left alone at a boy's house without supervision … This should never have been allowed …'

What about the time he left me alone at Josh's, I wonder.

'You're never to see her again,' he said too quietly and I wondered if I'd heard him right.

'What?'

'You heard me! That girl's a bad influence! You're not to see her any more!'

'But they catch the bus together,' Mum said.

'And whose idea was that? I don't like it Jean! Hanging out over there all the time, you never know what they're doing! Is the mother home? Who's keeping an eye on these kids?'

'I can't believe this is all you've got to say!' I shout over the fracas. 'You're not even going to ask me what it was like? Have you ever even tried it?'

'No!' Dad shouted.

I looked at Mum who was shaking her head, 'Oh no Katie, of course we haven't!'

'Seriously?'

I just assumed they had, they were always going to parties and had all these bohemian friends.

'No!' Dad said again, 'We haven't tried it and neither should you!'

I looked at them, Dad was going to send me to my room anyway so I might as well lay it on them. 'Well, pity for you,' I said, 'Because it was *great*!'

I don't understand my mother, she comes across as all hip and cool, yet she's such a square! I wouldn't be surprised if she'd never even had sex either, but of course I'm living proof that she has … gross. What a thought.

Later up in my room I lie on my bed and close my eyes, thinking about the night before at Michael's house, reliving every delicious moment. I know Danielle has the shits with me, she asked me if I like Michael, her boyfriend, and of course I said no.

'Yes you do,' she said, 'It's like soooo obvious. You're always looking at him …'

'I do not!' I said. I screwed up my face to make an 'as if' look, 'I'm going out with Flea, remember?'

Flea is Michael's best friend. It's true I didn't really choose to go out with him but whenever the four of us went out, Michael and Dan would go off somewhere leaving us alone. I quite like kissing him even though we both have braces and it's kind of awkward, but he has a nice smell about him and he's quiet and sweet. I'm much more adventurous than he is though. Dan is always telling me about the things she's doing with Michael and I wonder why Flea never really puts too many moves on me. Maybe it means he doesn't really like me that much, but then, he did give me a ring of his to wear which was really cute and he was so shy when he gave it to me.

Okay, but yes … I do have to admit secretly that Michael, Dan's boyfriend, is hot. Totally hot. I'd jump his bones in a second! But of course he's Dan's boyfriend so I shouldn't even be thinking these thoughts!

But they are always fighting … they might split up! And Michael did look at me and make a joke that only we understood last night. His eyes when he laughs twinkle and make him look even hotter, and he has the cutest smile. So maybe we will get together at some point. My stomach flips at the thought. Imagine getting with Michael! That would be so hot!

But of course I can't because he's Danielle's boyfriend and everything, that would be really nasty and I shouldn't even be thinking about these things…

But so what? He's hot! I'm allowed to *look!*

THE UNGUARDED MOMENT

Dor Dor's been having a few falls. She's eighty-seven and living alone has become dangerous. The last fall left her with an egg on her forehead the size of a golf ball and when she's released from hospital they send her to a nursing home. She hates it. She's sitting morosely in a chair when we visit, the bruise on her forehead faded to an awful green and yellow that's spread down around her eye.

I've never seen her like this; she hardly even acknowledges Dad and completely snubs Mum, who's brought a huge bunch of flowers she was given at a charity event. Even I find it hard to get a smile. Dad tells her she's on the waitlist for another nursing home that's supposed to be nicer but she just keeps looking out the window.

'Alright Mum,' he says finally, 'we'll come back next weekend.'

She gives a short nod and looks away as if to say 'You do that'.

When a bed finally becomes available in the next nursing home it's in a shared room.

'Dora will hate that!' Mum says grimacing.

The new place is a sprawling mansion in Greenwich with an extension on the back. Dor Dor has a corner in a large front room with decorative pressed ceilings and a bay window, probably once a sitting room for a wealthy family. There are four hospital-style beds in the room with identical bedside tables, four plastic covered armchairs, four chairs for visitors, the seats of which are lifted to double as their latrine.

A lady with jet-black hair and large glasses occupies one of the corners, she speaks with difficulty from a stroke, her body left semi-paralysed and incontinent. She has a proper English accent and sits surrounded by framed photographs of her dogs. Opposite Dor Dor's bed is a Chinese lady, her middle aged son arrives dutifully every afternoon to rub her arms and legs with a pungent liniment. In the final corner, a lady with dementia named Betty, who sits in her armchair playing Solitaire.

Dor Dor tells Dad she wants to go home. Dad says he's looking for another place but the waiting lists are long. The only privacy in this room is provided by the thin plastic curtains hung on rails, which are pulled around the beds when the ladies are sat on their latrines. Dor Dor, like my parents, have never been this familiar with the noises and smells of human bodies before. 'We have to get her out of there,' my father says in the car.

The nurses, however, are not shy of bodies or bodily functions. They whisk my grandmother away to the shower and shampoo her hair, smooth sorbolene cream on her and help with the myriad of things other people take for granted. 'Would you like me to cut up your dinner Dora?' they ask without a trace of awkwardness or condescension.

The food in the home repulses my parents. It arrives on a tray at 5 pm, gluey soups, watery vegetables and grey slices of meat hidden under gravy. My grandmother, however, seems to enjoy the food; she's been living mostly on cornflakes and powdered milk in her unit for years.

'How can she eat that?' my father says.

'It must be hideous!' Mum agrees.

The days take on a reassuring, predictable rhythm and by the time a vacancy at another nursing home has become available my grandmother has developed a tenuous bond with the roommates and staff. Of course she can't say outright to my father that she wants to stay, that would mean she approves of the place and nothing is ever up to my grandmother's standards, let alone a shared room in a dormitory with penitentiary food. To my parents she is as surly as ever but the nurses know how to get a smile. When my parents are visiting she pushes the plate of food to the side untouched, but this is all just for show.

One nurse is bossier than the others and when she starts her shift everyone knows. 'Ladies! Faces on!' is her catch cry. It's nice to be reminded of such trivialities and the ladies dutifully take their lipstick and blushers from their drawers. In the wan light of the fluorescent tubes the ladies sit in their armchairs, skin deathly pale in contrast to the violent gashes of awkwardly applied rouge, scarlet lips pursed in expectant smiles.

There's no television in the shared room, the drama unfolds at a much slower pace – visits from relatives become anticipated events. It doesn't matter that the Chinese lady doesn't understand English or the black-haired lady is deaf as a post, as much can be observed from a person by their dress or body language, how frequently they come to visit, how long they stay. Dora has never been one to make friendships easily, but eavesdropping on other people's conversations requires little effort on her behalf. Unwittingly the ladies in the room become intimately acquainted through overheard conversations and curtained bowel movements.

The end is inescapable, they're reminded of this daily, bodies that were once young and beautiful now obstinately fail them. Each of them has their own problems to contend with – recalcitrant bladders and disobedient bowels, arthritic knees and hips that no longer support their weight. But whatever the ailment, at least it's not as bad as Betty, who can walk unaided yet doesn't remember her destination. However bad it gets, at least it's not that.

***

Dor Dor's been at the nursing home at Greenwich for little under a year when her cousin Monica suffers a bad fall. Like wreckage washed from the same shipwreck, Monnie finds herself swept along to the very same home. We visit her when we go to see Dor Dor.

Monnie sits in an identical armchair, patched up and bandaged.

'You have to eat Monnie,' Mum says to her.

Dora was content living in her unit with Dad dropping in groceries once a month but Monnie has always prided herself on her independence. She caught public transport everywhere and if there was a bus that left from this nursing home she'd be out the door in a heartbeat. But she can't leave. She broke her hip in the fall, she's already had two knee replacements and knows there could be months waiting for surgery, then more months of painful rehabilitation if she has any chance of catching a bus again. There's little chance of this anyway because they're telling her she won't be able to live at home alone, just like they did Dora.

I've always liked Monnie's frankness; my father and grandmother's moods are complicated, requiring constant effort to navigate. Sometimes they say one thing when they're thinking the opposite and I've been slow to figure this out at times, have taken them at their word only to later feel confused and hurt, but Monnie has never been like this and her visits always brought laughter to our house. There's no laughter anymore though, at each visit Monnie talks less and less. Unlike Dora, Monica made up her mind not to stay.

***

My parents discuss whether they should tell Dor Dor about Auntie Monnie's death. My father decides not to. I still don't quite understand how she died.

'She stopped eating,' Dad says.

'She didn't want to live anymore,' Mum says and sobs. 'Poor Monnie.'

'Alright now,' Dad says, 'that's enough.' And that's the last anybody talks about it.

Later that night in my room I say a prayer for Auntie Monnie. I light a candle and put a photo of her beside my spirit house with a small carved elephant she once gave to me. Monnie had told me elephants have the longest memories, a fitting reminder to never forget her, her kindness and generosity.

TALK OF THE TOWN

The Copes are moving to Canberra. I'm desperately unhappy but nobody else seems to be. Everyone wants to sit with Danielle at lunch to hear where she's moving to – their new house is much bigger, the school is co-ed and the uniform is blue. 'I won't look like a grey elephant any more!' she says.

Danielle breaks up with Michael and tells him he's allowed to date anyone except me; he tells her he doesn't want to go out with anyone else anyway, that he only loves her.

'You will,' she says, 'you'll forget about me.' He looks sad.

Flea dumps me, tells me he's wanted to for a while. I go round to the Copes' house and watch the removalists scoop the mess of Danielle's room into boxes, take away the furniture that's always been too big for their rental house.

After the truck has driven off I sit down on the front step for a while not knowing what to do with myself. I feel lost and empty and completely alone, there's nothing to do but just go home.

My father and I are always fighting; everything, even the tiniest things make us erupt. We fight over what time I get home, what plans I've made for the weekend. He complains to Mum I don't help out around the house, that I have 'an attitude'.

'Your poor mother!' he shouts. 'Always picking up after you!'

'That's alright,' Mum mumbles.

'No! It's not Jean!' he roars over her. '*She* should be helping *you*!'

'I've got homework to do,' I say.

'That's right! Go off and leave your mother to do all the washing up!'

I go up to my room, thumping the stairs as I go. 'He doesn't help around the house either!' I think. I slam the door to my room just to make a point. I know he won't come up to reprimand me, he's too lazy. I go over to my stereo and open the drawer where I keep my cassettes. Madonna, Bros, The Bangles … all too happy. The only music I can stand listening to is The Cure.

I think of the fun times I used to have meeting up in the fire escape at Edgecliff station after school. How Michael would smile and try to hide his braces. It would look so funny, he'd do it on purpose to make us laugh, and then none of us would worry about how stupid our own braces looked.

We'd sit there smoking cigarettes, laughing, flirting, the most unromantic place ever – filthy and stinking like stale smokes and piss, everyone crammed in together on the steps, almost sitting on top of each other like seagulls squeezed on a shit-stained jetty, squawking and climbing over each other, jostling for space, elbowing and nudging and sticking our beaks into other people's business.

The four of us were like a secret club; the other kids in the fire escape looked at us with envy, could sense how exciting our lives were. I'd sneak out to meet them, three cigarette tips glowing orange on the corner. I run my tongue over my chipped front tooth, where I knocked it on the bottle of champagne we shared in the park.

Mum tells me not to worry, she says, 'I know you're sad,' and rubs my back, but that only makes me feel worse.

I start wearing black all the time and eyeliner. Most parents would be horrified at having a goth daughter, but not Mum. She rakes through her make-up bag and pulls out her darkest eyeshadow. 'Put more on,' she says, 'That's it, more!'

I tell Mum I want to get my hair cut, I need a drastic change. 'Really?' she says, 'Oh, your beautiful hair … I'd *kill* for your hair!'

I like Mum's hairdresser, Bruce at Toot in Double Bay. 'Let me just get Mum's bleach in Katie, then we'll do something wonderful!'

'How was your trip Dahling?' Mum asks.

'Terrible!' he says. 'I nearly died!'

'Ooooah really?!' Mum says, 'What happened?'

He went to Brazil for Mardi Gras – 'Fabulous!' – then up to Los Angeles to stay with friends. He started getting thinner and thinner. 'That's it, I thought, I've got the big A.'

'Oooah Dahling, No! No! No!'

I know what they're talking about; a number of people Mum and Dad know have got it, a new disease called AIDS. Rock Hudson died then suddenly it was all over the news. Everybody is terrified, talking in whispers if anyone looks like they've lost weight.

Bruce says, 'I booked my flight back to Australia, I'd get all the tests done when I got home. The flight, so hideous and long! It took me over a day to get back, I couldn't eat, I thought I was dying, I just wanted to get home, I was so thin and people kept staring at me …'

He keeps dabbing the bright blue paste onto Mum's scalp.

'When I finally made it home I collapsed on the sofa, then thought I needed to use the loo.'

'You're not going to believe this Jeanne!' one of the salon boys says.

Bruce continues, 'The next thing that happens is this terrible feeling of all my insides falling out, and I look down and MY INTESTINES HAVE FALLEN INTO THE TOILET!'

'What! *Ooooah what?*' Mum shrieks.

'Just wait Jeanne … Just wait!' another salon boy says. All the ladies in the salon have swivelled in their chairs to listen too.

'*So!* I thought … I didn't know what to do! I thought, I'll push my intestines back in and get myself to hospital!'

Mum's shaking her head now, her mouth gaping open. 'Oooah Bruce!' she keeps saying, 'Oooah *Bruce!*'

'So I grab my intestines – AND THEY MOVE!'

All the ladies clamp their hands over their gaping mouths. This story is their worst nightmare. 'What do you mean they *MOVED?*' Mum shouts.

'It was an enormous *TAPE WORM!*'

A collective shriek of horror erupts in the salon, Mum screams at top volume, '*STOP IT BRUCE!*'

'So, this *thing!* It's wriggling like crazy, trying to get back inside me. I hadn't eaten on the plane for twenty-four hours so it was *starving*, that's why it came out! I had to pull it out, it was over a metre long!'

'What? *WHAT!!!*' Mum's starting to hyperventilate, 'Oooooah stop it, STOP IT!'

'I put it in a pot with a lid on to trap it, and rang an ambulance! I was having chest pains and collapsed into cardiac arrest.'

Mum is clutching her chest, 'Oh! I'm having a heart attack just listening!'

'I was in hospital for nearly a month!' he says.

'Oh, I had no idea!' Mum says, 'I'm so glad YOU'RE ALIVE BRUCE!'

'It was a wake-up call for me, that's for sure!' Bruce says, and then leaving his audience with their mouths hanging open he turns to me with scissors in hand, 'So! Time for a big change, huh?'

'She got dumped,' Mum says.

'Nothing worse than a broken heart!' Bruce says and winks at me, 'Except maybe a metre-long tapeworm!'

The Tapeworm Story is the best story I've heard in my life, better even than Spontaneous Human Combustion. I can't wait to tell it to everyone at school!

I WANT TO BREAK FREE

I wake up with a small feeling of relief remembering I've got double art in the afternoon – it just might be a good day. I've been chucking a lot of sickies at school, putting my head down on the desk so I can be sent up to sick bay. I lie in one of the beds in the ward, relieved to be left alone, listening to the sounds in the old boarding house, the vacuum droning through the dormitories, the clatter of metal in the kitchen far below, the school bell punctuating the day into blocks of time and the hubbub of chattering students escaping when the bell rings for lunch.

By the time I've got my uniform on and come downstairs I'm running late. Mum says she'll drive me, she doesn't mind. She's poured me a huge bowl of cereal, much more than I could ever eat. 'Why do you give her so much Jean?!' Dad says, 'What a waste!' I close my ears, I've heard it all before.

Mum brings me my school shoes 'Quickly!' she says, opening the tongue for me to slide my foot in while I'm eating. Dad sees Mum putting my shoes on and shakes his head.

'No wonder she never learns!' he says.

Mum makes a face at me, and mouths 'Don't worry'.

At school in first period someone's left the window open where a new girl Sally usually sits and rain has come in. She walks across the room and dumps her books loudly on the table joining mine, where Danielle used to sit. 'You mind if I sit here?' she asks.

I'm surprised she wants to sit beside me. She's tough looking and has come from Vaucluse Public, she plays softball and sometimes hangs out with the cool athletic girls. Sally tips her chair back against the wall. I return to carving a broken heart into the top of the wooden desk and soon Sally takes up her project too. She pulls her sock down to reveal bloody cuts on her ankle where she's scratching the letters NZ with the point of a compass.

'Doesn't that hurt?' I ask.

The pain while she's doing it isn't that bad she says. It distracts her from the other pain.

'What does NZ stand for?' I whisper.

'New Zealand,' she whispers back. 'I went there last holidays, I felt like I belonged there.'

Sally's got a job working in the deli section of a supermarket so she can save up for an airfare to go over in the holidays. She tells me she has to break the wings on chickens to fit them on the rotisserie and slice ham, which makes her feel sick. She doesn't eat meat, doesn't like touching it either.

'Dead animals,' she says, 'I can't help thinking they're delivering truckloads of dead animals in boxes.'

I tell her I'm saving to go down to Canberra in the holidays. I've asked my parents if I can catch the coach but Dad hasn't made up his mind yet. I got a job at McDonald's to make money but almost got fired for putting too many pickles on the Big Macs.

'That's why you're in remedial maths,' Sally says, 'with me.'

***

I audition for the part of Mabel in the school musical of *Pirates of Penzance*, a combined production with Sydney Boys Grammar, directed by their head music teacher Mr McDermott. He's a brilliant yet frightening teacher who treats the young teenage cast like trained, seasoned professionals.

My costume is a virginal white dress with a baby blue sash. My co-star Chris, playing the part of Frederic, wears a tux. I find him quite attractive when I'm acting, but in real life he's as dull as a post. We're rehearsing a duet. I'm imploring him not to leave me and he rushes to the front of the stage to sing to the audience, then turns back to embrace me.

'*No! No! No!*' Mr McDermott shouts. Everyone is scared of him. If too many people disappoint him he gets in a progressively worse mood.

'You must embrace her like you *love her!*' he roars. 'Do it *again!*'

Once more the orchestra plays and Chris sings, his unbroken tenor voice pure and reedy. He has a look of terror in his eyes, it reminds me of Tiffy's pet rabbit that we used to let out of the cage from time to time. Chris runs across the stage and back again to embrace me, a lippety lippety Peter Rabbit run. He awkwardly puts his arms around me – '*NO! NO! NO!* Don't you know how to *embrace* a woman Christopher?'

Mr McDermott storms onto the stage. 'This is *you*,' he says, holding me at arms length, pushing his bottom out theatrically. 'That's not love!' he shouts.

The boys in the chorus snicker and Mr McDermott swivels around to include them, 'Isn't that correct?' he shouts, and they nod urgently.

'When a woman and a man love each other they hug from *here*!' he says. He thrusts his pelvis forward and points to his groin. The boys at the back of the stage go red-faced holding in their laughter. 'It's like a *magnet!*' Mr McDermott shouts.

'THIS IS LOVE!' he shouts and he runs across the stage and embraces me with his whole body. It feels more like a rugby tackle than an embrace.

'Now! Your turn Christopher! SHOW ME LOVE!'

Poor Chris runs again but faster this time, lippety lippety across the stage to embrace me.

'WHAT ARE YOU WEARING CHRIS – A CHASTITY BELT?' Mr McDermott roars, '*AGAIN!* YOU LOVE HER, REMEMBER? She's not your grandmother! She's your *lover*! What are you scared of?'

I wonder this too: what is everybody so scared of? And later at the afterparty, when the rest of the cast and crew are drunkenly pashing, and we're still sitting there feeling awkward … it would have been nice to have just one unrehearsed snog, I think, after all that effort.

***

'How was New Zealand?' I ask Sally in maths.

'Soooo good.' But the holidays are over and she's back in Sydney again. She looks pale and tired. 'How were your holidays?'

'Alright,' I lie. Visiting the Copes in Canberra was awful, I had nothing in common with their new friends.

'I hate my bedroom,' Sally says suddenly, 'It's pink! I didn't realise how much I hated it until I came home. Every morning I wake up and see it and feel sick.'

'But isn't your mother like, a feminist or something who wouldn't let you play with Barbie dolls? How come she painted your room pink?'

'I've got two older brothers,' Sally shrugs. 'Mum said the pregnancy oestrogen went straight to her head. Even she didn't understand it afterwards. Anyway, being a feminist is about having choice; unfortunately, her choice was pink.'

I tell her how I painted my room a different colour myself, 'Hey! Why don't we paint yours too?'

During the next maths lesson Sally leans into me with a worried look on her face.

'I need to talk to you,' she says, 'it's really important.'

'Of course,' I say. 'Hey, if you've changed your mind about painting your room …'

'It's not that …' Sally says. She takes a deep breath. 'I think I might be pregnant.'

My eyes go round, 'Oh, heavens!'

'I haven't gotten my period since I got back from New Zealand.'

'Oh …' I say.

'We didn't use a condom …'

'Oh shit …'

This is a problem much bigger than fixing a pink bedroom.

'Don't worry,' I tell her, 'I'll figure something out … Don't worry.' Sally nods, her eyes fill with tears.

'Is everything okay back there?' the teacher asks.

Sally wipes her eyes and sniffs loudly. 'Everything's fine,' she says, 'Sorry, I just had something in my eye.'

I take the pregnancy test to the counter of the pharmacy at Edgecliff, the lady looks me up and down in my school uniform. 'It's not for me,' I stammer. She puts a slip of paper in the bag with a phone number. I bury the paper bag at the very bottom of my school bag and go home, take it out when I'm safe up in my room and push it deep under the mattress. The next morning I smuggle it into Sally's hands.

'It's positive,' Sally tells me, 'Now what?'

My parents have told me so many times I can tell them anything, but the last time I told them something big, that I'd smoked a joint, they went crazy. I'm hesitant to confide in them again so I wait till the Colins are coming for dinner. Colin Johnston, being a pharmacist, has that doctorly way about him that grown-ups find reassuring in a crisis.

Sally comes home with me from school. Her mum's going to pick her up later I tell Mum as she climbs into the car with us. Actually, her mother doesn't know yet she'll be picking Sally up later, but I do, when the shit hits the fan.

It's the first time Sally's been to my house. I take her up the rainbow staircase and we climb out the bathroom window so Sally can smoke a cigarette. I sit on the masonry with my back to the wall, the tiled roof is steep and the ground is a long way down, but Sally walks fearlessly out to the chimney making my stomach clench.

Neat rows of terrace houses sprawl out below us, stretching towards the city with just a glimpse of the pale grey harbour.

'So, did you tell him?' I ask.

'Yeah, he'll pay for the abortion.'

'Sounds like a romantic phone call.'

Sally laughs wryly, 'Doesn't it.'

'Was it worth it?' I ask.

She takes a drag on her cigarette. 'Yeah,' she says finally, 'yeah, it was. Even though I'll probably never see him again … bastard.'

I go down to see my parents and the Colins.

'Hi Katie!' they say. 'You've got a new friend over your mother tells us! Where have you hidden her? She's not shy is she?'

'Well, that's one way of looking at it …' I begin. Once I've said it a chain of command takes over as I knew it would. Mum goes to find Sally and hugs her and tells her it will be okay. Sally cries, Mum cries. Mum always cries.

My father pours a round of Scotches and talks in low tones with the grown-ups. Colin Johnston makes the phone call to Sally's mother in the kitchen while we sit nervously in the other room.

'She's coming to pick you up,' Colin Johnston says. 'We had a good chat, she's just worried about you.'

HUNGRY LIKE THE WOLF

'If it feels good, do it!' says one article in the latest *Dolly*. Mum complains these magazines have a lot to answer for.

'What sort of advice is that?' Mum says to Angela Farrington.

'It's not the same as it was in our day Jeanne,' Angela says.

'That's for sure,' Mum says.

I've told Mum I want to go on the pill. Mum doesn't handle conversations like this very well. She tries to talk me out of the idea but I've thought it through and I have an answer ready for every argument. I've had a boyfriend for over six months and we're in love.

'We're both virgins Mum,' I say, and at this point I wish the floor would just open up and swallow me whole. 'We've waited and talked about it a lot. I'm sixteen you know.'

After all the build up, losing my virginity is a disappointment. We're both drunk and it's awful. My boyfriend apologises, he's just as crushed as I am. I go home and sulk. Mum comes to my room and asks me if I'm okay. 'I always thought sex was disappointing too,' she says, as if that will make me feel better; but it doesn't, it makes me feel worse. Now I feel weird and crushingly sorry for my mother too on top of everything else.

'Practice makes perfect!' says the headline in the next *Dolly* magazine. Thank heavens, I think, because my boyfriend and I are practising *a lot*. We have sex in odd places –

other people's houses when there are no adults at home, one time we even get sprung by the cops in his car – anywhere but my house since Dad made another rule.

'I don't want you taking boys up to your bedroom, Katie,' he'd said.

'What?' I said incredulous. I'd looked at Mum who'd just looked at Dad, this was obviously his call. 'But what am I supposed to do?'

'You can entertain them in the lounge room,' Dad said. Was he mad?

I'd laughed, 'First of all, you've never even let *me* sit in the lounge room, let alone "entertain" there. And what do you expect us to do? All my music and stuff is up in my room?'

'You can play music in the lounge room.'

I snorted. 'Dad, you've got a record player for starters – all my music is on cassette! Unless you want me to play Marlene Dietrich records!'

Without warning, I find I'm in excruciating pain. Convinced I'm about to die of an STD I take myself up to the medical centre. I'm too embarrassed to tell Mum but the doctor isn't worried. A urinary tract infection he says and sends me away with some satchels of fizzy powder and a course of antibiotics. I make the mistake of mixing one at my boyfriend's house and his sister comes round later to knock on my door.

'Oh my god,' she says, 'Mum is *freaking out*.'

'Why?' I ask, a shiver of panic going through me.

'That drink you made, Mum's a nurse, remember? She saw it and realised you guys were having sex.'

'I thought she already knew.' I say, but his sister shakes her head. 'Mum was actually crying.'

I don't know how to feel about this. Should I feel guilty? Grown-ups are always trying to make me feel guilty! We're both of legal age and we love each other! I'm so sick to death of being judged by everyone – at home, at school! Everyone has an opinion of how I should behave, what I should do, who I should speak to, what I should say. Even what I choose to read is criticised, just because I'd rather read Nietzsche over Jane Austen – I hate being forced to be something I'm not!

At home Mum and Dad have been arguing about something. She's gone out to work leaving me alone with him. It's one of those rare moments where my father tries to share something with me – there's nobody else to talk to. He busies himself with tidying up as he rants, talks out loud to himself, but loud enough for me to hear.

'Your mother, she can be aloof, so hard and unemotional at times.' He shakes his head as if he's about to give up.

'Go on …' I say from the other side of the room, as nonchalantly as I can, not to scare him off. He struggles to find the words. 'That can be hard for a man …' he says, then finally before going off to sulk by himself, 'Oh, you're too young, you don't understand.'

I think about what he says because I really want to understand. I think he's talking about the part of my mother that's separate from us. She's made from something stronger than Dad and me, moods don't seem to affect her like they do us, and she's always so determined, has such conviction and purpose. I wish I was more like her; life would be so much easier.

'Should you fake orgasms?' reads an article in the next *Dolly* magazine. This is of particular interest to me because I've been faking a lot of them. It's not that I'm not enjoying sex with my boyfriend, just that I kind of feel like it's the least I can do. After all, he seems to be putting in a lot of effort, and a few sound effects sometimes makes the whole experience feel a bit more … constructive.

Reading through *Dolly* I'm surprised to learn what I've thought was called sex is actually foreplay. Of course boys think intercourse is the most important bit because it's the bit with the big-bang ending! So I don't feel bad for faking a bit during that part. The article says only one in three women orgasm during intercourse, 'See? I'm not a freak!' I think to myself.

I find sex is like when I wanted to play the piano. I wanted to buy the piano so badly, I thought about it all the time and worked hard to save the money, and it was exciting at first, but after a while I found practising to be a bit of a chore.

Now that we're not virgins anymore my boyfriend wants to have sex *all the time*, which is starting to annoy me. When we meet up I know we're going to have to do it. Sometimes I string him out a bit and make him work for it, sometimes I want to get it over with straight away so that we can do other stuff without the sex hanging around, lingering like an unspoken question. Sometimes we get into an argument about it and then I tell him that I don't like him smoking all the time too, which is turning into an issue between us. And sometimes I go too far stringing him out and he gets the shits – but then we make up and it feels all romantic again, and then we end up having sex anyway.

'Boys!' Sally says knowledgeably, 'can't live with 'em, can't live without 'em!'

PARTY GIRL

Somehow, for my seventeenth birthday, Mum and I have convinced Dad to let me have a party in the backyard. We haven't told him how many people are coming of course. I haven't told him that I've invited *the whole year;* but he didn't ask me about that, he was only concerned with saying 'No boys!'

I said that was fine, almost – except that of course my boyfriend had to come because I'd asked his band to play. It would be their first official gig! And then I mentioned the boys from Sydney Grammar who were in *Pirates Of Penzance,* they had to come. He gave me a look but didn't say any more and I knew that would get him because he was impressed by their fancy school when he came to watch the show; it looked expensive.

I didn't tell him I'd already invited some of the boys from Cranbrook too, who were in the school play with me, and that I'd also been a bit sentimental and asked Michael and my old boyfriend Flea because the Copes were coming up from Canberra for the party. And then Tiffy asked me if she could invite Troy, this guy who looks like Patrick Swayze who she'd had a crush on forever! And a few of the girls asked if they could bring their boyfriends too.

To be honest I'm too scared to add up how many people I've invited, but it won't matter because it's all going to be down in the back garden and Dad will never go down there so he won't even know!

Mum asked me in the car on the way to school one morning, she knew it was going to be a lot of kids. 'More than a hundred?' she'd asked conspiratorially.

I grimaced and said, 'I hope not. I don't think so.' We're both nervous about that.

'Well, there's nothing that can get broken down there in the garden or anything,' Mum says, then she cheers up and says, 'So! Is everyone excited? Tell me, what's everyone wearing?'

That's Mum's favourite thing to talk about because it's a dress-up party. I'm going as Judy Jetson from *The Jetsons* cartoon and I found this fantastic stretchy orange dress in Mum's wardrobe.

'What's this?' I'd asked. I just liked the colour really.

'Oh! That's fun, I stuck a hula hoop in the hem of it. It's tight like a boob tube, but flares out at the bottom.'

That's when I got the idea of sticking more hula hoops in it so I looked like I had a slinky inside my dress! Then Mum dug around in her wardrobe some more and pulled out a silver wig like strips of metallic paper. She even had silver eyelashes. I think Mum's possibly more excited than I am!

On the afternoon of the party my boyfriend and his band come round to do a sound check. They lug their instruments in through the back lane and set up two enormous Marshall speaker stacks that they've hired for the night. It's starting to look very impressive.

Mum's busy sweeping the tiles in the yard and Dad's in his office making a barricade, putting up a big piece of plywood to block off the entrance to his office from the outside toilet.

Mum suggests we do a run to buy supplies for the party. We jump into her car and get the usual things – chips and soft drinks – and then as we're coming down the hill from Kings Cross Mum sees the bottle shop with the parking out the back and says in a panic, 'I suppose we'd better get a few drinks too!'

'Hi Jeanne!' the shop assistant says. 'Need any help?'

Mum tells the guy I'm having a party. 'What do teenagers drink?' she asks him, and rather than tell her teenagers aren't legally allowed to drink, he just laughs and shows us to the alcopops in the back fridge. 'Oh! West Coast Coolers, they look nice don't they Katie?' I nod my head, too scared to open my mouth.

'Alright then, we'll get half a dozen cases of those,' Mum says 'and a dozen Tropicana casks. It looks like cordial Dahling! Too sweet for me!'

The man in the bottle shop starts ringing up the purchases and I whisper to Mum about getting a bottle of Malibu too. 'What's that?' she asks, and I explain that it's coconut liqueur. 'Urgh!' she laughs to the bottle shop attendant. 'How revolting! Like drinking suntan lotion!'

'Sounds like it's going to be some party!' the man says taking the Malibu off the shelf.

We pull up in the laneway to unload the drinks. My boyfriend giggles when he sees the boot loaded up with alcohol. 'Are you *serious?*' he says. 'You've got the best mum in the world!' and I smile because yes, it's true, I do seriously have *the best mum in the whole world,* and in a few hours we're going to have the best party in the world! I'm so excited I could scream!

The band take up their instruments. 'One two, one two …' my boyfriend says into the microphone and the sound ricochets around the courtyard. They launch into a cover, the music blasts out in a wall of sound, I can feel the base vibrating through my bones. Mum comes rushing in looking a bit alarmed, although you can tell she's trying to look encouraging for the boys' sake, and then we hear the faint noise of shouting coming from upstairs, over the ruckus.

'*Turn that down! Turn that down!*' Dad is screaming.

Mum makes a face and starts shaking her head frantically and before we know it Dad is coming down the back stairs shouting his head off. The music is *too loud* he's saying, are we out of our minds! The neighbours will call the police! —*and!* —*and!* —*and!* —and then he sees the gaffer tape on his tiles.

'My tiles!' he shrieks.

'It's okay Barry!' Mum is saying anxiously. 'It'll come off! Won't it boys! It won't leave a mark!' Everyone nods enthusiastically.

Dad is huffing and puffing around the courtyard. 'It better come off Jean!' he's shouting. 'And what's happening with this music? I never agreed to anything like this! Where did all these speakers come from! This is *a residential address!* You can't do things like this!'

'They'll turn the music right down, won't you boys!' Mum is saying, and then Dad sees the back gate open.

'Who unlocked this!' he shouts, 'What's this doing open?!'

He starts pulling the gate closed. 'Hang on! Hang on!' Mum says, 'I need to get out to my car!' She rushes out before the metal gate slams closed and Dad threads the padlock through the chain.

'But Dad, you can't shut the gate!' I say. 'People need to be able to get in and out of the party!'

'Are you *crazy?*' He shouts back. 'You can't leave it open! *Anyone* could just walk in off the street! We'll have gatecrashers!' There's no point trying to argue, he's too worked up about the loud music and the tiles. 'Nobody's going in and out of the party and that's final!' he shouts, 'We're *responsible* for these kids, don't you understand?'

'But how's everyone's supposed to get in?' I ask.

'THROUGH THE FRONT DOOR!' he thunders back.

My face goes red and tears spring to my eyes. Now Dad's going to know how many people are coming – and the boys! It's going to be a *disaster!*

Dad storms off back upstairs and my boyfriend comes over to comfort me. 'Don't freak out!' he says.

'But Dad's going to see all the people I've invited! *Everyone's* coming! He'll have a fit! And what about if people want to get out again! My party will be like a jail!'

My boyfriend laughs and says, 'Hey, don't you climb over the back fence all the time when it's locked?' I nod and sniff away my tears noisily. 'Well there you are! If people want to get in or out they can just climb over it! As a matter of fact, the band and I are going to climb over it right now and go to the pub!'

'I wish I was eighteen already like you! I'm still trapped in that school and *this house!*' The tears start up again. 'I wish I had a fake driver's licence so I could go to the pub too!'

'You can't come to the pub!' he says laughing. 'You have to get ready. Remember Judy Jetson?'

I give him a small smile to show I appreciate him trying to comfort me, even if I still feel completely miserable.

'I wish … I just wish … Dad could be happy for me for once.'

'Don't worry about him!' he says. 'The party's going to be brilliant!'

The boys have no trouble scaling the fence. Their winklepicker shoes poke easily through the holes of chain link, they hoist themselves over and jump down into the laneway, landing on their feet with feline grace, like Kiefer Sutherland and the *Lost Boys*.

***

The tears have left me looking red and blotchy. I'm gluing on the silver eyelashes in Mum's bathroom, hoping my skin will look normal again soon when the doorbell goes. The Colins have already arrived, they're downstairs with Dad having a Scotch, listening to him ranting about the loud music and the gaffer tape on his tiles. Hopefully it will calm him down a bit. I wonder who's at the door now, the party doesn't start for another hour.

'Oh Dani!' Mum says. 'Come in! Come in! Katie's upstairs getting ready! Go on up!'

Danielle comes upstairs looking for me. 'I'm in here!' I shout.

'Oh wow, you look amazing!' she says. 'I look like a total idiot in this lion outfit of Adam's …' We hug, I'm so excited to see her, and then she looks at me with that special intensity and says, 'Can we go upstairs to your room? There's something I *really* need to talk to you about.'

'Oh! I've missed your rainbow staircase!' she says. We get to the top and I close the door of my room. We talk about who's coming to the party, she's excited to see Michael, of course. 'Oh Michael … that feels like a lifetime ago!' She's looking forward to seeing a bunch of girls from school, but not Kate McDonald, who she never got on with.

'You have to promise not to tell anyone … Promise?' she asks. I look at her curiously, of course she knows I won't tell anyone. 'You have to swear, *on your life,*' and then she just laughs like she always used to when things got too serious before handing me a photo.

'This is my son,' she says. I look at the picture, a tiny, red-faced wrinkly baby wrapped in a hospital blanket.

'Are you for real?'

'Deadly,' she says. 'I had a baby.'

And then the doorbell goes downstairs and the first guests start to arrive.

THE FUTURE'S SO BRIGHT, I GOTTA WEAR SHADES

For the Colins and my parents it's like watching a parade coming through the house, dozens of gorgeous young ladies in fancy dress are filing through the house on their way to the back garden.

'I can't believe how grown up you all look!' Mum shrieks. 'Can you believe it Barry?'

'Angela Fletcher! Is that you?' Colin Brees says, remembering the little girl from the spooky party at their house all those years ago. 'I thought it was Marilyn Monroe!'

'This is better than Mardi Gras!' Colin Johnston laughs and their good mood has the desired effect, my father starts to relax and enjoy himself too.

'Who's that? Who's that?' Colin Brees asks Dad, spurring him into action, and Dad's probably as surprised as they are by how many of the kids he recognises.

Kate McDonald enters dressed as Vivian Ward from *Pretty Woman* with thigh-high boots, Tiffy Farrington arrives as Cinderella in an enormous fluffy blue gown and blonde wig. Tiffy's mum Angela comes in for a quick drink, 'You're very brave Barry!' she says, and Dad laughs ruefully, 'Or stupid Angie! We'll see!' he says.

The line of guests trails through the house, winding down the back stairs and into the garden where I greet them with a plastic cup of Tropicana. Everyone is laughing, having a terrific time, sporty girls with the nerdy girls, boarders and arty kids getting along like the best of friends. This is the best bit that Mum and I have always loved about throwing parties, watching the guests mingle and have fun.

The boys start arriving upstairs, they're all polite, taking my father's hand to shake it, saying 'Pleased to meet you Mister Little.' My father starts to let down his guard, they all appear so handsome and well mannered.

'Oh look, there's someone dressed as Mr T!' Colin Johnston calls out. 'And there's the Pirate King from the *Penzance* musical Katie was in!'

'At your service!' the Pirate King says theatrically.

'Gosh, you're all so good looking and gorgeous!' Mum says.

Three boys dressed in trench coats with their collars pulled up and Ray Ban sunglasses slink in. 'Barry!' Colin Brees says, 'Who are those boys?'

The boy in the middle with the sculpted cheekbones flicks his hair and with a smirk answers, 'Michael.'

A huge exclamation erupts from the grown-ups, 'Ooooooh! So you're Michael!'

'Isn't he dishy!' Mum says.

'Who? Who?' Angela Farrington asks, and Colin Johnston leans over knowledgeably and whispers 'He's the politician's son!'

'Oh!' Angela replies, instantly more interested.

'He went out with one of Katie's friends! And she was dating his best friend, I think, that one beside him!'

'And who have you come as?' Mum asks.

'We're the Blues Brothers,' Michael says.

'What's under the trench coats!' Colin Brees teases and Colin Johnston gives him a hard nudge in the ribs. 'Shush Colin! You can't ask that!' he says.

'Why not?'

'Because! It's not appropriate!'

'Oh shut up Colin Johnston!'

Michael's eyes sparkle with mischief, 'Do you really want to know what's under the trench coats?' He snickers and turns to the other boys. This is a surprise they were saving for the girls downstairs. Flea is shaking his head but Michael, always with more courage, eggs him on. 'One, two, three!' The coats flash open for a second showing a glimpse of nothing but white boxer shorts underneath. The grown-ups laugh and Mum shrieks 'Oooooah! Aren't you all outrageous!'

It doesn't take long for things to get messy, most girls have never even tasted alcohol before and the alcopop goes straight to their heads. The band launches into their first number, a cover of a U2 song, the music is loud and live and the guests soon pick up the idea to shout 'Hey!' in all the right pauses.

'Hey, they're really good!' Danielle shouts into my ear and I glow with pride. 'Yeah! I know!' I say. When I look up even Mum and Dad and the Colins are at the window looking down, enjoying the music too. I smile up at Dad and give him a thumbs-up signal. Mum went and spoke to all the neighbours and told them the band was only going to play for thirty minutes. They were never going to play longer than that anyway, they don't know that many songs.

After the band finishes the stereo sounds tinny and small. The smokers head towards the laneway and the silver innards are torn free of the Tropicana boxes to squeeze the last few drops out. A few people disappear off into bushes to hold more intimate parties and a whiff of pot drifts through the garden. Every now and then a scream goes up as Michael and his Blues Brothers flash open their trench coats.

Tiffy runs up to me staggering slightly with a West Coast Cooler in hand, the enormous pale blue dress swirling around her like a meringue. 'Have you seen Troy Banks?' she asks, 'I've been looking everywhere!'

A girl is throwing up under one of Dad's camellia bushes. 'She'll be alright,' her friend says patting her back. 'She was just a bit too excited I think!'

Kate McDonald is holding centre court, laughing wickedly with a group of girls. 'Did you hear she got pregnant and had a baby?' she whispers too loudly. The other girls snigger and look around, shaking their heads. I wonder who else Danielle shared her secret with.

I try to look shocked, 'That must be a rumour …'

'Oh come on! Of course it's true!' Kate says. 'Trust her to do something like that!'

Down at the back gate a few people have discovered how easy it is to jump the fence. A crowd of kids are mingling out in the laneway with the band, smoking and laughing.

'I wonder if Troy went out there?' Tiffy says, sculling the rest of her West Coast Cooler. She throws her head back and when the bottle drains she tosses it carelessly into the back corner of the garden then attempts to climb the fence, but it's not so easy, she can't seem to coordinate how to get her awkward sparkly shoes into the chain-link holes. Finally she gets one in only for it to get stuck.

'Stupid shoe!' she says laughing. 'Hey! Who wants a glass slipper?' She pulls off the other one and chucks it over the fence, it ricochets off someone's head and is caught by The Pirate King. He runs to her aid, calling theatrically, 'A damsel in distress! How may I be of service?'

The enormous dress engulfing him, Tiffy is laughing uncontrollably, the more he tries to help the louder she shrieks with laughter. 'Hey, wait a minute! Are these *bloomers?* Are you wearing *bloomers* under this thing? That's a Pirate King's *fantasy!*'

I don't want to leave the party but I have to, just for a minute. I have to dash up to my bedroom to get the bottle of Malibu I stashed up there for later. I haven't had time for one drink myself all night, I've been flat out looking after everyone. In the bedroom I catch a glimpse of myself in the mirror and stop to take a look. I take a deep breath and pause: it's good to be seventeen! Soon I'll be free!

The party carries on noisily down in the garden. I put some lipstick on and glance at the photos stuck on my mirror. Tiffy, Kate and I dressed up for the *Rocky Horror Show*, a photo of Danielle wearing that beret after she burnt half her hair off, Sally and I painting her room …

Where is Sally? I haven't seen her for most of the night, since she turned up looking like GI Joe. 'I'm Sarah Connor,' she said, 'from *Terminator,* you know …'

'Oh yeah, right, of course! Cool,' I said. 'Actually yeah, your hair's perfect for that, and you really suit those khaki pants!'

'Thanks, they're my brother's, so's the fake machine gun and bullets and stuff. Thinking of taking a couple of boys hostage, know what I mean?'

'Actually I think it's your boobs in that singlet top that are gonna take a few boys hostage!'

'Yeah! Let's hope so! You can run but you can't hide boys!'

I wish Sally was up here now. As soon as I get downstairs I'm going to find her and pour her a Malibu and coke. The noise from the garden is getting louder, I peer down, there's a commotion of people around the fence. Several people are on it, either climbing out or climbing back in, and in the middle, propped up on the top like a tulle toilet roll dolly is Tiffy, tipsy and clinging to the fence with a group of boys either side ready to catch her if she falls.

She's attracted a crowd, a few people have started clapping in expectation. 'Cinderella sat on the wall! Cinderella had a great fall!' they chant and cheers erupt from the crowd.

Inside the party another commotion starts, two girls are screaming at each other and I realise it's Kate and Danielle.

'You should have come as a witch Kate!'

'Well at least I didn't come dressed as the tawny scrawny lion!'

'You've always been a bitch!' Danielle screams.

'Well at least I'm not a slut! Like you!' Kate screams back.

'I don't have to listen to this!' Danielle says, 'I'm leaving!'

'Good! Fuck off back to Canberra!' Kate yells, laughing.

Danielle runs from the party towards the back fence and launches herself up onto it. From upstairs in my bedroom it looks comical, like a lion escaping a zoo. The lion pounces up onto the side of the fence and the gate starts toppling over bringing the brick walls on either side down with it. The crowd staggers back and Tiffy is launched off the top with a scream, flying spread-eagled towards the crowd. The pale blue dress billows up over her head with white knickerbockers exposed for all to see and she lands like a seasoned crowd-surfer into the dozens of waiting arms and a huge cheer goes up!

I race down the stairs, faster than I've ever raced before. Dad's already in the garden by the time I get there, a raging bull ready to charge. 'That's it!' he's saying. 'Party's over!' He turns the lights on next to the outside toilet and sees the plywood board he put up has been moved.

'MY OFFICE!' Dad roars. 'WHO'S GONE INTO MY OFFICE!'

A crowd is gathering at a safe distance behind, they follow him into the office, terrified yet unable to resist watching what's going to happen. Moaning is coming from deep inside the office, it gets louder as they reach the door to his private study. The crowd behind Dad shuffles closer, peering to get a look. Dad flicks on the light to his room and somebody under the desk bumps their head. 'Fuck a duck!' the person mutters.

My stomach sinks, only one person I know says that.

'WHO'S UNDER THERE!' Dad shouts. 'COME OUT!'

Dad circles the desk but still can't see under it, he pulls the chair out of the way and it's like releasing the pin on the Melbourne Cup race, two half-naked figures make a break for it.

'Run for your life!' Sally yells, yanking up her army fatigues, and Troy Banks comes stumbling out behind her, too large for the confined space, accidentally upending my father's desk in the process. His treasured word processor comes crashing down, splinters into hundreds of pieces and the book that he's been working on, the ten-inch stack of carefully typed manuscript flies up into the air like a ticker-tape parade.

Tiffy, her mouth opening and closing like a fish out of water as Sally and Troy barge past her, suddenly turns pale and collapses into the arms of the crowd which caught her only moments earlier and Kate, enjoying every minute of the unexpected blood-sport entertainment, shrieks with laughter.

DON'T YOU (FORGET ABOUT ME)

The three of us are sitting at the little round table in the sunroom for dinner. As usual, I'm not really hungry. I push the food around my plate and chew on the same piece of steak for what feels like an eternity. Dad took about a month to cool off after the party. He's only just started talking to me again, which is lucky, because there's something I need to tell him.

Mum, as usual, is starving. She starts bolting down her food like a hungry dog.

'Slow down Jean!' Dad barks.

'Oh yes, I must,' agrees Mum. 'I forgot to have lunch.' She deliberately slows her chewing and takes a drink of water. 'So Dahling, how was your day?' she asks Dad in a deliberately formal manner.

He briefly recounts the trouble he's having with a client who's being difficult – the colour scheme she's chosen is awful! The carpet too bright! She keeps changing her mind and there are problems with the upholsterer and the painter. He was going to get his book published and become a writer, give up interior design for good and tell all his clients to go to hell – but that dream went out the window when his manuscript and word processor were destroyed.

He turns the conversation back to Mum. 'And how was your day Jean? Don't tell me ...n't give you anything to eat at that function? These people are unbelievable. I ...ou cab fare home at least!'

'A nice lady who works for a children's charity gave me a lift.'

Dad smells trouble. 'You didn't agree to do another charity I hope.'

Mum can never say no and is already stuttering, 'It's for children's leukaemia …'

'Oh Jean!' Dad puts down his cutlery too hard. 'Well, there goes another weekend. We haven't been up to Pearl Beach for months! What's the point of having it, we never use it! We might as well sell it!' Not this again, I think.

'Well, I told her I'd have to check with you …'

'I'm not getting you out of it! *You* can phone them yourself! You agreed to it!'

'It's children's leukaemia,' Mum repeats. 'Just imagine if it was Katie …'

There's no comeback to this, Dad can't argue, so he sits and stews instead, chewing in silence, angrily cutting his steak into pieces. Mum attempts to move the conversation on again. 'More potato Katie?'

I shake my head.

'Gosh Dahling, you hardly eat a thing.'

We sit in silence for a while longer, chewing. Then the phone rings. At the sound Mum automatically goes to spring from her seat. 'Don't answer it!' Dad says.

'But it might be—'

'They can *wait!* Sit and finish your dinner!'

We continue eating, studying our plates as the phone rings, and then the answer machine picks up downstairs. Muffled talking, a long beep, a person's voice being recorded on the tape. I take a swallow of my drink and clear my throat. 'I've got some news,' I say tentatively.

Mum and Dad look up, surprised. Dad wipes his chin with his napkin and erases the frown from his forehead. He makes an effort to look interested. 'Wonderful,' he says. He sits back in his chair grandly, puts his knife and fork together on the plate.

I feel like jumping up and running from the room rather than having this conversation.

'Well,' I begin, 'there's this program, someone came to talk to us about it at school, its called GAP, where you can apply to go overseas for a year, and work, when you finish school. It's called a working holiday, or something. You travel in the summer holidays, because their summer, in Europe I mean, is when it's winter here, so it's longer, the holidays that is, in the middle of the year, so you can travel longer …' I'm feeling breathless, this is all coming out wrong, I'm rambling. I suck in another breath and try again. 'Anyway, I applied, to go to England and work in a school and I got accepted.'

Dad looks confused. 'Pardon?' he says.

'She said she's going overseas,' Mum starts.

'Yes! I know! I know! I heard what she said!' Dad shouts then turns back to me, speaking quietly again, 'Now, what did you say? You're thinking of going overseas did you say?'

'Not thinking of,' I stammer, 'I got accepted. I'm going to England.' My voice shrinks, 'I thought you might be happy for me.'

'Of course we're happy …'

'Oh *be quiet Jean!* Stop interrupting!' He tries again, 'Now, let's discuss this rationally. What are you thinking of going overseas to do?'

'Teaching, I'll be teaching kids …'

'Teaching?' he looks to Mum 'Did you know about this?' She shakes her head. 'But you're going to university …'

'Well maybe …'

'What? Of course you're going to university, your mother and I would have killed to have gone to university, you just don't know what you want to study yet.'

'Dad, I've never actually said I wanted to go to university. I don't know. It's just for a year, to figure out what I want to do, and to go travelling.'

'Like an exchange program,' Mum volunteers, 'without the exchange.'

'Yeah …'

'I went overseas when I was young …' Mum says.

'Oh we know about THAT!' Dad roars. 'Shut up a minute, I want to hear about Katie's plans, not yours! Now … we'll discuss university later, where did you say you were thinking of going to?'

'England.'

'England!' Dad snorts. 'Why on earth would you want to go there?'

There's no way I'm telling him it's because my favourite band, The Cure, are English, which suddenly sounds ridiculous, even to me, so I just shrug and mumble, 'I just thought it sounded interesting.'

Suddenly Mum gets all teary, 'Oh Dahling, you're too young …'

'But what are you going there *for?* I don't understand.' Dad is flustered by Mum's emotions.

'I told you, just to kind of, experience … life, I suppose.'

'Life?' he looks blank. 'Life? But you have a life, here, living with us.'

'Well, that's *your* life.' I make an effort to explain, 'I just want to try having my own life, sort of.'

'Maybe you should think about it,' Mum says.

'I have Mum, it's a great opportunity. They only select a handful of students, I was drama prefect and I've done pretty well in my high school certificate, both my artworks have been chosen for ARTEXPRESS. I've got the money for the airfare, and then it's paid work, which I can save up to go travelling with. I leave in four weeks.'

'I see.' Dad serves the last of the creamed potatoes onto Mum's plate. 'Eat some more Jean, you're looking too thin these days.' He starts scraping the crusty bits off the edge of the dish, chipping into them with his knife. 'Well, it sounds like you've already made up your mind then, doesn't it? Not much of a discussion to be had is there?' The phone rings again, this time there's no argument about answering it.

I feel like I've let them down again. I always end up feeling like this, but what am I supposed to do? It's like when I was little they used to dress me up in the most ridiculous outfits when they took me to parties with them. One day I stood up to them, came down wearing my stars and stripes overalls and refused to get changed. Dad called me disobedient and spoilt, then went mad on Mum saying she indulged me too much and I screamed at him – I didn't want to wear the hateful clothes Mum had picked out for me, some stupid cream woollen jumpsuit that made me itchy and had a matching beanie that made me look like an elf! I didn't want to be called 'cute' and 'adorable', *that wasn't who I was!* Most of their friends were phoneys anyway, couldn't they see that? I didn't care about what other people thought of me, I only cared what Mum and Dad thought, if only they could just see *me* for who I was!

***

The days in our house after I tell them about my plans to go overseas are strangely quiet. No-one fights or argues about anything. Mum doesn't complain when Dad leaves the bread out, crumbs strewn over the countertop she's only recently cleaned. Dad doesn't comment when Mum leaves the bedroom untidy, sheets and doona in a crumpled mess. No-one shouts at me to turn my music down, or to get off the phone line, but then I find I am strangely respectful – hanging up when I hear a click on the line, listening to music on my Walkman instead of blasting it through my stereo.

Mum and Dad's friends have been complaining of children who won't leave the nest, they thought they had years still to endure me coming and going at odd hours, borrowing Mum's car and leaving it on empty, but now that I've effectively given notice, our time together as a family can be measured in weeks and days. Dad disappears down into his office, Mum gets on with her sewing, trying to remain cheerfully optimistic, but I know they both think I'm too young; I know they're wondering why. The house feels empty already, soon it will just be the two of them.

My adolescence has not been easy on anyone. The quiet little girl grew into a messy, outspoken teenager. I know I've been hard to bear, but the thought of me absent is unbearable to them, it's always been the three of us, even at my worst I've still been their little girl. 'It's just a stage,' I've heard Mum say numerous times to other parents, rolling her eyes theatrically when I dyed my hair black, got caught smoking or sneaking out. I know she's been waiting for this latest stage to pass, had hoped my rebellious streak would run its course like a fever. Mum can still see glimmers of me as I used to be – the quiet, fair-haired dreamer, the little girl who clung to her and cried when she had to leave me. When I leave, that little girl will go too.

***

'Jean! Put it away for heaven's sake! Katie is not going to England wearing a monkey coat!'

Once Dad told a few friends and clients about my acceptance into the GAP program he changed his mind. Everyone has been wildly enthusiastic about my plan to live overseas for a year so now he's even starting to sound boastful about it. Together, Mum and Dad have written up a list of essential things I need to take, and top of the list is a good warm coat.

So now I'm standing like a mannequin in front of the big ornate mirror in their peach coloured bedroom as Mum drapes her full-length black monkey fur over my shoulders. It is surprisingly heavy and the satin lining is cold, like the material inside a coffin. Mum is taller than I am, on me the coat brushes the carpet, my hands hidden inside the sleeves.

I stroke the fur, wondering how many monkeys were murdered to make it. I know that Mum deeply regrets buying it, but now it seems even more tragic that it never sees the light of day.

'Don't be ridiculous Jean, that coat's worth thousands of dollars!'

'It's just sitting doing nothing in the closet!'

'Jean!'

'But it's lovely and *warm*! It will be *freeeezing* over there! In the middle of winter!'

Dad's going red in the face, his blood pressure rising again.

'Don't worry Dad, I'm not taking the coat.' The last thing I want is to look like Chewbacca. I slip out of the gruesome coat and give it back to Mum.

'Poor monkeys …' she says. She puts it back on a hanger and buries it in the back of the wardrobe. 'No-one thought about things like that back then. We just didn't know.' She takes out a brown fur, 'What about this one?'

'Jean! She's not wearing a fur coat!'

Mum starts talking about the cold again. 'Honestly, you won't believe how cold it gets! It gets into your *bones*! When I lived there we all had to share a bathroom. A hot bath – that was the only thing that could warm me up but I hardly ever had any money and you even had to pay for a bath! There was a slot on the wall and you had to put coins in it to get hot water – truly! No-one has showers over there, they all just have baths all the time.'

I look at her skeptically, then to Dad, but he's busy moving piles of books around on his bedside table. There are dozens of them, towered up around the lamp, and more in piles on the carpet. 'I must do something about these,' he's muttering, wiping the aptly named dust jackets.

'Barry tell Katie it's true! She doesn't believe me!'

'Well that's hardly surprising when most of the time you talk such rubbish!' he says and winks at me.

'Good one Dad,' I say.

Mum is offended. 'I do not!'

'Oh stop carrying on Jean, can't you take a joke?' Dad continues wiping down his dusty books and Mum goes back to her wardrobe, pulling out another unsuitable coat with feathers sewn onto the collar. 'I could take these off … try this one on.' I put the coat on as instructed, black ostrich feathers curl up around my face and tickle my nose.

Dad laughs, 'Jean! She can't wear *that*!'

'Without the feathers though!' Mum says holding them down so she can see what it would look like without them.

'Take it off her! It looks ridiculous!'

'I was just thinking Bar,' Mum says, 'of that old story I used to tell, about the bath in my English hostel.'

'Oh yes,' Dad says.

'Katie's probably never heard it, have you Dahling? I used to have to leave the water running for ages to fill the bath up. So I'd go do something else for half an hour and then come back, and when I returned the bath would look all cloudy, and then later when I emptied it there would be all this white flaky stuff left in the tub. I didn't know what it was but someone told me the water in England was very hard, and I thought, "Good heavens! That must be it!" But then one day I came back early because I was in a rush and caught this old Indian man who lived on our floor rinsing his rice under the tap! Golly! I couldn't believe it!'

Mum shrieks with laughter at the memory and even Dad snorts though he's heard it so many times.

'All that beautiful boiling hot water! I suppose he couldn't resist! No wonder my hair always stood up on end like chicken feathers! It's never recovered!'

Finally they decide to give me a coat of Dad's to wear, which is much more sensible than anything Mum owns. Mum convinces Dad to let me borrow her Italian leather gloves and they take me into town to buy me a new black felt hat that I don't really like but it's easier just to go along with them than to appear rude and ungrateful.

My boyfriend laughs when I show him and says I'm going to look like Charlie Chaplin. I don't dare show him the two full-length tartan skirts Mum's made me or – heaven forbid! – the puffy tartan shorts that make me look like a court jester. I had to try them on for her, carefully stepping into them while they were still full of pins. 'You can tell me if you hate them,' she'd said, but of course I couldn't! I didn't want to hurt her feelings.

So now I'm going to England with more than half of my suitcase taken up with clothes I don't want to wear. I'll stand out alright when I get there, but not in a good way.

And that's the last thing I want, to stand out. The real reason I'm going is to just experience living some place where I'll be completely anonymous, where no-one will have any preconceptions of who I am or what I should be like, what I should live up to or how I should behave. For once, I won't have any nagging doubts about people wanting to befriend me for any reason other than they like my company … I'll just be Katie, not 'Jeanne Little's daughter'.

***

'This might be your grandmother's last Christmas.'

Dad says this every year, each year, I think, suspiciously sounding a little more hopeful. I've never taken him seriously of course when he's said it, but this year a twinge of worry goes through me. I'll miss Dor Dor a lot. I'll write to her but she's too old to put pen to paper and reply. For her birthday Mum made a cake and covered it with dozens of candles, which she hated. It made her look old, she said.

'Well you are *ninety* Mum!' Dad said, which was totally the wrong thing to say, and thankfully Colin Johnston started going on about how wonderful her skin was and how good she looked for her age, which put her in a good mood again.

Tiffy has always ended every phone call to her parents with 'Love you!' The only person in our family who says things so blatantly sentimental is Mum, she's constantly telling strangers how divine they are too or kissing them, which is even worse. For years Dad and I have rolled our eyes at each other and winced at Mum's emotional excesses, we don't cry in sad movies and we'd never be caught *dead* behaving like that. If Mum says something mushy Dad will tell her to stop mollycoddling me and I've always sided with Dad because I don't want her treating me like a baby.

You should have seen Dad's face the time he overheard Tiffy hanging up saying 'Love you!' He's taken her off ever since, ending every phone call in a falsetto voice. Mum laughs in the background when he does this but I wonder if secretly he actually means it too, that's just the only way he can bring himself to say it.

When I'm overseas we'll have very little contact. Mum said she's going to write me big, newsy letters and put them through the fax machine, placing an international phone call will be too expensive. I wonder if Dad will still say 'Love you!' in his falsetto voice at the end of the call. I wonder if I'll miss them.

PART 3

YOU'D BE SO NICE TO COME HOME TO

'Make sure she eats,' that's the last thing my father says before he hangs up. Mum is coming to stay with me for five days while he goes into hospital to have a knee replacement – and I can't wait! I've made up the spare bedroom with fresh sheets and stocked the cupboard with Lan-Choo tea, the brand Mum drinks. I'm decluttering the house and making everything as tidy and organised as possible for her visit, which is a challenge with two small children!

Time with my mother is always measured; I almost never get to spend time with her alone. Dad makes all the decisions – if and when they're free to meet up, how long they stay for. There's always some excuse, and yet there's never an excuse when it comes to work. Work is always their priority, and I understand that, showbiz is a fickle business.

Dad finally retired from interior design a few years ago, his energy now goes into helping Mum with her cabaret shows. After the success of Mum's first show *Hello Dahling*, they wrote another based on the life of Marlene Dietrich. They're still performing this show and working on a new one about Marilyn Monroe. Dad sources the music and writes the script while Mum designs and makes the costumes. When Mum's not touring she's got a regular gig on the panel of *Beauty and the Beast* with Stan Zemanek, alongside ladies such as Ita Buttrose, Carlotta and Maggie Tabberer.

Beauty and the Beast is filmed at Foxtel and the studio is less than ten minutes from my house. Several times I've put a cake in the oven when they've said they'll pop round afterwards, but they haven't turned up. Dad is vague over the phone. 'Your mother was tired,' he says, or, 'We had to get home, she had a radio interview.' He gets irritable when I tell him the kids were looking forward to seeing them. I don't mention I'm disappointed too, that would be giving too much away.

The only time I see my parents is when we go to their house. It's always nice being cooked for and looked after but my son Tom, who has the same boundless energy as Mum, never sits still. It's exhausting being there any longer than a couple of hours. Dad is always stressed Tom will break something so my husband Tim and I have to take turns being 'helicopter parents', not letting him out of sight. Both our children are active, but Charlotte who's still crawling is at least a little slower.

'Tom's not touching those bronze heads is he?!' Dad will call out, and Tim, who's just worked ten or more hours at the office, with a Scotch in hand that Mum made him the second he walked in, will catch my eye and raise his eyebrows before calling out, 'No Barry! He's not touching anything, just climbing up and down the stairs!'

'It's a wonder you survived, growing up in that house,' Tim will say privately to me in the car later, and I'll laugh because someone finally gets it.

The story of me being brought home as a baby has already been told for Tim's benefit at least once as dinner-party conversation. How they came home from Paddington's Royal Hospital for Women, how Mum didn't have any milk.

'They gave me a needle to make it go away!' Mum squawked. 'I didn't want to look like Dolly Parton!'

'And when you got home you screamed and screamed,' Dad said.

'We fed you Carnation evaporated milk from a tin,' Mum said, 'Ooooh, we didn't know what to do!'

'And your intestines seized up *like a brick!* A client told me to give you a little spoonful of peanut butter—'

'Peanut butter!' Tim said, horrified at the thought of a baby going into anaphylactic shock, and Tom, who was still little, and rarely off the boob till he was two years old, swivelled round, nearly twisting my nipple off to see what all the fuss was about.

'It's a wonder you didn't *die* Katie!' Colin Johnston said chuckling.

'—and then there was this loud *POP!* Dad said (this was his favourite part of the story), 'and you stopped screaming, and when we opened up the nappy there was this tiny little rock-hard pellet of poo the size of a bullet!'

'Poor Katie!' Mum said, 'Having us as parents!'

***

Colin Brees has been designated with the task of dropping Mum at my house when she comes to stay. Colin is always doing things like this, as if he still works for my father. These days Colin Brees runs errands for Colin Johnston's pharmacy and looks after the house. Their house with its enormous manicured tropical garden looks like something out of an international *Vogue* magazine; it's Colin Brees' pièce de résistance.

My father rarely trusts my mother with anything practical, for these things he enlists Colin Brees. In return for continually being imposed upon, Mum is always trying to return the favour by inviting them over for roast dinners or looking after their dog when they go on holidays. Colin's beloved dog Cindy died long ago, replaced by Rusty, who is equally as spoiled. Mum is scared of Rusty; it attacks their old dog, takes over the couch and claims the end of the bed when it stays – Mum hardly sleeps for fear of it attacking her feet.

'I know what I'd do with that dog if it tried to bite me!' my husband says. 'I'm not scared of it!' And like a dare, Tim puts his hand out towards the small, scruffy dog that's taken over the sofa, laughing as it bares its teeth and growls menacingly.

'Horrible dog!' Dad will say as Tim's hand gets closer and the growling grows louder. Mum hides behind the doorframe saying, 'Ooooh! Tim, be careful!' Finally, an inch from the snarling jaws, Rusty erupts into a terrifying howling frenzy of snapping teeth and screeching barks that makes even Tim jump and pull his hand back.

By contrast, my two dogs, bigger but not spoiled, circle Colin excitedly as he comes through the door carrying Mum's small suitcase. Mum's following, making a fuss, telling Colin that she should be carrying the bag, and Colin ignores her, talking to the dogs instead. 'What's in here?' he asks them and I notice there's a plastic shopping bag in his other hand. 'What is it?'

My black dog, Curly, leaps right up onto his back legs and prances, and Colin laughs appreciatively.

I put a pot of coffee on and Colin deposits the bag on the counter top. Inside are a few sad looking lemons and a withered carrot, the contents of my parents' refrigerator crisper by the looks of it. Colin shrugs his shoulders and says, 'Barry gave it to me to pass on. There's also a kilo of bacon in there.'

No wonder the dogs are going absolutely bonkers.

'Ahhh, you do know we're vegetarian, right?' I give Colin a look and he smiles back wickedly.

'Barry was worried Jean would go hungry.'

My father's still meddling with my life even from hospital and I'm secretly furious as I pull the offending bag of bacon out, wondering what to do with it.

'I told your mother she should ask to be taken through the drive-through, *didn't I Jean?*'

Mum, who's been looking at the kids' artwork stuck up on the walls turns around when Colin calls out her name, 'What's that Dahling?'

'If you get hungry! Tell Katie to drive you to McDonald's! There's five dollars in your handbag for a Big Mac!'

Mum looks confused for a minute and Colin shouts, 'IF YOU'RE HUNGRY!'

'Have I lost my handbag?' Mum says looking confused. 'No Dahling, it's here!'

Colin groans and turns back to me.

'She's going deaf!' I say. 'I've told Dad she needs her hearing checked. Why doesn't he make her get her hearing checked?'

Colin shrugs.

'What am I going to do with this bag of bacon?' I say. 'Will you take it?' I push it towards Colin, who looks pleased.

'Good. I'd only have fed it to the dogs,' I say.

Colin looks apologetically at the dogs and says, 'Doesn't she feed you either?'

TIME HEALS EVERYTHING

When Tom was born we started going round to my parents' house for brunch on Sundays with the Colins. As a new mum I was always exhausted and starving hungry – for the first time in my life I was grateful to have Mum dote on me in her over-the-top way, bringing me cups of tea and propping cushions behind my back.

I'd always felt I had to fight Mum's excesses, proving I was capable and independent in every way. Leaving home the minute school ended had been a rite of passage, I'd had to get away from my parents' sphere of influence to discover what really excited me. My parents, my father in particular, had always had such strong ideas of what I *should* do, but I didn't know if their ideas matched up with what I felt in my heart. Most of the time it seemed what I had to offer wasn't what pleased them, and finally I concluded it was easier to live with a safe and civil distance between us.

I'd travelled a little, partied to excess, followed my passions of music and art and been thrilled to discover the emerging technologies of graphic design and electronic music, which had led me down a rabbit hole into the Sydney dance music scene. I'd had some small success as a DJ, music producer and promoter, and my father had not been impressed with any of it. Nor had he approved of my new boyfriend, a Brisbane boy turned Sydney rave promoter who I started a business with, whom I would eventually marry.

Part 3

To say that Tim and I lived hand to mouth in the early years is an understatement, but we were young, reckless and unencumbered, and we were having fun. And then suddenly the 'underground' dance music scene exploded into the mainstream and electronic music was everywhere, on the radio, in brand new enormous clubs and international record labels, and what we were doing suddenly became legitimate. Our business grew and our hard work began to pay off. We went from living in a rundown share house with mattresses propped up on milk crates to buying a converted warehouse and taking on staff. I bought myself a Cherry Hood watercolour, Tim bought a Porsche.

And now at thirty years old I was ready to turn the page on the next chapter of my life – starting a family. It felt like I'd run a mile and come full circle, and whether it was the postnatal hormones that swelled me with new gratitude, or the first glimmer of maturity being wrung out of me now that all my energy was being devoted to caring for the life of another, in this chapter of my life my family was my priority. My beloved grandmother Dor Dor had died a few months before I fell pregnant, so now my parents and the Colins, who I thought of as uncles, were the closest family I had.

* * *

A new baby really is a bundle of joy – everyone was so excited to see Tom! He was a tiny baby, wrapped up like a loaf of bread, his face creased with wrinkles. 'An old soul,' Mum said, and while he slept in my arms the expressions that passed over his face as he dreamt were so captivating that all of us, Mum, Dad and the Colins, would just stare and watch.

What do babies dream of? One moment Tom's face would darken like a thunderstorm, bottom lip quivering in a whimper, the next his face would light up, a giggle erupting from his tiny lips.

'Oh, look at him, isn't he just divine!' Mum would whisper and then Colin Brees, growing impatient, would cut in and say, 'Poke him! Jiggle him a bit! Wake him up!'

When he did wake, the translucent eyelids fluttering, blue eyes squinting painfully against the bright light, every annoyance seemed to be magnified a thousand times in his expressions. His mouth would open into a yawn and he would stretch, his back arching, unravelling like a glow worm from his muslin wrap, revealing minute toes with tiny paper-thin toenails, skinny bow legs, still moulded from the shape of my belly, skin so pale you could see the network of veins inside like a tender leaf held up to the light. Suddenly exposed, Tom would let out a cry – startlingly loud!

A high forehead and eyebrows so pale they were barely visible, the bright blue eyes, baby Tom was cut from the same cloth as Mum, and there were similarities in his personality too – he was loud, *really loud*, had no 'off switch' and thrived being the centre of attention.

Mum and Dad had built an extension onto the back of their Paddington house, the tiny room where the three of us had sat to eat dinner had been extended into a large, comfortable sunroom. Furniture from the property at Pearl Beach, sold long ago, had ended up here, the long, L-shaped cream lounge stretched across the back of the room under windows that showed glimpses of hot pink and apricot bougainvillea, accentuating Dad's collection of Hawaiian Pegge Hopper watercolours.

Tim would drop me off with the baby and I would lumber in with all of my new baby belongings while he circled the block trying to find a park. Inside, there was the dark hallway, the familiar lounge room and the smell of delicious foods wafting from the kitchen as I made my way towards the back of the house.

'*Yooohooo!*'

'Oh! Is that you Kitty Kat!' Mum would call back, rushing out to help me, cooing over the baby, fussing over me. 'Heavens, here, let me take that!'

I'd collapse onto the lounge in the sunroom, which was always covered with sheets so it would stay clean for photoshoots. At one end their ancient black poodle dozed, and after brunch Dad would take up the other end, emitting a snore every now and then while the conversation continued on regardless.

Mum would ask, 'Are you warm enough?'

Mum hated being cold, hated even the *idea* of anyone being cold. There was no point in saying anything because even if I shook my head and said I was fine, she wouldn't believe me, she'd already be reaching over me for the cord to pull up the blinds. The warm sunlight would stream in over my shoulders, falling onto Tom's face. He would wince theatrically and Mum would panic, hurriedly grabbing cushions to prop against the window behind me, building a strange, awkward tower to block the sun from his face.

'Would you like a cup of tea?' Mum would ask. 'Of course you would! I'll make you a nice hot cup of tea!'

I'd never much cared for tea, until I became a mother. And then the very idea of it became the most lovely gesture in the world. The steaming hot liquid was a miraculous antidote to weeks of sleep deprivation and baby-brain confusion, aching muscles and mastitis, complete and utter physical and mental exhaustion like nothing I'd ever experienced. And that lovely warm couch in the house I grew up in, a daybed where humans and animals retired for midday siesta – what paradise!

But Dad would not be napping just yet, he'd still be prepping the meal, bustling about in the kitchen, annoyed with Mum encroaching upon his domain to make the tea.

'Go out and see the baby,' Mum would say. 'Say hello to Katie! Go on!' and Dad would come out and be stopped in his tracks, not by the sight of his grandson, but by the horror of the higgledy-piggledy blinds and the sun pouring in directly onto his Pegge Hopper watercolours.

'Jean!' he would shout, *'My paintings!'*

He'd reach for the cord behind me muttering, 'What is your mother doing? What are *these* doing here?' noticing the cushions propped up on the window just as Mum came back in with the tea.

'Oh no Barry,' Mum would say, 'Katie's *cold!*' but of course I'd never actually been cold, I just knew there was never any point debating her when she'd made up her mind.

'Cold! She's *not* cold! You're not cold, are you?' Dad would say, and I'd shrug my shoulders half-heartedly, knowing better than to get drawn into another one of their Seinfeldian debates.

'See Barry, she *is* cold!'

'Don't be ridiculous!' Dad would say, pulling down the cushions, unblocking the sun, and this time a howl would erupt from Tom as he tried to move his face away from the light.

My mother would be horrified, 'Barry! You're waking the baby!'

Dad would lower the blinds quickly trying to look nonplussed, but you could tell he was rattled. From the minute Tom arrived he had all of us on our toes and everyone on their best behaviour – my parents' bickering would be magically silenced, my mother's usually loud voice hushed to a whisper, nobody was tipsy or loud and Colin Brees especially didn't drink too much. Everyone made an effort to be nice to each other.

That's not to say, however, that my father and I didn't continue to exercise our sarcastic wit, and as usual, my mother's ditsy antics presented us with plenty of opportunities. Sitting on the L-shaped lounge on one of these Sunday brunch mornings I decide Mum needs a grandparent name, one of those silly nicknames you overhear little kids in cafes calling their grandparents.

I christen her 'Ninny', short for nincompoop, and it's so sweet and mean at the same time that everyone laughs – the Colins, Dad, my husband Tim, and best of all Mum, who never takes herself too seriously to have fun. The name sticks and Mum wears her new name like a badge of honour, telling all the shopkeepers in Paddington, laughing along with them, and everywhere she goes people are so overjoyed and excited for her because they can see how completely and utterly *over the moon* she is about becoming a grandmother.

FALLING IN LOVE AGAIN

If I'm happy that Mum is coming to stay while Dad has his knee operation, Tom who is four now is literally *bouncing off the walls* with excitement. Tom loves Ninny more than anything. It could be because she keeps Tim Tams in her handbag, or it could be because the last two times I left him at their house she made pancakes for him and let him eat so many, with maple syrup and nearly a whole tub of ice cream, that he threw up afterwards.

The first time it happened was in bed in the middle of the night and I didn't think that much of it; I was still half asleep staggering around just trying to survive a night of pure hell and didn't *want* to think about it. But the second time he threw up was on the way home from my parents' house, and too late I realised a pattern was emerging.

I'd gotten angry on the phone with Dad, 'I *never* ask you to babysit and the two times I do I end up having to clean for hours afterwards! Vomit, Dad! He vomited two litres of ice cream, *in the car!* You have to keep an eye on what Mum's doing!' I pictured Dad dozing on the couch with the dog leaving Mum to 'entertain' Tom by cooking with him. 'Don't let her feed him all that stuff! He just keeps eating it and he never says no! He's just like Mum – the two of them never know when to stop!'

The afternoon I brought Tom home from preschool telling him that Ninny was waiting he ran into the lounge room like it was Christmas morning knowing he had the biggest present of all. He ran towards Mum full speed with his arms out and as she bent down to catch him the two of them bowled over backwards onto the couch and lay there laughing and hugging each other.

Mum did smuggle a packet of Tim Tams over to our house in her handbag, I knew it straight away because they were suddenly so quiet when I left them to go to the kitchen to start dinner. I popped back in again and the two of them were sitting suspiciously side by side on the sofa, Mum holding her black handbag in her lap, and neither Tom or my mother are ever quiet or still.

'What are you two up to?' I'd asked.

'Nothing!' Mum had said too quickly, and then Tom had smiled with teeth full of chocolate.

'Look, I don't want to be the boring person spoiling all the fun,' I'd said, 'just don't feed him *the whole packet* Mum! Please?' But Mum never knows how to say no.

I'd gone back to the kitchen to continue with dinner. Charlotte was sitting in the highchair with me eating crackers and I could hear them laughing and the sound made me feel happy. Usually Tim didn't get home for hours and the afternoons were the loneliest time of day. The laughing grew louder and more hilarious, and I started worrying about the biscuits, but when I went in I was laughing too because there was Tom sitting on the floor calling out, 'Stop!' 'Go!' 'Stop!' 'Go!'

Mum was walking around and around the living room freezing and walking on his command like a giant life-sized robot. And I laughed even harder because I had the sudden thought that Mum looked like C3PO because she was wearing a gold belt and high-waisted, tight-fitting pants, her short blonde hair combed back smoothly. I knew that this image would stick with me even after this game was over because of the way Mum walked, a kind of stiff awkward shuffle, and the way she held her head on the side at times, so naive and proper, just like C3PO.

Charlotte joined in, copying what Tom was calling out, and the game only looked to be getting more hysterical until I started worrying again, this time about Mum not knowing when to stop.

'Alright kids,' I'd said, 'you'd better let Ninny relax now, you don't want to break her on the first day!' but it took some perseverance to quiet them down. Mum looked a bit tired, I thought.

'You want me to put the news on for you or something Mum?' I'd asked.

That's what Tim's mother had done when she came down from Brisbane. She'd sat with the newspaper at the kitchen table in the morning, and in the afternoon had watched the news on the telly.

'Oh no Dahling, I'm fine! I'm fine!' Mum said, but I'd put the news on for her anyway, in case she was just saying that like I knew she often did, when really she wanted to say yes.

'What about a cup of tea while dinner's cooking? Or glass of wine?' but Mum wasn't interested in a drink and she wasn't interested in the news either. When I came back in again moments later Tom had taken over the TV and put his favourite movie *Finding Nemo* on with the funny, forgetful fish and Mum was sitting on the couch with the kids watching it.

'You don't have to watch that Mum, come and hang out in the kitchen with me for a while!'

I poured Mum a glass of wine and she perched herself on a stool at the bench. We talked briefly about Dad's operation, which was probably in progress right at that moment, and what I was cooking and then Mum said, 'I'll just go check the children are alright,' even though I assured her neither would even flinch while the electronic babysitter was going.

Dinner was coming out of the oven as Tim walked through the door. Usually there was a mad welcoming party, but not tonight. 'Where is everyone? Where's your mum?'

I shrugged, 'She's in watching telly with the kids.'

'Who's drinking this?' he said pointing to the second glass on the counter.

'Nobody, I poured it for Mum but she didn't touch it.'

'Good, I'll have it!' he said, and then after taking a large swallow came round to embrace me like Gomez Addams, saying, 'Don't tell me I can spend five minutes *alone* with my beautiful wife?'

***

Late that night when everyone is in bed my mobile rings. The voice on the other end is direct and emotionless: there's been a problem with the operation, the knee replacement went well but Dad has suffered a stroke on the operating table.

'How bad?' I ask.

I have that peculiar feeling of hearing myself speak calmly when I should be screaming. The registrar is blunt: Dad probably won't talk or walk again, he's in intensive care.

Tim sees the look on my face when I come back to bed, my mind still reeling from the call. Should I tell Mum now I wonder? No, I decide not to, better to let her sleep peacefully and try to get some myself. I'll tell her on the way to the hospital when I drive over first thing in the morning.

Tim puts his arms around me. 'It's going to be okay,' he says.

My mind is full of thoughts, and the last words Dad said over the phone: 'Look after your mother, make sure she eats.' I'm too stunned to cry. Dad and I have always had a difficult relationship, I just can't believe this is how it ends.

In the morning Tim stands on the front step holding Charlotte, Tom's hand in his. Mum waves to them from the passenger seat window and Tom wails, 'I don't want her to go!'

'Don't worry buddy,' Tim says, 'Ninny's not going home yet, she's coming back!'

I catch Tim's eye and he gives me a grim smile, 'Drive safely,' he says.

Neither of us has slept and focusing on driving is going to take all my concentration. We gave up on sleep at the first hint of dawn, wandered out to the garden and sat in the grey light watching the dogs running around sniffing the dewy grass.

I don't know if it was Tim or I who first started weeding a couple of patches near the steps, it was what we always did I suppose when we came down to the garden, but already we were sizing the house and garden up, looking at it differently, an asset to be put on the market. We'd need a bigger house if Mum lived with us permanently, let alone if Dad moved in too.

I pull up at a set of traffic lights, Mum is sitting primly in the passenger seat beside me with her handbag.

'Mum, there's something I need to tell you before we get there,' I start. I take a deep breath, 'Dad's operation didn't go too well ...'

She's surprisingly calm. 'Ooah, I thought so,' she says. 'Is he alright?'

'He's had a stroke ... I don't know how bad it is.' I don't want to burden her with any more.

I'm struck by how beautiful the intensive care ward is, all pale blue glass, polished steel and white linen. Everything looks calm and orderly, silent apart from the gentle beeping of machines. The nurse behind the desk looks up as I walk in with Mum, 'I'm here about my father, Barry Little, I got a call last night ...'

A few clicks in her computer and she locates him and smiles, 'Bed four, he's feeling much better this morning.'

She leads us to his room, he's sitting up in bed with an oxygen mask on, a tray of half-eaten breakfast not far away.

'Oh, are you alright Barry? Oh Barry ...' Mum says, taking his arm.

He raises a hand to take off the mask and talk.

'I was told he'd had a stroke,' I say stupidly to the nurse.

'Not by the looks of it,' she says matter of factly. I look at Dad's eyes just to make sure, watch as he lifts his other arm to take Mum's hand.

'Oh Bar! We were so worried …' Mum says suddenly tearful. I seem to be having trouble doing simple things like swallowing. My mouth has gone very dry.

'Are you feeding her?' Dad croaks in my direction. All I can do is nod.

***

The minute I get home I throw my shoes off and make a beeline for the sofa, I'm suddenly totally and utterly, exhausted.

'He's fine!' I say to Tim on the verge of laughing as the kids barrel past us to get to Mum.

'What do you mean he's fine?' Tim says following me, 'I thought he'd had a stroke!'

'They don't know, they think it might have been a reaction to the anaesthetic.'

'They don't know? *They don't know?*'

I let out a strange kind of giggle. It occurs to me that this is the second time something like this has happened to us. 'Remember that ultrasound before Tom was born?' I say to Tim.

When I was heavily pregnant a stony-faced technician had done an ultrasound and said the baby had 'holes in his brain', that he would probably be stillborn or die shortly after birth. We'd gone back to the hospital car park and walked around for thirty minutes, unable to remember where the car was parked.

Luckily Tom had moved around a lot in the last weeks of my pregnancy to let us know he was well-and-truly alive. We'd had to make regular visits to the paediatric wing after he was born but there was never any question his brain wasn't developing properly, and by eighteen months we were dismissed for good. I'd sat in the waiting area with Tom and smiled at the other little children, determined not to show a trace of the horror I felt at the sight of their misshapen heads, shaved in patches and crisscrossed with huge zippers of stitches. I was so thankful for Tom being healthy that just like now with Dad's wrong diagnosis, I hadn't thought to question why we'd been put through such stress.

While Tim and I talked Mum went out to attend to the washing. I'd told her yesterday not to worry about it, if the clothes I'd hung out on the rack didn't dry by the afternoon I just brought the whole thing inside. But Mum hadn't been able to leave the clothes alone. She'd layered wet clothes over the top and then started dragging the whole rack around to keep it in the strongest patch of sunlight. It was one of those situations with Mum where I knew it was better to turn a blind eye for the sake of my own sanity. And now she was out there again, layering the wet clothes; they'd never dry that way!

I shake my head as she starts dragging the heavy rack up the deck.

'Hey Jeanne!' Tim calls, jumping up from the sofa, 'Don't do that!' but Mum can't hear and keeps dragging, cutting a big ugly scratch mark in the brand new decking. There are scratches all over the deck I notice now, the deck that was only built and freshly stained a month ago. Tim runs out to show her the damage. 'Oh sorry Dahling, Sorry!' she says.

Tim sighs heavily and tells her it's alright. In light of what's happened – or not happened – with Dad, a few scratches seem like nothing worth getting upset about. We're all exhausted and Mum's only been staying less than twenty-four hours.

'How about I put a pot of coffee on?' I call out. 'Want to make some muffins kids?' Caffeine and sugar, that should get us through the afternoon.

PISTOL PACKIN' MAMA

Before having Tom I was doing some work for a girl I'd been to school with whose father owned a big company. She'd approached me to redesign the brand and we kept in touch after we'd both gone on maternity leave. I was excited when she invited me to afternoon tea with another close friend of hers, and the conversation eventually gravitated to househunting.

Like me, she was devoting hours upon hours to real-estate websites and viewings. We bemoaned the frustration of finding a potential property only to watch the price skyrocket at auction.

I was changing Tom's nappy on the floor behind the sofa when my friend said, 'I just can't find anything I like for under six!'

Gosh, I thought, feeling rather smug, my budget was eight hundred thousand, for six hundred thousand she'd be lucky to even buy a garage in Sydney! Building our business was sure paying off I thought proudly. All those years of coming in early and meeting clients' impossible deadlines!

My friend kept chatting away to her friend, she discussed the suburbs she was looking in near where we'd gone to school, and then it dawned on me: she was talking about *millions*.

'I just can't find anything I like for under six ...' MILLION! I nearly threw up.

On the days I took Tom for check-ups at the hospital I'd often go back to Mum and Dad's and Tim would join us after work with the Colins for dinner. Mum would fix Tim a Scotch and ask him all about the business, revelling in the drama of Tim's storytelling – the difficulty with clients, the problems with staff, funny stories like the girl who worked for him with hairy underarms that he couldn't stop looking at.

Mum was also excited to hear about Tim's latest hobby, car racing. He'd started driving in a national racing circuit and Mum thought it was a bit scary but terrific that he was pursuing a dream he'd had since childhood.

'Ooooah Tim! *Tim!*' she would say. 'Aren't you terrified? Be safe won't you!'

Dad, however, who'd inherited more than a few of my grandmother Dora's genes, thought fancy cars were showy and a ridiculous waste of money, racing them even more so.

'What's all this car racing nonsense?' he'd ask me later over the phone, taking any opportunity to bring up the fact we didn't own a house yet. 'Tim should be over all this silliness, he should be at home with you and the children, not off gallivanting around the country.'

The problem was though that we'd been househunting for well over a year and were struggling to find anything within our budget. We cast our nets wider but Mum, who wanted to be a hands-on grandmother, still clung to the hope we'd find something near them. Paddington, the suburb I remembered, with a pub on every corner, broken glass and stray cats in heat had been transformed from an ugly bohemian duckling into one of the swans of Sydney real estate. The auction prices got higher and higher while the houses seemed to get smaller and smaller, and Tim being a tall man who grew up in the sprawling suburbs of Brisbane refused to even look inside most of them.

Undeterred, Mum saved the local courier that landed on their doorstep every week, swelled to nearly an inch thick with overpriced real estate, and would throw it down on the glass coffee table. With the meat out of the oven resting and the potatoes having a final blast in the oven, Mum leafed through the dozen or so earmarked pages, finally stopping at one – this week, a shell, completely blackened by a house fire.

'Look!' she said. 'Here's a fabulous *dump* dahlings!'

Tim and I were not afraid of renovating, but a total knock-down rebuild was way out of our league. Mum of course was always optimistic, 'What about if you just replaced that bit of roof there and painted over the rest?'

Colin Johnston laughed, 'Jean! You wouldn't even be *allowed* to do that, the place is *condemned!*'

He pointed to the official tape stretched around the house warning people to keep out.

The other dumps Mum earmarked were usually at least livable, and for fun we'd take turns scribbling over the floor plans, fantasising what we'd do with them. Tim and Mum both loved dreaming big – Dad called it 'raving' – and was thankful to have the excuse of dinner to get us moving to the dining table. He knew as well as I did there was no chance in hell we could afford even the dumpiest property.

Colin Brees joked my parents' house wasn't far off being called a dump in Paddington too. Apart from the sunroom extension they hadn't renovated anything for thirty years.

'The place is falling down around us!' Dad said. 'I've given up!'

The house needed painting and a new roof, the front verandahs were rotting, and that was just the exterior. They'd been talking about downsizing to an apartment and retiring, but the idea of that seemed even more terrifying – there were rooms upon rooms full of my mother's clothes and fabrics, enough books accumulated by my father to fill several libraries, and furniture and antiques collected over a lifetime. But one night Mum and Tim came up with a brilliant idea.

It had been a frustrating week. Tim and I had missed out on another property at auction and the townhouse we were renting in Redfern was becoming more unsuitable to raise a family in. The tenants next door were throwing parties with loud music every second night and there had been a knife fight in the block of units opposite that had made me think twice about even walking to the supermarket with the stroller.

'Oh I wish you could just move in here,' Mum said, 'this house is big enough for ten people!'.

'What if,' Tim said, 'instead of buying our own place, we used our deposit money to renovate this one?'

Mum's eyes lit up, 'Oh Tim!' she said. 'That's *a brilliant idea!* Did you hear that Barry?'

Dad always became nervous when Mum started sounding too excited about anything; he was used to downplaying Mum's enthusiasm. 'Mmmmmm,' came his non-committal reply as he disappeared into the kitchen; but it was too late, the idea had already sparked to life and was multiplying with the rapidity of an algal bloom.

'If you think about it,' Tim said, 'you're not even using *half* the space here…'

'You're *right* Tim!' Mum exclaimed, 'Most nights Barry doesn't even go up to the bedroom, he just sleeps on the couch!'

'I can't manage the stairs with my knee!' came Dad's rebuke from the kitchen. He was obviously still listening to the conversation.

'Oh we know that Dahling!' Mum assured him, 'There's no need to be *embarrassed!*'

'And what do you use the downstairs office for?' Tim said.

'*Nothing!!*' Mum said, 'Barry just has the answer machine down there!'

'Wow! That is crazy,' I said laughing at the insanity of it. 'Imagine using *a whole floor* for an answer machine!'

Thinking about the rest of the house though I said, 'You are aware, both of you, that it would take *a shit load* more than our deposit to renovate this place?'

'Kate,' Tim said (I hated it when he called me Kate), 'We're paying six hundred and fifty dollars *a week* in rent where we're living now—'

'Money *wasted!*' Mum cut in.

'—we can take out a loan instead of a mortgage …'

And now my eyes began to sparkle too.

I *loved* the house I grew up in! As a child I'd drawn endless plans of the house, I knew every floorboard, every quirk! I'd climbed under the foundations, explored the manholes above the ceilings.

'Imagine how great it would be,' Tim said, 'not to have to sell this place.'

These words Mum and I had not even dared to say aloud.

Mum loved living in Paddington Street, she walked up and down to Oxford Street with the dog at least twice a day, stopping to talk with everyone. This was her home, and it was my home too, I had a history here, I felt *connected* to this neighbourhood and the land it was built on.

'This is … a totally brilliant idea.' My mind was whizzing and popping with all the modern architectural elements I could add to the old terrace – a mix of old and new! Contemporary tiles and fittings, a light filled atrium! Imagine even putting a chic plunge pool in the back! The possibilities were endless! And Mum had become so excited at the thought of us living together and her being part of her grandchildren's life *every day* that she'd had to stand up and was squawking, waving her hands around as if she might take flight. 'Oooah! Oooah! Oooah! Yes dahlings! Yes!'

Dad roused on Mum, he ordered her to quiet down and told us to go to the table with a note of sternness in his voice, 'Now Jean, let's not all get carried away here. This is something that will need to be discussed.'

But it was like trying to hold back an avalanche with a hand fan, the momentum of the idea had us all next to exploding. We sat at the dining table like naughty school children smiling conspiratorially at each other until Mum started jumping up and down finding things that needed to be brought out to the table – water, mint jelly, a serving spoon, the salt …

'*Sit down Jean!*' Dad called out, but Mum could only sit still for a second before bouncing up again.

'Oh! The butter!' she said, and then from the kitchen, 'Does anyone need anything else?' to which we all shouted back, '*No!*'

'JUST YOU JEAN!' Dad boomed.

Having dinner at my parents' house was always like being part of a pantomime, and just as long as everyone stuck to the script it was fine.

The script ordered we spend a suitable amount of time discussing Colin Johnston's pharmacy and Colin Brees' renovation plans, after which Mum delicately brought up the subject of renovating Paddington again. She took a bite and chewed carefully, then dabbed her mouth with a napkin before clearing her voice. 'What do you think about the kids renovating Paddington, Colin Johnston?' she asked.

Bringing Colin Johnston into the conversation was a smart thing to do because he was always seen as the sensible and financially savvy one, the bedrock of good advice. Dad sat down the end of the table pretending not to be interested.

'Well …' Colin Johnston said, 'I think you'd need to all think it through. Your parents are getting on Katie, would you really want the responsibility of living with them? You're a young family, you might have another baby and your parents are too old for all that …'

'Oh Christ yes,' Dad said.

There was no chance of that; Tim and I were only planning on having two children!

'And *if* you all were serious about it, you'd have to renovate the place so you had completely separate living areas, with separate front doors and everything – otherwise you'd drive each other mad.'

ANYTHING YOU CAN DO I CAN DO BETTER

'Is that Tom on the Bega Cheese ad?' Colin Brees asked. When I nodded he exclaimed, 'True!'

The Colins raised their eyebrows, my parents looked as proud as punch, and everyone wanted to know how this came about.

We'd all barely seen each other apart from the brisk fortnightly meetings with the architect to commence drawing up plans to renovate Paddington; there hadn't been a chance. The Colins had been overseas on holidays again, Tim had been busy with a new employee whose expectations were way out of line with his experience, and my parents had been spending every spare minute being interviewed by a woman who was writing a biography about Mum.

It was the book launch that had sparked the idea to sign Tom up with a casting agency. I'd had my hands full at the party, held on a rooftop in Crows Nest. It had been a beautiful summer's evening, the champagne was flowing and everyone laughed and talked while I ran around after Tom and Charlotte.

Mum had been invited onto the stage to give a speech and the crowd had moved inside to listen. I'd been relieved that fewer people made it easier to watch both kids, who ran around and climbed over the wooden benches like it was a playground. Finally able to relax a little I took a gulp of my own glass of champagne and winced as the bubbles fizzed up the back of my nose.

'OOOOOAAAAHHH! THANK YOU THANK YOU THANK YOU EVERYONE FOR COMING!'

Mum's voice blasted out through the speakers, she really didn't need a microphone, I thought to myself. The crowd of people laughed and applauded, squeezed closer to the stage to be nearer to her, packing the room tightly. I could see Mum up on the stage inside, sparkling in an orange sequined jacket, combed back platinum hair luminous under the spotlights. Scared of the noise, Charlotte lifted her arms asking to be picked up. I noticed too that Tom had stood up on the wooden bench like a meerkat, strangely still until Mum's voice blasted out again and I realised he was looking for her.

'OH DAHLINGS AREN'T YOU ALL DIVIIIINE COMING OUT HERE TONIGHT!'

She said a few more words but sounded like she was faltering, she was putting her index finger to her forehead saying, 'OH BARRY, WHAT WAS I GOING TO SAY AGAIN?'

'THE BOOK!' someone yelled out from the packed room. It sounded like Colin Brees.

The crowd was laughing, thinking it was all part of Mum's dippy act.

'OOOOAH YES! YES DAHLINGS – THE BOOK!'

'Ninny!' Tom shouted. He jumped from the bench and bolted in the direction of the stage.

'Shit!' I whispered under my breath. I upended the champagne and ran after him with Charlotte on my hip. I managed to grab his arm as he neared the crowd but he threw himself forward with unstoppable determination, twisting his little wrist from my grasp. 'Tom!' I gasped. He disappeared into the forest of legs. Within seconds there was a commotion down near the stage, people were exclaiming in surprise as Tom pushed through the final grown-up legs, then unperturbed hoisted himself up onto the stage.

'Ooooh! Tom! Is that you Tom!' Mum laughed in surprise, 'Oh, this is my grandson everyone. What are you doing here?'

He leant forward to speak into her microphone and said, 'I'd like a book Ninny.'

Both Mum and the audience laughed. 'OH DAHLING, AREN'T YOU ADORABLE!'

Mum told the story of being called Ninny, short for nincompoop, and the delighted audience applauded and lined up to get their books signed. As I drove home I laughed at the realisation – that's the first time *ever* anyone has upstaged my mother!

***

It's in his genes I'd said to the girl at the children's casting agency by way of explanation. I'd sent them some photos we'd taken in Japan – Tom surrounded by young Japanese girls who'd practically mobbed him because of his high forehead and big blue eyes. The photos were gorgeous but the holiday had been a disaster, Tom screaming every time we tried to confine him to the stroller. It had been our first and last attempt at a holiday since becoming parents.

I'd taken Tom to a casting – a packed waiting room full of smartly dressed little boys playing Angry Birds on their mother's iPhones. Like always, I'd been pressed for time getting there, we'd come straight from preschool and Tom was wearing his jeans with the tears on the knees, a beaten-up khaki jacket and hand-me-down sneakers with the velcro straps stuck on 'criss-cross', the trend going at preschool.

I'd explained to Tom in the car what we were doing. 'Would you like to be on the telly?' I'd asked. 'They're making an ad for cheese.'

'I hate cheese!' Tom said.

'What are you talking about? You like cheese!' I said.

'No I don't, *I hate cheese!*'

'Since when do you hate cheese?' I asked incredulous. This could be a problem.

'You *know* Mum! I've *always* hated cheese!'

'Well … Maybe today you could just *pretend* to like it, huh? That's called acting!'

Tom looked at me sceptically in the mirror.

'You don't have to eat it okay? They just want you to say something—'

'What do I have to say?'

'In – my – pocket.'

'What's in your pocket?'

'Not *my* pocket, *your* pocket. "In my pocket", that's what you have to say.'

'What's in my pocket?'

'Well, the cheese, I suppose!'

'But I hate cheese! Why would I want cheese in my pockets! Yuk!'

'*Who knows!* But it's not in your mouth okay? You don't have to eat it! So just stop saying you hate it! You can tell *me* you hate cheese, but for heaven's sake, just don't tell them! It's called acting!'

'Acting is lying?'

'Sometimes! Well, I suppose, yes … Yes! Acting is lying. Just lie, say you love cheese!'

'But I—

'Or just say maybe, or sometimes, *sometimes* you like cheese!'

'But I ha—

'Or just don't say anything! *Say nothing!* Just look cute and say the words "in my pocket"! That's all you have to do, got it? Just look cute and say "in my pocket!"'

This was the trouble with having a brainy kid I thought, as I reverse parked into a space that was meant for a smaller car, at four years old he was already smarter than me.

After sleeping in the car Charlotte was full of beans. She walked up and down the corridor holding onto my fingers while each of the boys were taken in. Tom was the last to be called, 'Sorry we went overtime!' the girl said as she called Tom's name, and I laughed and said, 'No problem!' even though my back was aching from being bent over like a hunchback. I thought also of the long-expired parking meter downstairs and the peak hour traffic we'd catch on the way home. I smiled at Tom encouragingly and gave him a nod as the girl stood by the door.

'I hate cheese!' Tom said.

I grimaced but the girl just laughed and said, 'Well you're a bit of a cheeky one aren't you!'

She opened the studio door wider and squatted down to his level to welcome him in. The glare of professional lights against a white backdrop inside the room, a video camera trained on an isolated stool – it must look intimidating to a little person I thought.

'Ready?' the girl asked. Tom nodded, hesitating at the door.

I was starting to think this was all going to be a total waste of time when suddenly he shot into the room like a bullet and climbed up onto the stool to claim the spotlight.

'I'm Tom the bomb!' he said, and I overheard the director exclaim, 'Well this one looks like a *real boy!*'

Before I could wonder what a 'real boy' was, Tom had claimed his first job – a ten-second close-up sitting on the stoop of a suburban picket-fenced house. Filmed at dawn in an Annandale laneway he'd taken to the job like a duck to water, seemingly unfazed at being led to his mark on the step by the director, past back-to-back filming trucks and a generator, enormous lighting rigs and a partition of huge, black, trampoline-looking screens set up to block out the reflections.

When the advert aired it was a medley of iconic Australia promoting dairy industry goodness. A soothing male voiceover asked the question, 'Where's the cheese?' and Tom whispered direct to camera with his winsome grin, 'In my pocket.'

TAP YOUR TROUBLES AWAY

Dad asked if I could help them one day by driving them to the hospital. Mum had an appointment with a specialist.

'Sure,' I said over the phone, marking the date on my calendar.

'You won't forget?' Dad asked.

'No Dad, I've written it down. When do I ever forget?' Luckily he couldn't see me rolling my eyes; I was still furious at him. The plans to renovate Paddington had turned into a catastrophic failure.

We'd spent a significant chunk of our deposit savings drawing up plans, and Dad hadn't wanted to go ahead with the idea. Worse still he hadn't told us. He'd made up his mind and only complained to Mum until finally she'd told me, blurting it out in a stuttering mess over the phone.

I couldn't believe it. All those meetings with the architect! Our plans for a life together, aborted! The situation had opened up old wounds. Dad had always hated talking about the future, he'd never valued my opinions or trusted my judgement! I felt as small and angry as I did when I was a teenager. I'd reacted by putting my defences up, determined not to show him how deeply hurt I was. Shutting down was the only defence that worked because arguing with him never went anywhere – it just sent me insane.

There was only one person who could change Dad's mind – Mum. She was the only person stubborn enough to stand up to him! And for the life of me I couldn't understand why she'd backed down now. I *knew* Mum wanted us to move into Paddington as badly as I did, yet when I tried talking to her she stuttered and said she didn't want to upset him. And so I closed off from her too, because she betrayed me – she'd chosen him over me, again.

If they'd just told us earlier it wouldn't have been so bad! It was heartbreaking – the money that we'd worked so hard to save, wasted on architect meetings, and all those phoney cups of coffee, the charade of talking over the plans in their lounge room, just like when they entertained journalists and people they wanted to impress – except this time they'd duped me! Their only child! What sort of relationship was that? I resolved to keep them at arm's length again; it was easier for everyone.

Although months had passed Tim was still furious. I hardly dare tell him I'd agreed to drive my parents to the hospital. He thought it was about him, the reason they'd pulled out of renovating Paddington.

I felt sorry for my husband. There'd been a time, particularly just after we'd gotten engaged that Tim and my father had seemed to really get on. Tim's father had died when he was very young, and Dad of course had never had a son. Tim had even jokingly called my father 'Dad' a couple of times, and rather than run a mile my father had actually smiled and laughed like he'd enjoyed it.

***

The drive over to pick up my parents was peacefully quiet and easy without the kids in the car. I couldn't remember the last time I'd driven anywhere alone.

I put some music on and tried to think about something else beside my parents' weird behaviour, but something else was bugging me – why had I been called upon as chauffeur? Colin Brees must have been busy, I thought.

If only I had parents like my friends: grandparents who adored seeing their grandkids, who took them out for milkshakes and picked them up from preschool, or had them for sleepovers while they went off to grown-up dinner dates. We'd stopped going out to restaurants with the kids because it was just too stressful, Charlotte pulled everything off the table and Tom wouldn't sit still, jumping up to talk to diners all around the restaurant, reminding me again so much of my mother! Tim got angry and complained that nobody else's children were so badly behaved while I worried a waiter would trip over Tom.

Dad opens the door for Mum to sit in the back then gets in beside me. Mum comments on the traffic, 'So many cars!' she keeps saying. Dad remarks what a good driver I am. They're trying to be extra nice to me. At the hospital I navigate them through the nondescript corridors. I'm reminded of all those visits to the paediatric wing, thankfully now I'm going in the opposite direction, towards geriatric medicine.

'Aren't we lucky we've got Katie here to show us where to go!' Dad says.

'Yes, isn't she clever!' Mum says. I roll my eyes again.

The specialist is a tall, thin man who looks like Quentin Blake's inspiration for the BFG. He shakes our hands and welcomes us into his office. I sit farthest away. What a strange doctor's visit I think, watching the proceedings, it's more like a chat. He doesn't measure or weigh anything physical, there are no readings of blood pressure or temperature, no peering into crevices of the body with a flashlight.

He asks what's been going on in my parents' lives and my father explains they've been moving house into an apartment. I grit my teeth.

'It's nearly killed us!' Dad says.

'Shocking!' Mum agrees laughing.

'Four storeys of belongings—'

'Barry's books!' Mum says.

'Jeanne's wardrobes!'

I picture the Paddington house, the rooms empty and sad.

'And how about you, Jeanne?' the doctor asks. 'Are you still working?'

'Oh, yes Dahling, I love work!'

'And what are you working on at the moment?'

'Ooooh a stage show I think, aren't we Barry …'

'Marilyn,' Dad finishes.

'Yes! Marilyn, about the life of Marilyn Monroe. I really love it.'

'And how's that going?' the doctor asks Mum.

'Oh terrific Dahling! Isn't it Barry?' Mum says.

'For the most part pretty well,' Dad says, 'But Jeanne's been forgetting some of her lines …'

Mum looks annoyed but laughs, 'Oh! Have I? How terrible! That sounds awful!'

'It's the stress,' Dad says. 'Moving house has been very stressful for both of us.'

Friends of my parents have been ringing to tell me they're worried about Mum, they've seen her forget lines on stage. She's always been known to play up the ditzy persona but Mum is extremely professional, forgetting lines on stage is not like her at all. I've told the callers what I know – they're selling Paddington and supposedly retiring, but Dad's still taking bookings on the show.

But then someone rang to say Dad had sent Mum to Brisbane overnight for a book launch. She'd lost her luggage and gotten upset at the airport; the trip had been a disaster. What the hell was going on? At least if we'd moved into Paddington I'd have known! I'd have been there! *I* could have taken her up to Brisbane on the plane – Tim's family lived there!

'Tell me about your new place Jeanne,' the doctor says. 'Have you moved into an apartment, a house…?'

'Oh, an apartment, haven't we Barry? Where is it again?'

'Double Bay,' Dad says.

I hate the apartment they've bought, a sprawling maze of dark rooms in a security building. Dad and the Colins love the grand entrance with tropical gardens, looking more like a resort than a unit block. The rooms look silently out into trees through double-glazed windows – perfect for Dad and his antiques, who likes cool, quiet darkness, but not for Mum who likes activity and sunshine.

An assistant takes Dad away while Mum does some tests.

'Alright Jeanne,' the doctor says. 'I'm going to ask you to remember three words: cow, hat, ball.' They sound like words Tom practises writing at kindergarten, tracing letters in lead pencil at a miniature desk.

The doctor asks Mum about her new cabaret show but she seems confused without Dad cutting in to finish her sentences, 'Oooah! Oooah, what was I saying again?' she stutters. I'm struck suddenly by how lost Mum is without Dad.

'That's okay Jeanne,' the doctor says. 'It can be difficult to remember sometimes I know. Let's move on, I've got a worksheet here, I'm going to ask you to draw a clock face if you can.'

Mum's always been great at drawing; this should be easy! I watch her draw a wonky circle. She hesitates and adds some abstract lines.

'Oooah,' Mum says laughing nervously, 'I've kind of mucked that a bit haven't I?'

My mind is reeling. I'm still stunned from the realisation of how often Dad's been finishing Mum's sentences, I can hardly believe what I'm seeing.

The doctor points to a simple drawing. 'Can you tell me what this animal is Jeanne?' he says.

'Oh … What is it again?' Mum concentrates, it's on the tip of her tongue.

'*Duck!*' I feel like screaming, 'It's a *duck!*' How can she not know what a duck looks like!

'That's okay,' the doctor says, 'let's try the next one …'

'Oh! Oh, a lion!' Mum says. She sounds relieved but also annoyed, 'What am I doing this for again?' she says. Hearing Mum angry worries me even more. Mum only very rarely gets angry.

'It's just a little test Jeanne, to see how your brain's working.' He smiles and asks, 'Do you remember any of the words I told you a while ago?'

'What words? Where's Barry? Where is he?' Mum asks.

I feel like I've woken up in a horror movie.

EVERYTHING'S COMING UP ROSES

'Aaaand – *cut!*'

Tom is standing at a kitchen bench dressed in an apron, making biscuits with a mother who is the on-screen version of me.

I'd sat in the waiting room of the casting for the Arnott's commercial flipping through dog-eared magazines, rocking Charlotte's stroller with my foot. Tom had only been gone a moment when the casting agent, a young bearded hipster I'd grown to like, popped his head back round the door.

'Excuse me, Tom's mum?'

I looked up, 'Is Tom behaving himself?'

The casting agent laughed, 'Yes, he's doing a great job! Actually, we were wondering if you'd like to try out for the part of the mother?'

I stared and blinked, '*Me?*'

'We're assuming you know the script …'

Of course I knew the script! Tom and I had practised it together, it was cute, a little boy asking his mother if she knew how old she was, telling her to look at the tag on her underpants. I felt like Cinderella being invited to the ball!

'I'd love to have a go!'

On the drive home I'd phoned my old friend Danielle, who lived in Canberra. 'Guess what?' I said. 'I just got asked to audition for a commercial!'

'No way!' Danielle exclaimed. 'How'd you go?'

'I nailed it! I reckon I've got a shot!'

'Wow!'

It was particularly exciting because grown-ups got paid good money to appear in commercials. Children, like employing monkeys, usually got peanuts.

Tim had been harping on for some time now about how much financial stress was on his shoulders. After my father had backed out of renovating Paddington we'd wasted no time in buying a run-down house with the little deposit money we had left; the mortgage and renovation bills now seemed to be never-ending. Adding to this our business seemed to be under constant stress, there were more problems with staff, and a big client had gone into administration.

When Tom was a baby I'd set up meetings with clients assuming I could keep working, just as Mum had with me, but each time it had been a disaster. Tom demanded constant attention making talking about anything work related next to impossible. Finally tired, he'd latch onto my boob and drink too fast then sit up screaming before spewing the lot over me. I even started wearing cream clothing from head to toe so if I got caught out it wouldn't look so obvious!

The alternative of leaving him was also disastrous. Besides putting nappies on backwards, Mum looked awkward even holding a baby – she'd carry Tom at a strange angle, arms and legs hanging out all over the place. I tried expressing milk, the pumping torture device that sounded like a distressed cow crossed with a vacuum cleaner pulled on my poor overworked nipples, turning them purple and threatening to snap them like elastic bands, with barely any milk to show. Tom knew the second I even let Mum take over pushing the stroller and would start screaming, and after hearing the stories my parents told about my childhood, Tim agreed, it was just too risky to leave a baby in their care.

Two years on I'd fallen pregnant again. I struggled with unrelenting morning sickness and tried to keep up with the unstoppable toddler Tom, and with little alternative succumbed to the very traditional role of stay-at-home mum.

The new phase of my life devoted to motherhood was challenging, at times terrifying, being left in charge of a living, screaming baby with no instructions! All I had were books that left me riddled with anxiety, feeling more confused than ever. It was also desperately lonely, mindlessly repetitive and completely, utterly, exhausting.

All the things I'd been appreciated for in my previous grown-up life became obsolete – my creativity and managerial skills, my gift with words, even my dress sense, none of it mattered! In the chaos of babies and young children I couldn't seem to finish even the simplest of tasks. I was lucky if I got as far as changing out of my pyjamas.

Running a business felt like a distant memory. I didn't have a card with a title anymore, in fact, as soon as I was carrying a child the midwife hadn't even called me by my name – I was just 'Tom's mum', or 'Charlotte's mum'. But the sacrifice was worth it. From the minute I'd held my first baby Tom in my arms, his big eyes blinking open slowly in the semi-darkness of the birth centre like a possum, I was in love and I knew being a mother would be the most important job of my life. In practice, however, I often forgot. As I stumbled through days of disorganisation and confusion I found my greatest challenge was how to be wholly content with the simple, mundane exercises of life; domestic bliss for me did not come easily.

I started a blog and humorously called it 'Going to Seed', I volunteered to run the local playgroup and started fundraising for the preschool. Unfortunately, however, my new interests weren't helping to pay our bills, a fact that kept rearing its ugly head. In a recent argument Tim had shouted, 'I just don't understand why you devote so much time to all these things that don't help us!'

'Of course they help us!' I'd shouted back. 'Fundraising for the preschool is contributing to our community!' But volunteering and the new found love I'd developed for gardening didn't pay rates or petrol.

'You're always exhausted!' he shouted. 'Devoting all your time to these things instead of to us!'

'What are you talking about? I never stop doing things for us – shopping, cooking, cleaning! Three loads of washing just today!'

Tim had been forced to fire one of his employees the week before. It had been yet another financial blow.

'Don't you understand?' Tim shouted, 'I need you back at the business! I can't do it all!'

'Well that's how I feel too!' I screamed. 'I do *everything* around here! You don't even hang a bloody towel up!'

'*Fuck* hanging the towel up! Employ a cleaner!'

'And who's going to look after the kids if I'm at work?'

'Send them to daycare – like everyone else does!'

'And how much will that cost? Sending Charlotte to daycare full-time, getting a nanny to drive Tom to and from preschool, getting a cleaner in, and who's going to cook?'

'Oh it's not that hard to cook a meal for god's sake!'

'So I'm *expendable*, is that what you're saying? That everything I devote my time and energy to means NOTHING!' I shouted so loud my voice cracked.

How could I explain that I couldn't give up the preschool council or writing because they were the only things keeping me sane!

The logistics of me going back to work seemed impossible, between organising renovations and builders and driving Tom to preschool every day, I barely had time to put on a load of washing before going out the door again. Plus my father seemed to be on the phone every second day asking me to do something for them as well. Tim stayed at the office working longer and longer hours while I continued looked after the house and children.

'Don't wish it away,' Tim's mother said over the phone from Queensland, which only made me feel more desperate. I didn't want to wish it away, of course I didn't – but at times I felt like I was being strangled! There was no point arguing with Tim about our situation, we could never seem to find a solution, the reality was we had to put our differences aside and just get on with the lives we'd made for ourselves.

The last thing I needed to do was pursue yet another unprofitable activity – Tom's fledgling acting career. I knew full well the reality of filming – it was not glamorous, it was tiring and relentless, the hours were horrid and the pay was pretty often miserable, unless you were lucky enough to strike the big time.

But! I was thrilled to have hit on something Tom had a knack for and, truth be told, I loved it at as well, because on a film set I felt at home. The wardrobe departments with their sewing machines and starch reminded me of Mum's sewing room. The big padded chairs in make-up took me back to the *Mike Walsh Show*. The easygoing banter of the crew and the excitement of scripts and lighting and direction!

So what if Tom, at preschool age, was earning the wage not me! Mum had always said to follow my heart and I could see I wasn't the only one who felt at home on a film set, Tom did too.

He landed one job after another – an ad for Tip Top filmed at midnight in a supermarket playing opposite a man dressed up as a giant loaf of bread, infomercials for toys and review shorts for movies, a promo for Nickelodeon where he and a little co-star were dressed up to go dinosaur hunting in front of a green screen. The little girl's father complained about the ordeal his daughter was being put through – the weight of the book she was expected to hold up, the endless takes and repetition of cues – but I said nothing, I just waited in the wings to give Tom encouragement, a reprimand or a bribe, and stepped into my new role of stage mother with aplomb.

And this time, I thought, I nearly landed a job myself!

Playing Tom's mum in an Arnott's biscuit commercial would have paid enough to take us all on a decent holiday to Daydream Island, probably with money left over. What a dream that would have been! By now Tim and I were living separate lives and we had no idea how or when we'd ever match them up again.

On the shoot I dunked a Scotch Finger in my cuppa and consoled myself that although my career appeared to be presently bogged in a stagnant maternal backwater, Tom's star was on the rise! He didn't care about the pay cheque, filming life was full of perks for five year olds – skipping school, cans of creaming soda and ice cream from the catering truck, and on this occasion, the unthinkable – eating biscuits all day!

I watched as tray after tray of butternut biscuits oozing with melted chocolate were placed before him. Yes, I thought, I'd very nearly landed that job – the brunette playing his mother was the on-screen version of me! A wholesome happy interpretation, taller and more beautiful, complete with bountiful C cups!

'Your undies tell you how old you are,' Tom mumbled through another mouthful of biscuit, 'mine say five to six!' and his on-screen mother tousled his hair and laughed with large, perfect white teeth.

'Cut!' the director called. 'That's a wrap!'

I'VE GOT YOU UNDER MY SKIN

When Tom came home from preschool I'd find worksheets crumpled in the bottom of his school bag. I'd straighten them out to stick up on the wall, laughing at his name scratched backwards in the corner – MOT.

The worksheets the doctor shows to Dad at the hospital looks just like these I think, but they won't be going up on anyone's wall. Although odd at times, Mum's behaviour hasn't struck me as unreasonable. If anything I'd just found her a bit more annoying! But as the doctor talks pieces start falling into place, and a nightmare begins to take shape.

He says Mum might get worried in unfamiliar places, background noises might upset her.

The weather! The traffic! The planes flying over, I think. She's always commenting on them!

She might become attached to certain objects, or worry about losing things.

Her handbag – she never lets it out of sight! And her silver rings! She'd been convinced they were stolen when they moved from Paddington!

The doctor talks about spacial awareness. She might have difficulty getting dressed.

She was always putting the nappies on backwards and we laughed, thought it was funny!

Or she might get lost easily.

Heavens yes! Mum had asked me a ridiculous number of times where the bathroom was at my house. One time she'd even asked where the front door was and I'd said 'Downstairs!?' and pointed to the stairs like she was off her trolley.

'It's stress related Doctor,' Dad says. 'The move was incredibly stressful for both of us.'

The stress of moving house has played a major part in accelerating the disease, he agrees. His diagnosis is Alzheimer's.

The word triggers an alarm inside me. Alzheimer's is the butt of old-people jokes. Little old ladies with grey hair – Sophia in *The Golden Girls*, Ruth Cracknell's character in *Mother And Son* – but that's not Mum! She's not that old, she's still in her late sixties. She doesn't even have grey hair!

Truthfully though I don't know Mum's exact age because she's always lied about her age, even on her driver's licence and passport. When someone official asked for her date of birth – a policeman or a customs officer – Mum had to guess it in front of them. If anyone else had pulled a stunt like that they would have been arrested or strip searched, but because it was Mum – and there was only ever one Jeanne Little! – everyone *knew* it was her, they just laughed and found it hilarious.

'It's important for Jeanne to have routine and familiarity,' the doctor says. She shouldn't drive anymore and they should look into getting help at home. Dad's hired a cleaner who waves a feather duster around once a fortnight, but they need more help than this, someone to change sheets and clean out the refrigerator, do things Mum's done for years that Dad's never even noticed.

'Will she still be able to work?' Dad asks. He's taken bookings for shows well into next year.

The doctor smiles kindly and says now would be a good time to retire. 'Routine and familiarity,' he repeats, 'an orderly environment, structured days …'

I know this, I think.

I've read enough parenting books to know exactly what he's talking about. I can help! I can do this! Like when I helped Mum learn song lyrics in the car, practised tap dancing with her in the kitchen for *Jerry's Girls*.

'We were planning on taking a holiday, a cruise …' Dad says.

The doctor shakes his head, 'Best not to at this stage.'

'Maybe if we wait a while she'll recover,' Dad says. 'The move was so stressful … A ten-day cruise …'

The doctor shakes his head. I feel like screaming: *haven't you been listening?*

My father just doesn't seem to get it. What is wrong with my parents? They never listen to sense!

It's like when their old dog Polly went blind and kept bumping into the furniture, Mum wanted to get the dog's eyes operated on but I warned her the dog was too old, the best thing would be to just stop moving the bloody furniture around. As long as they kept things in the same place the dog knew where to go. But Mum had gotten the idea into her head by then and did the operation and the dog was dead less than six months later. Meanwhile, I was still wearing glasses!

The doctor talks about a medication that has only just become available, he doesn't know if it will do anything, but it's worth trying. Anything's worth trying.

Nobody talks while he writes out the prescription; the room is deafeningly silent apart from the scratch of his pen. Then finally Dad speaks.

'My wife's a party girl, Doctor,' he says. 'When I met her, she was the life of the party … I just want some time with her, to retire and enjoy our lives together.'

These are the saddest words I've ever heard.

The doctor reassures Dad by talking about the new medicine; there have been good results in clinical trials. Just take it easy, he says, no big changes, just enjoy simple things together.

His calm mannerism reminds me of Colin Johnston, and for some reason I think of the awful story Colin once told us at dinner. He'd been reassuring one of his good customers at the pharmacy who was terrified of going into hospital the following day to have a leg amputated.

'You'll be fine. Just take it one step at a time,' he'd said, horrified at the words he heard coming from his mouth.

The doctor shakes our hands as we leave and we walk across the corridor to wait for the lift.

'What a charming man!' my father says.

'Wasn't he lovely!' Mum agrees.

In this nightmare world everything is wrong – there are so many urgent things to talk about I think, yet here are my parents, giggling as they wait for the lift. Dad gossips he's heard the doctor is quite a ladies man.

'At his age!' Mum says.

'Yes!' Dad says. 'He looks like he could be in a nursing home himself – no wonder he's in geriatric medicine!'

'Oh! Stop it, Barry!' Mum says laughing. 'Stop it!'

I WANNA BE LOVED BY YOU

Amidst the chaos in my house the phone seemed to always be ringing and more often than not it was my parents.

'Oh, did I wake you?' Mum would ask. 'Were you having a rest?'

'How could I *possibly* be having a rest Mum? Charlotte's been awake since 5 am, she had a tantrum that lasted an hour, one of the dogs nearly ate a guinea pig we're minding for a friend, and Tom opened a beanbag so there are styrofoam balls everywhere!'

'You need a rest Dahling, you sound *exhausted*. Can't you go and have a lie down?'

Mum had absolutely no idea what my life was like. A sleep! In the daytime! I let out an hysterical laugh.

Mum rang all the time and never seemed to have anything to talk about; I dreaded answering the phone. After the let down of Paddington I just wanted to get on with my own life, if they chose to be part of it, fine, but they didn't, except when Dad needed something. They were driving past my house every week to film *Beauty and the Beast* at Foxtel, yet instead of dropping in like normal grandparents Mum was posting things to me in the mail. Odd newspaper clippings kept arriving in envelopes with their 'Please note new address' sticker on the back.

There were so many important things I wanted to talk about, yet when I brought up anything I'd been thinking about or investigating that would help Mum, Dad brushed me off. As usual it felt like I didn't know anything and had nothing to offer.

And still the phone kept ringing: Mum calling, only ever to talk about superficial things like the weather and how cold it was, before stuttering and putting Dad on – it was enough to drive a person insane! I hated all these pointless conversations, I wanted to spend real time with them.

I'd heard the doctor's diagnosis, but to me Alzheimer's was still just a word that I had no experience with. I hadn't grasped the myriad of implications, I didn't understand Mum was having trouble talking on the phone because she couldn't see me, and when a parcel arrived in the mail, a pretty cotton skirt for Charlotte that was ten times the wrong size, I took it only as evidence of how little my parents saw their grandkids.

I kept telling myself it didn't matter, soon I would be spending real time with Mum when the back wall of our house was knocked out. Tim would be away and I'd arranged to take the kids to stay at their new unit for a couple of nights. I was looking forward to it, thinking finally we might put the dramas of the failed attempt to renovate Paddington behind us. They'd only been in their new unit a couple of months and I knew they still had a lot of boxes to unpack. I couldn't wait to be helpful and help them settle in.

It would be fun I thought as the time grew near. I packed the Uno cards and a DVD set of a new series called *Game Of Thrones* that I knew Dad was going to love; it sounded like the plot in the medieval novel he'd been working on all those years ago.

Mum is excited when I tell her over the phone about the back wall being knocked out in a few days time. Dad starts asking in the background what she's agreeing to.

'Katie and the children are coming to stay for the weekend!' Mum says, before stammering into the phone, 'Oooah, here's Barry, I'll put Barry on …'

'I don't think that's a good idea,' Dad says stonily. 'Your mother and I can't cope, we don't have a spare bedroom set up yet or enough sheets or anything like that.'

'What are you talking about?' I ask him. 'I organised this with you weeks ago.'

I tell him I've got a blow-up mattress I can share with the kids, we bought one for Tim's family when they came down from Brisbane once. 'I'll bring all the sheets and things, nobody has to cook, we'll order pizza …'

But Dad is adamant, he doesn't want to discuss it, we can't stay with them.

White-hot fury surges through me. 'I thought the whole reason you bought a three-bedroom unit in Double Bay was to have a room set up "for the children"?'

Dad had sold the idea of buying the unit to Mum by saying Tom and Charlotte would have their own room, but the spare room had been turned into a TV room crowded with antiques and a wall of books.

Dad is angry too. 'Don't you understand?' he says, 'We moved out of Paddington because we had to—'

'Well no, you didn't *have to* actually,' I interrupt. 'Remember? We spent a bloody fortune having plans drawn up! Oh, but that's right, you didn't tell me you'd changed your mind until we'd spent most of our deposit money on an architect! *For nothing!*'

I hate confrontation more than anything; my whole body has started shaking.

'I don't have time for this!' Dad snaps.

'What am I supposed to do?' I shout at him, 'We have to move out of our house for *two nights*, what's the big deal if the kids and I stay with you?'

'Stay in a hotel!' Dad shouts.

'I can't *afford* that and I don't *want* to stay in one anyway! I want to stay with my *family!* The kids and I barely ever see you and Mum, you don't want us at your place and you don't like driving to my place. Mum can't come over to help me with the kids for a few hours – not even to help, just as company – and yet you *send her on a plane* to Brisbane to stay with some person she hardly knows!'

I can hear the surprise in his voice. 'That was work!' he says quickly, 'That was a book launch!'

'No, that was a *disaster*, that's what that was!'

'Well you're not staying here and that's that!' There's a crash as Dad slams his phone down.

'Fuck YOU!' I roar at the empty receiver.

***

It's strange looking back on life's twists and turns. The kids and I took our blow-up mattress and stayed at Kate McDonald's house. Her kids had only just gotten over a stomach flu, which Charlotte, still crawling, picked up. She couldn't shake it, couldn't even keep water down, and was in hospital three days later. Nobody could do anything, we just had to wait for the virus to run its course, and pray. For six days I sat in a silent, quarantine room watching her little body lie limply in the enormous cot. I thought she might die and I wondered if I'd brought this all upon myself by wishing for a moment of solitude.

Tim kept running the business and a preschool parent we'd only just met offered to take Tom home with her daughter every afternoon and feed him dinner. My parents phoned of course, but they didn't visit the hospital. When my battery went flat I didn't ask Tim to bring in the charger. It was a relief not to have to answer it.

THERE'S NO BUSINESS LIKE SHOW BUSINESS

Rumours are flying that Mum isn't well after a mention was made in a newspaper gossip column. Journalists are phoning for comment but Dad is adamant he doesn't want to discuss her diagnosis.

Instead they've done a big article with *New Idea* about how much Mum loves being a grandmother. The photoshoot is done at our house with the kids and dogs photobombing. Journalist and friend Craig Bennett has written the article and working on it with him has been fun; it's got us all talking again and at least pretending like we're a family who gets on with each other. 'Fake it till you make it', as the saying goes.

I've known Craig since I was nine, when I was dragged along to his twenty-first birthday party. Expecting to have a dreadfully boring time I was shocked to discover that, like me, Craig loved animals, particularly snakes – he had several pythons roaming free in his bedroom! I spent the day in rapturous delight, popping out into the party with a few of the snakes draped around me from time to time to show Mum, who squealed in terror. Craig loved my enthusiasm and laughed at Mum's reaction along with me – our friendship was sealed.

Thirty-something years later I'm enjoying his company just as much. He invites us to his house perched on stilts in the bush overlooking Pittwater, although now I'm wrangling children over reptiles.

Craig is one of the only people who knows about Mum's illness, his close friend, singer Helen Zerefos, recognised the signs long before anyone twigged something was wrong. Helen knew because she'd cared intimately for her mother who died from Alzheimer's. She knew exactly what lay ahead, while I was still as clueless as the card in the newsagency which read 'Dementia may cause memory loss, or worse, memory loss'.

Craig and his guests love asking about little Tom's acting gigs. A second series of *Rake* is about to commence filming, Peter Duncan's witty sitcom about the playboy barrister Cleaver Greene, who is constantly getting himself into hot water. Everyone wants to know what the leading man Richard Roxburgh is like and I tell them he's just as good looking in real life, and twice as charming!

They laugh at the story of Tom being directed to pretend hit 'the Rox' with a toy monkey in the first series. On his cue Tom had exploded into life, taking a swinging hit with the stuffed monkey like he was batting a baseball out of the pitch, landing hard below the belt! Richard Roxburgh had doubled over with a howl and nobody on the set had known how much was acting. The scene was so hilarious that when the director yelled 'CUT!' the whole studio had erupted with laughter like a cap released from a shaken soft drink, and to my eternal delight, little Tom had taken a high five from the master, Peter Duncan himself.

I love being on the set of *Rake* with Tom, it's more like theatre acting than a film set. Two other terrific actors, Danielle Cormack and Russell Dykstra, play Tom's on-screen parents. Russell has seen the recent publicity I've done with Mum and tells me he adores her.

'How is she, really?' he asks with concern.

When I've seen Mum at Craig's luncheons she's been surrounded by people and conversation, she's sipped champagne and laughed – everything has appeared normal. My parents and the Colins seem happy to keep up this charade but I feel unsettled, like I'm stuck on the deck of the *Titanic* and the music keeps playing. There's no time to linger on these thoughts though, I'm too busy watching the kids at Craig's – Tom will jump straight into the deep end of a pool while Charlotte climbs over the balcony.

Late at night, after the kids are asleep, I sit on the internet looking up places my parents might think of moving to when they need help. It seems like the logical thing to do, like researching future schools for my kids. I ask Dad for Mum's ACAT score, I can't make any real headway without it. There's a towering pile of paperwork on their dining table – what used to be fan mail and invitations is now medical bills and inch-thick forms – but Dad would rather be asked to walk over broken glass than look through that pile. He snaps that he's too busy or hasn't had time but I persevere and, finally, I'm able to answer the first question when they ask me – my mother's Aged Care Assessment Team score is low, I tell them!

Ring back when she has a high score they say.

My parents' unsolvable problems are driving me crazy. I'm thankful to have Tom's jobs to focus on. His filming jobs become a lifeline, a small escape for the two of us where people are productive and life feels normal. I love practising the scripts with him. He gets small parts on *A Place to Call Home* and *Puberty Blues* and I'm a good dramaturge. Once again I feel like I have a shred of professional ability, albeit unpaid!

Call times for filming days only come through the evening before, sometimes we're expected somewhere at 6 am, sometimes not until 6 pm and I've never got any idea how long we'll be needed for. I rely on a battalion of friends to babysit, who insist they're happy to help. One day I'm dropping Charlotte with a tray of muffins before sunrise, on others I'm scooping her in pyjamas from a sofa close to midnight.

One commercial sees Tom and I running to catch a plane to New Zealand less than forty-eight hours after the casting. On another job to be aired in winter he sips hot chocolate beside a fireplace in a heavily air-conditioned room for days on end while I push Charlotte up and down the steep hills of Avalon in pouring summer rain and steaming humidity.

It's true what they say, there really is no business like show business – perfecting such a grand illusion takes a lot of work.

LOVE AND MARRIAGE

After so many years of searching and all the time and money wasted on the idea of renovating Paddington, Tim and I had been so excited to finally realise the dream of owning our own home. The run-down old house had been passed in at auction, a battleaxe property with poky rooms, cobwebs and so much wooden cladding it looked like a scene in *Twin Peaks*.

'Maybe Laura Palmer's buried under the floorboards!' Tim had said. That was before we'd ripped up the hideous salmon-pink tiles. Our modern furniture had looked odd in the mismatched rooms but it didn't matter. After years of living in the concrete jungle we were keen to start renovating to make the place our own, and revelled at having a garden, planting trees and putting in a veggie patch and chook run. The vegetables were so pretty I let them run to seed and the chickens flew up into the trees.

The time had come to put all my energy into making a home for my family. I slid a cake into the tiny oven, marvelling once again how low the bench tops were in the original kitchen, as Tim and the kids gave my parents and the Colins the first 'grand tour'.

When we sat down for afternoon tea Colin Johnston said, 'You're just round the corner from Maria Venuti. She's in Gladesville.' He took a sip of coffee then said, 'You know, we're actually lucky the sat nav in the Jag could find your place, you told us the address is Hunters Hill.'

'It is Hunters Hill,' I said, but Colin Johnston shook his head.

'No, I'm afraid not,' he chuckled, 'It's *Gladesville*.'

Tim spoke next, 'Our postcode is 2110.'

'Maria's address is Gladesville ...'

Tim started explaining, it was a different municipality three streets away, but Mum put a stop to the discussion and interjected, 'It's a fabulous place, isn't it Barry! Isn't it a wonderful place to live!'

Part 3

Nothing was going to dampen my mood that day. 'Cake's ready!' I called out.

My parents rarely visited our new house unless Colin Brees drove them over, and they didn't want us coming to their new apartment that Dad was filling with more antiques and breakable things. One time we took a box of toys for the kids to play with but my father shouted, 'Don't leave that stuff here!'

'Wouldn't it be easier …' Tim had started.

'No! Take it with you, I don't want the place cluttered with *junk!*'

I didn't miss the constant stress of worrying about the kids when we visited their place, and I certainly didn't miss driving home afterwards. I'd loved sleeping in the car when I was little, but my children did not – they screamed blue murder every time. Tim, being a man, liked solutions; if there was a problem he wanted to fix it, but our screaming children would not be fixed. The unrelenting screaming, so unbearably loud in the confined space drills straight into Tim's skull every time, tweaking at a primitive nerve. His foot presses down incrementally on the accelerator, pushing the speed limit. A red light is a disaster. The pain from the screaming is physical, like thumbscrews twisting into bone. Sweat prickles under my armpits. A second in that car feels like an hour.

On the green light the car takes off, it rockets down the dark streets. I press my foot instinctively against the carpet as Tim turns hard into our narrow driveway and shoots down the long, uneven driveway terrifyingly fast, yanks up the hand brake and bursts out of the car, running from it like a man escaping from a building on fire.

When he's calmed down he'll come back out to help me with the kids. 'I'm sorry,' he'll say, 'that noise … I can't bear it.'

I thought Tim and I had a hardy relationship – we'd lived together ten years and managed a business – but nothing prepared us for Tom! Such a tiny baby, he never slept longer than a single sleep cycle, would wake screaming, starving hungry, sucking down milk like he was stemming the flow of a fire hydrant, would spew it all up and start screaming again. Tom was like throwing a hand grenade into our life.

From the beginning, Tim couldn't stand the interrupted sleep and the surprisingly noisy breathing of the baby. He'd moved into the spare bedroom within days of Tom coming home while I skated close to insanity with sleep deprivation. Nearly six years later he's still in the spare room, and I've always been fine with this arrangement because we were flatmates for years before were married, and even after starting a relationship we'd kept our rooms – and our laundry – separate!

Who wanted to sleep next to their lover in bed every night anyhow I'd always reasoned. I liked my personal space and argued not being too familiar with each other's unconscious habits preserved some of the mystery of romance. The trouble was, nothing about raising babies is sexy.

Sleep deprivation and irritability are catastrophic mood killers, leaking boobs and a body like a gym treadmill worn out from years of pounding service, a mind lobotomised by The Wiggles singing 'Fruit Salad' on repeat … what Tim and I needed more than anything was a night off – a date night! But there were never any date nights because my parents never babysat and every cent we had was going into renovating.

I was astounded to realise I had fallen into the trap. I knew fairytales were fiction, I knew the literal meaning of the word mortgage was 'death trap'! Yet still I'd bought into the advertised dream – I'd expected the happily ever after! Tim and I took ourselves to see a counsellor.

'Are you here because you want to break up, or because you want to stay together?' the counsellor asked.

'I don't know,' I'd answered truthfully.

Maybe it's because we were friends first, or maybe it's just because we're both so damn stubborn, we don't give up on our marriage.

Maybe, I think, this is really what being soulmates means and I should wake up to the fact that lessons of the soul aren't painless. Like anything worthwhile, It takes work to make it work.

***

When Dad called to ask if Mum could stay with me for a few days when he went to hospital to get a knee replacement I was thrilled because finally I'd get the chance to spend time with her. The drama and heartache of Paddington being sold, the loneliness and confusion of Charlotte ending up in hospital, I could put all these things behind us. Now, finally, after waiting so long I was being given the opportunity to show my mother the life I'd made for myself.

My husband – my handsome, outspoken, hardworking, dynamic, somewhat eccentric, never-boring husband! My remarkable, spirited, inexhaustible children! And my house, evolving every day into a beautiful, eclectic, sophisticated home, and the garden with its exquisite myriad of flowers and colours!

All the things I love most in the world. I can't wait to share them with the person whose approval means the most to me above all others, the woman who brought me into the world – Mum.

THANKS FOR THE MEMORY

I forgot how many annoying habits my mother has. *How could I have forgotten?!* I thought having her stay would be fun – it's anything but! It was *so lonely* looking after the children all day, the thought of having Mum here, someone to talk to and share the never-ending repetition of inane chores – feeding, bathing, changing, washing, vacuuming, driving, folding, shopping, cooking, cleaning – repeat, repeat, repeat! I thought Mum would be company, that conversation and laughter would brighten the days! But the only conversation we've had since she arrived ten days ago is about the weather and the noise of the planes going overhead. Over and over again Mum comments on 'the awful wind', 'the dreadful cold', and the planes.

'There's *another one!*' she says. 'So low!'

In the beginning I'd laughed, said that was nothing compared to the inner west planes that flew past Kate McDonald's window! But with each repetition I got vaguer until I scared myself by answering so abruptly I sounded like my father. When Mum complained about the cold early one morning I'd barked, 'Of course it's cold – PUT A COAT ON!'

The conversations I was looking forward to never seem to eventuate. Maybe, I start to think, the truth is we never had much in common.

I do things with her that make me happy. I take her to the park with a picnic, down to the garden to work on the vegetable patch – the trees, the flowers and insects, my children's laughter and the boundless, joyful energy of the dogs as they tear across the grass. The vividness of the green leaves, the brightness of the sun glinting off the water in Tarban Creek. So much inspiration blossoming miraculously from the earth. But it's hopeless; Mum hates the outdoors, she always has! She hates fresh air, hates the dirt, flinches at even the idea of an insect and can't be persuaded to sit on the grass. And she won't sit down with the kids at home either unless I give her something specific to do with them.

Dark thoughts start to fester in my head. The excuse for us never spending time together had always been work, and now I've started wondering, I keep returning to the same question – if she never had much time for me as a child why would I expect to have much of a relationship with her as an adult? I feel so confused. I had wanted Mum to stay with me more than anything in the world, to finally have time with her! How could this be going so badly?

'What's that Dahling?' Mum says.

I must have been muttering something aloud. I feel horrible. I'm jumpy and nervous and wracked with guilt.

'Nothing!' I answer quickly. 'I was just saying I didn't get much sleep last night, the kids came into the bed again … I'm just tired!'

'Oh you must be! You never sit down!' Mum says.

She's said this before, she's said this many, many, *many* times already.

'Why don't you go up and have a lie down?' she says.

Having Mum stay was supposed to lighten my load but it's even more work, more exhausting, there's no rest because there's never any down time, Mum never stops. The kids never stop! None of the people in my house ever stop!

At dinner, the accomplishment is sitting down to eat together; coordinating my children and my husband so we can share a meal is like herding cats. Now I have Mum to contend with as well. She bolts her food and jumps up to start on the dishes, usually she's up like a jack-in-the-box before I've even lifted my fork. She prefers to wash everything by hand rather than putting them in the dishwasher and I've let her because it's easier than arguing, and really, what sort of a miserable whingeing git could complain about someone washing up! What is happening to me, I start to wonder, *I'm turning into my father!* And then, taking the plates to the sink one night I see the colour of the water is bright blue.

'Mum, that's Windex!' I say alarmed.

'Isn't it wonderful?' she says. 'It cleans everything!'

'But it's for cleaning *windows* Mum!'

'Oh I use it on everything, I keep it in my handbag.'

'Mum, it's probably *poisonous!* You're not even rinsing it off!'

'I thought your cooking had a funny taste,' she says.

The last thing I want to do is get angry! I know she means well! And seeing Mum upset has always made me feel so utterly, utterly dreadful. The only solution I decide is to keep a closer eye on her, but it's draining living like this, constantly checking nothing bad is going to happen.

I've been thinking over these things while I pull out the last of the straggly tomato plants. I glance over to Tom and Charlotte, who are happy playing in the sandpit. Mum is standing stubbornly beside it, too nervous to sit on the grass where creatures might be lurking. I'd caught a glimpse of myself in the mirror earlier, my hair looked like a bird's nest, my face too pale.

'You know what Mum?' I say suddenly, 'I might actually go and take a lie down, just for half an hour, if you're sure you don't mind watching the kids?'

'Of course Dahling!' Mum says, thrilled to help as always.

I doubt I'll sleep, I can never sleep in the daytime.

I put a pillow over my face to block out the light, the silence in the bedroom is magnificent, the mattress so cool and soft. The fluttering spin and ecstatic relief as my conscious mind detaches, and then – a noise! Nails down a faraway chalkboard – I must have drifted off.

The noise, there it is again! I lift myself wearily and plod to the window. Mum is dragging the clothes rack up the deck again, a load of heavy wet washing piled over it, she pulls awkwardly, like an ox dragging a plough through mud. Deep grooves run the length of the deck. Tim will not be happy. The rack catches on an exposed nail, it lurches as Mum pulls, then finally gives way and collapses.

Down in the garden Tom and Charlotte are shrieking and running stark naked through a rainbow of water. The sprinkler has been turned on full, their wet clothes lie strewn in muddy puddles all around the yard. I chuckle to myself; heaven knows how long the water's been running, I won't have to water for a week! The chickens have gotten loose again and I can see one already over the fence in a neighbour's yard tearing up her lawn. Tom runs to catch another, it squawks and flutters out of his reach then squats down, cornered, ready to be picked up. Tom walks slowly forward, hemming it in with arms outstretched. The bird eyes him warily, this strange child streaked with mud – then the feathered head darts forward and an ear-piercing scream erupts from Tom.

I gasp, 'It's pecked his pecker!'

Tom's scream goes on and on as I race down the stairs, Mum and Charlotte are screaming too. It's pandemonium in the garden, the sprinkler going full bore, the dogs have followed me down and are now running and barking, the chickens flapping and clucking! Finally I reach Tom and hug him to me tightly, both of our hearts racing, threatening to burst out of our chests. I brace myself to look, release the breath I've been holding without even realising, and shout above the ruckus: *'It's okay, you're fine! We're all fine! Everything's okay!'*

I'M ALWAYS CHASING RAINBOWS

I'm having that dream I used to have as a child; the one where I'm in my old bedroom on the top floor of Paddington and the house is falling over. I can feel the vertiginous sway as the room starts to tilt, then the drop as the tower begins to fall, collapsing like a house of cards. I wake with a jolt, my heart hammering.

It's still dark and Tim is beside me in bed. As I catch my breath I become aware of talking. There's no mistaking Mum's voice. I fumble for my glasses to check the time – nearly 4 am. What on earth is going on?

I slide out of bed and creep into the hallway, a bright bar of light shines under the spare bedroom door. My eyes hurt as I enter the room. 'Mum … Mum, what are you doing?' I whisper.

She looks anxious, she's stuttering and apologising to whoever is on the phone, she didn't mean to wake them up.

'Do you know what time it is? It's too early …'

She gives me the phone, she doesn't know how to hang up. How did she even make the call in the first place? When did she get the portable handset from downstairs? Nothing makes sense.

Mum fumbles with her handbag, putting scraps of paper back inside. 'I was just phoning Colin,' she says, and all I can say again is, 'It's too early Mum …' and lead her back to bed.

Hours later, when Tom and Charlotte are at the breakfast table, Tim comes down looking cranky and dishevelled. If anything I'm the one who should look annoyed, I think, after being woken at 4 am! He grabs the cereal and starts dumping some in a bowl.

'I thought you were sleeping in this morning,' I say.

'I was going to!' he barks. 'Your mother came in and woke me up!' He pours milk into his bowl too fast and it splashes onto the counter. 'She started making the bed – *while I was still in it*!'

The kids and I start laughing but Tim doesn't find it funny. 'I was sound asleep! And then I felt someone tugging on the sheets. I thought it was you! And then she pulled the sheets right up over my head! I woke up and said, "What the fuck are you doing?"'

'I hope you didn't say that!' I gasp.

'I didn't swear!' he says, annoyed.

'Daddy said the f-word!' Tom says, lighting up with excitement.

Mum hurries in, 'Oh Tim! Tim! I'm sorry Tim! I didn't mean to wake you!' Mum is clearly embarrassed, she laughs awkwardly, her hand flutters from her throat to her mouth. 'I didn't know you were in the bed! Oh, I got such a fright!'

'Don't worry about it,' Tim grumbles.

* * *

I decide to put Mum in the kids' bedroom so Tim can have his own bedroom again. He's been complaining he can't function properly if he doesn't sleep well, and he needs to be on the ball running the business; he's worried our main employee is talking about taking time off.

'What?' I say alarmed. He's been with our business almost since the outset and he's Tim's right-hand man. 'But he's got a mortgage, and a baby!'

'Don't panic,' Tim says. 'He says he's only thinking about it at this stage. His wife's pressuring him because she wants to go back to work, but he loves his job.'

Just the idea of our main employee leaving is alarming. Our business is still shaken from a large fashion client going bust and Tim had been delaying employing any new staff until it had recovered a bit. We're in a precarious position. Plus it just seems out of character; we've always thought of him as family.

'He's changed since he met his wife,' Tim says finally. 'He's not the same.'

A deep feeling of dread goes through me. 'You don't think he's thinking of starting his own business do you?'

The stress is evident in Tim's face. 'That's what I'm worried about too, I asked him point-blank and he said no.'

'Oh gosh,' I say, suddenly feeling sad, 'I hope he doesn't leave …' It would feel as if a huge chapter of our business was ending.

'I hope he doesn't leave too,' Tim says. 'We're fucked if he does.'

***

Putting Mum into the kids' bedroom turns out to be a good idea. She never retired to her room, she's always up before dawn and never sits down, let alone relaxes!

At least now Tim has somewhere to retreat to. Meanwhile, the rest of the house is only becoming more chaotic. Mum is constantly picking things up and moving them. Piles of random things – kids toys, magazines, a hairbrush, pencil case – are growing like haphazard stalagmites in odd places around the house. It's bizarre how crazy this is making me feel. I go to put my shoes on only to discover one is missing. Nothing seems to be where I've left it or where it should be. The bookshelves too are being transformed as Mum takes books out and piles them back in again at odd angles.

I start putting the kids and Mum to bed earlier to get a break from the madness. By five o'clock I'm already drawing down the shades and their bedroom has the comforting smell of bubble bath and talcum powder. Mum's mattress on the floor looks like a bigger version of the children's cots. Tom and Charlotte clutch their teddy bears, Mum holds her black handbag to her chest. I'd pictured Mum reading bedtime stories to the kids before she came but I realise now how far from the mark that idea was; maybe she can't read anymore.

Charlotte has chosen a story I know by heart. I turn the pages automatically, thinking through the events of the past few days that I haven't had time to process. Tom's teacher had wanted to speak to me about 'a behavioural issue', teacher-speak for saying he'd been very emotional lately. I'd laughed out loud and had to apologise. A physiotherapist had rung from the hospital to give me an update about Dad's recovery, along with the bad reaction to the anaesthetic they'd found blood clots in his lungs and legs, they also suspected diabetes and were worried now that Dad was having trouble swallowing. And I had hardly seen Tim all week. I wondered if it was the problems with the business or if he was trying to avoid coming home. On the weekend something awful had happened. Tim had gone upstairs to take a shower and Mum had walked out of the bathroom completely naked.

Tim had entered the kitchen ashen faced. 'Jesus, I've just seen what you're going to look like in thirty years!' he said.

I'd run upstairs to check Mum was alright. She'd always been so modest, she must have been mortified! Couldn't she find a towel? But rather than being upset Mum laughed. She hadn't been able to find her bedroom, she said. I'd worried about Mum at the time but it seemed to be Tim who was most affected, even though he'd been trying to defuse his embarrassment by making jokes.

'Mum! MUM!' Tom says interrupting my reverie. ' "I'll huff and I'll puff and I'll blow your house down!" The *big bad wolf* says that, silly, not the grandma!'

'Oh! Sorry – what was I saying? Which story are we reading again?'

Tom and Charlotte laugh. They think I'm mixing up the stories on purpose.

I look over to Mum, who has the doona wrapped up around her ears. The person in the bed looks and sounds like my mother, but I don't seem to be able to get truly close to her and I'm continually fighting the same trivial annoyances that have needled at me since adolescence. I feel angry and disappointed in myself more than anything, for never seeming to be able to love her, just the way she is.

DANCING WITH TEARS IN MY EYES

Nobody at the rehabilitation facility seems to know when Dad will move home.

'I can't give you a date,' I say to Tim when he asks me again.

'Well, they must have *some idea*,' he says.

I don't know what to say, so I don't say anything, instead I concentrate on the task I came out to do – hose the dog shit off the driveway before Tim leaves for work. Except there's a tangle in the hose and I'm trying to work out how to unknot it, I don't want to have to unravel the whole damn thing.

'How can nobody know how long he'll be in hospital—'

'Rehab.'

'—Rehab! Hospital! Fucking whatever! How can *nobody know* how long they're keeping him for?'

'What difference does it make?' I ask.

'*What difference?* Are you mad? We've had your mother staying with us for *nearly four weeks* and it's driving us all insane!'

'You got your bedroom back—'

'It's not about the bedroom! I want my house back! I want *my wife back!* The only time we talk to each other is out here on the driveway at 6 am! Can't somebody else take your mother for a while? What about the Colins?'

'I don't know …'

'*Well ask them!* I've got a business to run! We've got two young children! Your mother will have to stay with somebody else—'

'There is nobody else! *I'm it!* I don't have brothers and sisters like you do!'

'Oh I forgot, *the poor only child*. Your family is fucking mental! You're expected to just drop everything for them!'

'I'm not *dropping everything!* I'm just looking after my mother for a few weeks—'

'*You say!* How do you know it's going to be a few weeks? It might be *months!* Who knows what's going to happen to your father. What if they don't let him go home? What then? What if *they both move in!* Well, you'll be looking after your parents *without me*, I'll get an apartment in the city somewhere, I'm not going to live like this!'

I'm suddenly furious. 'I don't understand why you're taking this *out on me!*' I shout.

'Oh *grow up* Katie! Take some responsibility for your life for once!' He slams the car door and reverses maniacally up the driveway.

I take my anger out on the garden hose. I wrench the whole looped mess off the hook and yank at it like mad when suddenly the kink untwists and the hose comes alive, shooting out water, twisting viciously like a snake. The brass nozzle whips down and hits my bare pinky toe, spraying me with a jet of cold water in the process and I don't know what's worse, the freezing shower I've just been given or the surprisingly enormous pain from injuring such a small body part.

Tim has no idea what my life is like, I think. At least he gets to leave and go to work each day. Imagine functioning in an orderly place with no distractions! No constant mess to clean up. No screaming or inane, endless talking. Imagine starting something and finishing it before moving to the next thing!

I'm halfway through looping the hose when I hear Charlotte start wailing inside the house. *Not again! Not already. Not so early!*

Yesterday Mum got upset with Charlotte for tipping out a box of toys. She'd turned and shouted, 'I just picked those up!'

It's not like Mum to get angry; it startled me. I'd run over to take Charlotte away from the toys and she'd exploded into a tantrum – they were her toys and she wouldn't calm down! The tantrum lasted well over an hour and she wouldn't let me out of her sight for the rest of the day, screaming anytime Mum came near her.

Even Tom, who used to love doing jigsaws, has gone off them since Mum took over doing the last one on the dining table.

'These are all the pieces you mustn't touch!' Mum had said to him, and Tom was confused because in this house he was the *king* of jigsaws – he thought it was a joke.

'Touch! Touch! Touch!' he'd said, putting a finger on each piece, and Mum had gone berserk!

'Ooooh no! No! *NO!* What are you doing?' she'd cried. 'That's *naughty!* You're ruining it!' And Tom, who loved Mum to bits, burst into tears and pushed the whole thing onto the floor.

The only friends of my parents I've seen or heard from are Shirley and Terry, who took Mum out for dinner with them last Saturday night. I make a mental note to call them to see if they can go with her for dinner again on the weekend, and I will ask the Colins if Mum can stay with them for a weekend when I see them at Dad's rehabilitation centre.

The front door opens, Charlotte has come out looking for me. She spots me from the front porch and stands there whimpering, too scared to go back inside, scared of Mum. Could things get any worse?

'Wait there Charlotte!' I call out. 'I'm coming now!'

Thank heavens playgroup is on this morning up at the council hall. It's the only place in the world where life feels normal! The noise and cheery chatter. Charlotte rejoices in the mess of toys and children and Mum can talk and laugh with the sleep-deprived mothers who adore her, clustering around her as she stands doing dishes with them in the kitchen. They talk about the same things every week: the weather! the sleep deprivation! the *insanity* of motherhood!

And I can relax knowing everybody is safe and occupied and sneak away for a minute by myself. I can sit in the sun with a cup of hot tea and pretend life is normal, that nothing is wrong with my mother and my marriage isn't falling apart. I can focus on the gentle warmth of the sun on my back, the comfort of the hot liquid warming my insides; I can practise mindfulness or gratitude or whatever the women's magazines call it these days. For a few minutes I'll concentrate on those small pleasurable sensations, a brief distraction from the overwhelming ache in my heart, for a grief that is too big to swallow.

A SPOONFUL OF SUGAR

I'm hanging the freshly washed sheets on the balcony on a windy day when I have a sudden vision of being lifted away like Mary Poppins, a wind filled sheet as my umbrella. If only I could be lifted and taken to a faraway land where things are gentle and kind. A fairy godmother, that's what I need. If only Dor Dor and my aunties were still around, they'd know what to do; but I have no-one to talk to. It feels like I have no-one at all.

I had no idea Mum was so unwell before she came to stay, I just had no idea. The blood clots have cleared from Dad's lungs and legs but he's still struggling to walk. They're talking now about Parkinson's and a heart condition.

I had nothing left to say to anyone. I went through the motions of the day, feeding my children and my mother, cleaning up, stripping the beds and hanging the sheets on the balcony. The wind was comforting. It made me feel like nature was still there for me, like it might pick me up and take me away …

It wasn't until my phone alarm went that I realised the time – I was late to pick up Tom from preschool! I'd called for Charlotte and found her asleep on the couch. Mum was tiptoeing around her, picking up toys from the floor.

With her hair splayed across the lounge and her pink cheeks, Charlotte looks like an angel, so peaceful. She rarely sleeps during the day.

'I put a blanket over her,' Mum whispers. 'Isn't she beautiful …'

Part 3

The preschool is ten minutes away yet I hesitate before asking the question, 'Mum, can I leave Charlotte sleeping while I run out and get Tom?'

Mum lights up, thrilled to be of help and whispers, 'Of course! Take your time! Don't rush!'

***

There are still a couple of rambunctious children in the playground and as I run up the path, a mother I know calls out, 'See you Sunday!' My memory is jolted back to ordinary things like children's parties.

'Oh! James' birthday, yes!'

'Great!' she says. 'It feels like ages since I've seen you!'

It feels like ages since I've seen anyone too; my life has been completely swamped by what's going on with my parents. It feels like the longest month of my life.

Tom is waiting at the door with his teacher. 'I finally saw *Rake*!' she says, 'I went out and bought the DVD. Oh, I laughed and laughed when I saw our Tom belt poor Richard Roxburgh with the monkey!' She laughs and ruffles Tom's hair. 'Cheeky boy!' she says to him.

Tom is full of news on the drive home. There were cupcakes for James' birthday and Oliver got in trouble for throwing sand. He has a new song to sing me too, something about frogs jumping in a pond.

'Are you listening Mum?' he asks.

'Mmmm-hmmm,' I say.

'Listen Mum! You're not *listening*!'

As I turn into the driveway I feel an uneasy sense of dread – the electric gate is open. I would never have left it open. The front door is wide open too. My hands are trembling as I unbuckle Tom's seatbelt. I usually help him out, but not today. I leave the car door open and start running.

'Mum!' Tom calls. 'Wait for me!'

At the top of our driveway is a busy road. I didn't see Mum or Charlotte on the street. They must be in the house, they must be!

I soon discover it's not just the front door that's open, *every door* is wide open. The lounge where I left Charlotte sleeping is empty.

One of the dogs, the faithful one, is still lying in his bed but the other, the wanderer, is missing. Would Mum have taken one of the dogs for a walk? Why would she only take one?

Suddenly breathless, I run onto the back deck and look down into the garden. It's empty.

'*Charlotte! Mum!*' I call out, and running through the house I see the blanket Mum had put over Charlotte lying on the stairs.

I take the stairs two and three at a time. The bedrooms appear empty at first glance but then I see her, just the top of her head, she's on the floor beside my bed, pulling things from the bedside drawer. 'Mumma!' she says, throwing her hands up when she sees me. I hold her tightly, try to steady myself so as not to scare her.

'Did you come up here looking for me?' I ask.

She nods. 'Sweetie, I need you to tell me something really important. Do you know where Ninny is?'

***

The old Mum, the real Mum, would have left a note; she wouldn't have just disappeared. In Paddington there would have been a note in the kitchen with her big, loopy handwriting, 'Kitty Cat, Gone to the shop, back in a minute! Love Mumma xxx'.

Would Mum even know the way to the shops near my house? I doubted it. She couldn't find her bedroom two steps from the bathroom.

How did she find the button to open the automatic gate? Why were all the doors wide open? Maybe she was opening them all trying to find the way out.

'Dad's going to kill me,' I think. 'I've lost Mum …'

I load the kids into the car. She couldn't have gone far. 'Right!' I say to them strapped in the back. 'You two are going to be my special lookouts! This car is actually a pirate ship and we're looking for Ninny!'

A bag of recycled craft bits that I've been intending to take to playgroup is still on the floor of the passenger seat. I pull out two cardboard tubes and hand them to the kids. 'If one of you see her you call out "Ninny ahoy!"'

At least she'll be easy to spot, I think. Today she'd been wandering up and down the hall by 6 am, fully dressed in a bright pink sequined jacket and matching pants. Strangely, I'd wondered how she cleaned these clothes, before reaching for my old jeans that were so tired I was ready to burn them.

My mobile rings through the car bluetooth making me startle. It's the vet calling to say someone has brought in my wandering dog.

'Do you have my mother too?' I ask, and the lady on the phone laughs. If only my mother was microchipped! Can they microchip humans?

My phone rings again, 'Katie, it's Terry here! We're at your house to drop your mother home, we took her out for a quick coffee, but the gate's closed and nobody seems to be home. Your mother doesn't think she has any keys …'

Relief floods through me, tears are welling up in my eyes already. 'Oh Terry!' I say. 'That's wonderful!' I must sound half crazy; I'm overreacting. I must lower my voice and dull down my reaction – I'm sounding like my mother! 'I'll be there in a minute,' I say, 'sorry to keep you waiting!'

I wipe the tears away hurriedly, breathe and blink to get myself under control. My mother isn't a child! She can go for coffee with her friends! But leaving Charlotte like that … It's my fault, I think, I shouldn't have left her!

'Ninny ahoy!' Tom calls out, and there she is, smiling and waving to us in her bright pink jacket as we near the house.

'Oh gee it's nice to see you all!' she says. 'What a lovely surprise!'

AFTER YOU'VE GONE

After Shirley and Terry left I put the TV on for the kids and escaped to the garden. Usually I took them down with me, but not now. I needed space and air; I felt like I couldn't get enough oxygen into my lungs. That wind was still blowing and when I looked up at the house with the sheets hung on the balcony it looked like a ship about to set sail.

I'd taken a packet of silverbeet seeds with me but the seeds stayed in my pocket, I just knelt on the ground and put my hands in the dirt, desperate just to hang on to something solid.

Mum had followed me down and she lingered on the bottom step. She'd always hated the outdoors and just seeing her there looking helpless irritated the hell out of me. And then she made some small remark about Tim, how my husband wasn't home much, it sounded like something my father would say, and it was like putting a match to an oily rag. I exploded.

'HOW DARE YOU INSULT MY HUSBAND!' I screamed.

It was like uncorking a bottle, every vile thing came pouring out of me – the money we'd lost on the plans to renovate Paddington, the anger of them never visiting Charlotte in hospital and the blame for her getting sick in the first place. Everything I'd pretended not to care about.

'YOU NEVER WANTED US TO LIVE WITH YOU!' I screamed at her. 'IT

WAS ALL A LIE!'

'Of course, of course I did,' Mum stammered.

'Then why didn't you STAND UP TO HIM! Why didn't you want us to be A PART OF YOUR LIVES!'

Mum couldn't answer, she just kept stuttering. C3PO had short circuited, and so had I; I had become a deranged, screaming lunatic. Nothing could stop me. 'PACK YOUR BAG!' I screamed. 'Get out of my house! Get out! GET OUT! GET OUT OF MY HOUSE!'

I had put her suitcase in the boot of the car, thrilled to be finally putting an end to this nightmare – but there was nowhere to take her. I'd phoned the Colins, but like every other time I'd tried, I only got their answer machine.

The voice I spoke in sounded high-pitched and unnaturally formal; I was a hostage reading a ransom note. Could Mum stay with them for a few days? We were meeting for a family conference the following day at the rehabilitation centre. Mum could go home with them.

I took Mum's bag out of the car and returned it upstairs, went to the fridge and skulled one of Tim's beers, then opened a second one.

***

The last time I'd visited Dad at the rehabilitation centre he'd been sitting up in a chair beside the bed. He'd smiled as we walked in, so evidently pleased to see us. He was wearing a grey T-shirt that was too big.

'You're shrinking,' I'd said to him.

The surgical stockings had gone and Charlotte had been awed at the enormous pink scar down his knee. He'd pulled out some chocolates to share while Mum sat on the bed and held his hand.

The Colins turned up and we talked about Dad's progress using a walking frame; he'd fallen over again using a walking stick. The Colins were talking about putting a chair lift into the apartment, where half a dozen steps separated the entrance hallway and the lounge and they'd been collecting pamphlets about home help and food delivery. I'd been telling Dad I could shop for him on the internet, but he'd have to shop more practically.

'He shops like a French housewife,' I said, 'only buying groceries for one meal at a time!'

Dad was stubbornly refusing every suggestion but Colin Brees was insistent. 'Well

I know you don't *want to* Barry, but you're going to *have to*, isn't that right Jean?'

On the drive home Mum had been strangely quiet. Charlotte had fallen asleep and I was enjoying the time to think without interruption. It surprised me when Mum suddenly let out a sob.

'I don't think Barry needs me anymore,' she said.

'What?' It was such a strange thing to say, it sounded so archaic.

'What are you talking about?' I'd said, 'Of course he needs you …'

It must have been all that talk about getting extra help at home; Mum looked so sad and confused.

'Of course Dad needs you!' I'd said again.

I'd put my arm around her but the light changed. The driver behind me beeped and I had to drive, keeping one hand on her back with the other on the wheel.

I already had a suspicion of what the family conference would be about. Dad was refusing all suggestions to make any kind of change to his life – he wouldn't entertain the idea of wearing a personal alarm around his neck and he didn't want to drink thickened fluids. He was taking up a bed in a rehabilitation centre and making little or no improvement. A battalion of professionals headed to the conference room holding folders and clipboards.

'Aren't you coming to the meeting?' I asked Colin Brees. I'd just assumed he would.

'No,' he said, 'It's not my place. I'll stay here with your mother instead.' He smiled at Charlotte; maybe I could leave the stroller with him too. But Charlotte didn't want me to leave her. She'd become so clingy since Mum was staying and I couldn't even go to the loo by myself anymore.

The seats around the conference table filled up and my father was the last to be brought in, sitting in a wheelchair, wearing a tight smile. One by one the staff gave accounts of Dad's problems, the difficulties with balance and coordination, with swallowing, blood pressure and bladder, on and on it went. The idea of moving back to their apartment looked ever more remote, and that wasn't even factoring in the seriousness of what was going on with Mum.

Yet with every prognosis Dad only became more stubborn and determined; he would return to the apartment with Mum and he would walk again, they would manage. The awkward pauses grew longer as each staff member failed to dent his determination. Finally they turned to me.

I was still reeling from loosing my temper at Mum the day before. Strangely, I noticed my hands were trembling as I opened a packet of Tiny Teddies for Charlotte. She'd been pretty good throughout the meeting but was now starting to get restless, echoing the sentiment of the room. I'd had time to think throughout the night and after all the horrible, horrible things I'd said I was cautious each time I opened my mouth.

'Dad … If I were you, I'd just pack a bag. One for you and one for Mum, you could move into a place with assisted care. I know how much help Mum needs, or you can move in with us …'

Dad laughed. 'We couldn't live *there!*' he said, 'What about our things?'

'We could move somewhere larger, more suitable, somewhere we'd all be happy—'

Dad cut me off, 'Don't be *preposterous!*'

I felt like I'd been slapped in front of this roomful of strangers. I'd offered the most precious thing I had to my father – my home and my life – and been rejected.

There was an awkward silence before one of the physiotherapists spoke. 'Well, it's nice to be asked,' she said.

My face was still burning red as I followed Dad in the wheelchair back to his room. I couldn't wait to get away. I felt so embarrassed but I wasn't going to cry in front of my father. My mother would stay with the Colins for the weekend and I'd have time to sort things out with Tim.

Colin Brees was waiting with Mum in Dad's room. I was scared to even talk in case I fell apart; I couldn't fall apart until I was alone.

'I've got Mum's suitcase in the car,' I said, but Colin shook his head.

'Colin Johnston's nephew is coming from New Zealand, it would be awkward having your mother stay with us too,' he said.

Tim rang as I was walking back to the car and I gave him the news.

'They live in a *six bedroom house* with a separate granny flat!' he shouted, '*What's awkward about that?*'

RUN RABBIT RUN

Becoming a War Pup in the latest *Mad Max* movie had been like taking part in a secret ritual. Tom and another hundred or so boys were herded like sheep through a sheering station, transformed and stripped of their individuality one by one. Huge army-style tents had been set up to accommodate them with rows of hairdressing chairs lined up before mirrors framed with light bulbs, the buzz of clippers continued like a drone of rapacious insects.

The boys' eyes widened as the hair fell in clumps to the ground, their mothers laughed nervously and reached out to touch their exposed babies' scalps, surprised at the jagged roughness, like sharkskin.

Tom had been asked to perform in a scene with Hugh Keays-Byrne and we were both in awe of the scale of this enormous George Miller production. The incredible wardrobe department! The mind-boggling sets! Neither of us had really given much thought to the requirement to shave his head. It's only after it's shaved I realise I didn't think they were going to take all his hair!

The next day was Saturday and I was running to get the kids to their swimming lessons on time. Cars had stopped to let us cross to the entrance of the aquatic centre, the receptionist had opened the gate before I'd even taken out our card – it was like we had some kind of magic power. A father stepped back to allow me into the coffee queue and the barista had given the kids marshmallows. Everyone was being so nice. Finally, it dawned on me – they thought Tom had cancer!

Before my parents sold Paddington Mum had fallen down the stairs. She'd gone from the top of the first flight, lost her footing on that tricky corner, the same spot I'd fallen as a four-year-old but insisted she was fine and our plans to meet later at

Balmoral had gone ahead. I hadn't known about the fall; I wasn't told until later.

It had been a cold, blustery day. Tom had run along the sand while we followed on the boardwalk with the stroller. Tim had gone to buy fish and chips with the Colins and Mum, stylish as always in an oversized black Issey Miyake jacket, her cheeks red from the wind, had put her arm through mine as we walked and found a seat to watch the kids on the sand. Seagulls had rushed at Mum's feet, all orange beaks and arched white wings, cawing loudly.

'Back! Get back!' she shouted but they kept coming. Colin was throwing chips near her feet.

'Oh is that you doing that Colin!' Mum said in an accusatory tone, but she could never stay angry and laughed along with the rest of us. It had been funny until Mum had said she needed to use the ladies; but suddenly it was too late. It was strange more than anything. Colin Johnston took over with his calm, reassuring manner. There was a towel to sit on in the car he said, she'd be home and washed in no time. It was only then they told me about the fall, and later that night the phone rang. They'd taken Mum to hospital Dad said.

When I arrived it was near midnight, Mum was sleeping. In a hospital gown with no make-up she looked much older. I smoothed the hair back from her forehead the way she'd done for me as a child and whispered I was with her. I'd brought a book with me but couldn't read. It was strange to be awake at this hour, away from my husband and children.

A young guy, off his chops, was brought in and they left him to sit on a chair while the drugs wore off. He was terrified, nearly out of his mind, and nobody would go near him. Finally, I took a chair over to sit with him. I couldn't do anything for Mum.

'Just breathe,' I said. I smiled and tried to hold his gaze while his eyes darted maniacally. I tried to help him focus, 'Sometimes breathing's all you can do.'

Hours went by until finally Mum was wheeled down into the labyrinth of the hospital for a brain scan. She woke with a fright as she was being wheeled into mouth of the huge machine.

'Keep still!' the attendant shouted. 'KEEP STILL!'

He called for another worker to restrain her and I was surprised at how rough they were. Just another geriatric who'd had a fall; deaf probably and demented. When the scan came up showing a large haemorrhage at the back of her brain everything changed. The workers were suddenly sympathetic and concerned. After hours left lying in a bed in emergency, an oxygen mask was suddenly put over her face and they rushed her to intensive care. It was strange how differently people treated you I thought, depending on what they saw.

***

From the outside our lives looked normal. Mum looked healthy and when Dad was finally allowed to go home, nearly two months after his operation that was supposed to take two days to recover from, Mum went with him.

She went downhill rapidly in the dark apartment. She couldn't get in or out of the security block so she walked around and around the dining table. On one occasion she'd gotten locked in the garbage disposal room for hours before another resident found her. Mum could no longer use the toaster or the kettle and lost the ability to use her beloved sewing machine.

I hadn't found out any of these things through my father or the Colins though. Dad still didn't want to admit anything was wrong with Mum, and he'd never admit he was wrong to move into the apartment.

There were a couple of incidents with Dad too – a phone call in the middle of the night and a groggy voice telling me he'd fallen in the kitchen. It looked like a murder scene when Colin Johnston and I arrived. We helped him up into a chair and I looked for a mop and bleach to clean up the mess. It was a simple accident he said, he'd been heating something in the oven and turned around too quickly. The food in the oven had been reduced to a lump of charcoal. There was a bump on his head the size of an egg that Colin Johnston patched up, but he refused to be taken to hospital and leave Mum, who slept through the whole thing.

The charade of pretending things were fine went on. Interactions with my parents were kept to civil platitudes and I was surprised when they made the effort to come to the preschool Christmas concert. I'd dutifully mailed Tom's invitation to them, still damp with glitter. They were given a royal welcome as Dad pushed through with his walking frame, Mum at his side, but I found, strangely, I couldn't look them in the eye.

I invited my parents and the Colins and our friend Maria Venuti to dinner at my house. I made two courses and had gelato in the freezer for dessert. Charlotte and I set the table with fresh flowers and cloth napkins. The kids were so excited to see everyone when they arrived. Maria was a welcome addition to our dysfunctional family. She'd become like an aunt to Charlotte since we'd moved so close to her, dropping around for afternoon tea, bringing cupcakes and little presents with her. Maria livened up the atmosphere, propping up the theatricality, which was sadly lagging at our family dinners these days.

The kids ate early and went off to the lounge to watch a movie and now it was the adults' dinner and the familiar script started to play out – the discussion about Colin Johnston's pharmacy and Colin Brees' latest renovation, Dad's lamentation about something that wasn't quite to his liking in their new Double Bay apartment, but his first-world complaints were half hearted these days.

Mum sat at one end of the long dining table, Tim at the other. I listened to the conversation and watched Mum eating salad with her hands; she must no longer know how to use a fork. I wished I'd thought to sit beside her so I could help. Why did I always think of these things too late?

I cleared my throat and held my hands in my lap to keep them from shaking. The last time I'd spoken up was at the family conference, but I had to try again.

'I'd like to say something ...' I said.

I took a breath and forced myself to look at the faces of the people around the table. Maria patted my hand reassuringly. 'What is it Darling? What do you want to say?'

'I think ... I think we need to talk,' I said, 'about Mum going to live somewhere she can be properly cared for.' It took all my courage to look my father in the eye. 'I know how bad things are Dad ... she's eating dinner with her hands.'

I caught a glimmer that could have been the start of resignation in my father, but there was no time to pursue it. Colin Brees put down his wine glass and narrowed his eyes. I felt the blood in my veins turn to ice.

'You!' he said vehemently. 'How dare you! You should be over there helping your parents!'

The dining room erupted. Tim shouted to defend me, Colin Johnston turned on Tim, and Colin Brees started an unceasing tirade about the many ways I'd failed my parents. The dogs were barking, my mother was stuttering and my father kept saying, 'Now hang on ... now hang on ...'

'It's time you left!' Tim shouted at Colin Brees.

They stood up, it looked like Tim might hit him, but Colin Brees wouldn't stop – the venomous words continued unabated, he spat them out at us, everything he detested about our 'millennial lifestyles'.

I started screaming to block out the words. I stood up too fast, the chair fell over backwards, I ran into the lounge to get away from them. I couldn't breathe, I couldn't breathe, I couldn't breathe! It was like that scene in *Raiders Of The Lost Ark* with the snakes slithering through the walls of the temple, and I was being sealed in with them!

I'LL BE HERE TOMORROW

Dad phoned the next day but I didn't answer. The noise of the phone ringing made me jump, and I recoiled when I saw it was my parents' number. He left a message, 'I'm just ringing to make sure you're okay. Call me.'

But I didn't call; there was nothing left to say.

By Christmas our main employee had not only left our business but taken our two biggest clients with him. I couldn't believe another person I'd trusted and loved had betrayed us. The walls had come down alright; we'd been infested with snakes. We downsized and cut back on every expense but it wasn't enough. We moved the essential equipment home and it was like when we were starting out ten years earlier, just Tim and I designing again at a shared desk, but now we had Charlotte with her colouring pencils who we could no longer afford to keep sending to preschool, and a shitload more overheads.

Christmas Day was a couple of packets of chips and a six-pack of beer on the beach. Drained from the past year, thankful just to have survived, we sat back and watched Tom and Charlotte jumping waves. About midday, when I knew my parents would be at the Colins', I rang and left a message on their machine. It was the first Christmas I hadn't spent with them.

One of the first things to go had been Tim's car. After it was towed I told him maybe letting go of all this stuff would make room for new things to come into our lives, and now, as Tim and I sat on the beach he kept commenting on the sky.

'You're starting to sound like my mother,' I said, 'always talking about the bloody weather!'

'It's the clouds!' he said. 'I've never noticed how amazing the sky is!'

It was the start of a new obsession that would see him travel to the far reaches of the globe and win numerous international awards for his spectacular landscape photography.

For Tim's milestone birthday I threw him a big dinner party, after what we'd been through I was determined to seize every opportunity to celebrate. I sent out formal invitations to an evening at 'Poulty Towers' (a humorous play on Tim's last name, Poulton), photoshopped my face on Sybil Fawlty and Tim's on Basil Fawlty. I cobbled together tables along the balcony and dressed them up with borrowed tablecloths and my finest op-shop crockery. I made three courses and told everyone to bring a bottle of champagne. It was a riot of a night!

Craig Bennett followed me to the kitchen, his arms laden with plates. He grabbed a tea towel as I quickly washed up a few plates to reuse for dessert. He was deeply upset about what was going on with my parents.

'It's just so dreadful!' he said, his words slurring sadly. 'When I think of your beautiful mother locked up in that ridiculous apartment, walking in circles around and around the dining table, it's too awful for words!'

Craig took another gulp from his wine glass. 'Oh Katie …' He rested his head mournfully on my shoulder for a minute before reviving with anger, 'I don't blame you cutting off Colin Brees, to think he cheated on your father too –'

Suddenly he clamped his hand over his mouth, his eyes were wide.

'Oh good gracious!' he said. 'You did know?' He looked panicked.

'Of course!' I lied and reached for my wine glass.

***

Learning my father had been in a relationship with Colin Brees before he married Mum was a shock that took a few days to process. I rang my old friend Kate McDonald to talk it through.

She got straight to the point, 'Surely you're not upset your father was bisexual?'

As always, I appreciated her directness. I could answer truthfully and I was relieved – no that wasn't it. So what had upset me? I guess I wondered why they had never told me.

'Maybe it was just none of your business,' Kate said.

I wished I could talk about it with Mum – so I did the next best thing, I looked up Toot Hairdressing. Although it had been probably twenty years since I'd seen him, Mum's hairdresser Bruce Macdonald had hardly changed, he was still tall and charming with a sonorous voice and kind eyes that welled with sadness when he asked after Mum.

'Of all the people …' he said.

We had coffee on the verge of a busy Double Bay cafe, the conversation peppered with laughter as he recounted stories from his salon's heyday. Finally I brought up the subject I wanted to discuss.

'Ahhh,' he said, 'so you've finally heard.'

Bruce told me he'd known my father and Colin Brees long before he met my mother and they'd lived together until my father came home to find Colin with another man.

'That was it. Your father didn't stand for that. It was over. Then I heard your father was dating a woman,' he laughed. 'I thought – well this will never last! Another gay man trying to convince himself he was straight!'

He took a sip of coffee and said, 'But then, I met your mother!'

The story goes that my father had met Mum at a party – she'd worn feathers and little else, topless apart from pasties attached to her nipples. 'Your father couldn't take his eyes off her. They were inseparable after that!' Bruce laughed.

Talking with Bruce I could now hear the echo of my mother's voice, I remembered her joking on a few occasions, 'If it wasn't for me Dahling, Barry would be gay!'

'Shush Jean!' Dad always said.

My father's relationship with Colin Brees was probably never meant to be a secret from me at all, it was just a page of history that Mum had never felt the need to clarify.

I had to take into account too that although my mother and I would never have blinked an eye, Australian law told a different story – homosexuality had still been illegal in New South Wales until 1984 – shockingly, ten years after I was born! The first Gay and Lesbian Mardi Gras Parade, which had blossomed in 1978 in Paddington's neighbouring suburb of Darlinghurst, had been more than just a parade, it had been a flamboyant protest march where police had arrested fifty-three people.

I understood my father's reasons for keeping things hush-hush, but I still felt a mix of emotions. Growing up, we had been such a close little family, the Colins, my parents and me, now I looked back and had to rethink the way I saw our relationships.

My father, mother and Colin Brees had all worked out of the house in Paddington, Colin by my father's side in the basement office, my mother in her sewing room up the top. And although my father's affair with Colin Brees was long under the bridge I still found it remarkable my mother had been completely fine with this arrangement. I don't think many women would have lived with their husband's ex in the basement.

Again I thought how interesting my mother was as a person – so traditional and conservative in many of her views, particularly about marriage! Yet so pragmatic and open-minded in the way she saw the world. She had been the glue that had held us all together and when she got sick our family fell apart.

***

A few months later Dad left a message on my phone, Mum was going into care. I tossed and turned worrying about her the night she went in – would she be scared and confused in a strange place? Would she be even more lost now without my father? Would she think she'd been abandoned? I wondered how much more of her was gone since I saw her last at that final disastrous dinner.

I looked up the address and drove over early with the kids, hoping to avoid seeing my father and the Colins. A lady at the desk issued me with a card that said 'Visitor' and showed me through a labyrinth of doors. The institutional smell of stewed vegetables reminded me of the years I visited my grandmother Dor Dor in her nursing home – was my mother really in here somewhere?

Surprisingly, when I found her, she was fine. Tom ran to hug her. I asked her how she was settling in but it was a cheery nurse that answered, 'Good Jeannie, aren't you? She's doing fine!' Mum's blonde hair was growing out, her roots were dark brown now like mine. Her hand when I took it still had the same long fingers, the same cool, papery skin, the same scar that Mum used to joke was a stroke of biro.

Mum looked at me blankly when I visited. I felt like I'd been erased and I thought I deserved it; I'd finally got my comeuppance. Charlotte was still scared of Mum and all elderly people and she held close to me when we visited, but Tom always got a smile. She continued to recognise him long after she forgot me. The kids and I often sang to her, music reached her when nothing else could.

Usually I had the kids with me and there were always people around, but one time when I'd been out to dinner with friends I dropped in before going home. I found her in bed, just quietly lying there staring up at the ceiling, tucked in like a child.

I leaned in and whispered, 'I'm sorry Mum. I'm so sorry. Please, forgive me.'

Tears flowed silently down my face. I wished Mum could tell me not to cry, that everything was going to be alright.

Mum had always forgiven all the horrible things I'd done as a child; as an adult she'd only told me how clever I was, how beautiful, or creative. She'd always had such a gift for looking beyond people's limitations to only see their best qualities and what they were capable of achieving. Maybe that was the reason Dad used to say sometimes that Mum was a saint.

Life without Mum went on; my children demanded it. But frequently, particularly when I was without them or my husband was away, I felt completely lost and would start crying. Running to the market to quickly grab a missing ingredient for dinner I'd become unstuck, overwhelmed in front of a shelf of products with too many choices. Lost with no idea of how to find my way back.

LIFE IS JUST A BOWL OF CHERRIES

Dad had declined all requests to be interviewed, but when Craig Bennett asked me if I would speak to *New Idea* I said yes, and then Laura Sparks came round with a film crew from *Today Tonight*. The interviews were easy but the still photos were hard because Mum wasn't there. She'd always been so ridiculously embarrassing, standing behind the camera, waving her arms around like a loony trying to get me to smile, singing out 'Ta-daaa! Ta-daaaa!'

When the story breaks the effect is immediate – suddenly everywhere I go people tell me they have experience with dementia too. They tell me about losing their mother, their father, a sister, a friend and I can see in their eyes how raw their grief is. It's scarred them too. It seems like everyone has been affected by this devastating disease. I wonder why, when it's obviously so prevalent, people aren't talking about it more often.

Maybe, I think, it's because it's so terrifying – you can't amputate or transplant or blast it with chemo – your brain is you. It doesn't matter if your body goes on, without your brain at the helm you might as well be dead. I knew Mum thought the same way, I remembered a conversation from childhood, which stood out in my mind like it was yesterday.

My parents had returned from seeing a friend in hospital who'd been in a motorbike accident. Mum had called him 'a vegetable' before saying, 'If that ever happens to me Bar, put a pillow over my face.'

Dad was horrified, and even though they were alone talking behind closed doors he said, 'Shhhhh! Jean! You can't say things like that!'

'Why not?' Mum said, ever practical and unafraid of speaking the truth. 'I'm serious!'

And now, as Elon Musk blasted a car into space and we had phone conversations beamed via satellites orbiting the earth, people still continued to talk about dementia in whispers. Maybe it was because the brain was still so much a mystery and a miracle – and where there were miracles, spirits and demons lurked. Previous generations had always been terrified of dementia, and rightly so I supposed; only something of pure evil could kidnap your loved one from under your nose, leaving their eyes vacant and staring.

The survivors I meet reach out to me, they squeeze my shoulder or put a firm hand on my forearm, they look me in the eye and say 'I know what you're going through. It's *hard*.' And each one of these people reaching out, sharing their own stories with me – their grief, their guilt, their regret – reels me in.

* * *

Craig Bennett invites me to a party at his house. So many people I recognise from long-gone TV days are there: Miss Helena from *Romper Room*, actors and entertainers. A taxi pulls up with retired news presenter Brian Henderson. 'Brian told me so!' the taxi driver calls out as he drives off. But the most lovely surprise is seeing Marcia Hines. She looks younger than she did thirty years ago when we shared the flat for *Jerry's Girls*. That Royal Jelly sure was amazing!

'Tell me, how's your mother?' Marcia asks in her thick, velvet voice.

'She's okay,' I say. 'She just sleeps a lot of the time now.'

That was almost true. The truth was, most of the time when I saw Mum she was just lying there with her eyes open. 'Are you in there Mum?' I'd whisper, 'Mum?' Sometimes she talked gibberish back to me. It was easier telling people she mostly slept.

'Your mother loved you, you know,' Marcia said.

Really? I couldn't remember back that far, before the mess.

But Marcia knew; she knew because she had a daughter too, and love was always there between mothers and children, strong like a silver umbilical cord that stretched across any distance or obstacle. Marcia was right! Mum *did* love me, how could I have forgotten? What a blessing to be reminded of that love. And god my heart ached – how I missed it!

***

'Gee Ninny's got a lot of slaves,' Charlotte said one time as we left the nursing home.

I snorted, 'Yes, but they call them nurses La La.'

What a relief to laugh! I suddenly saw Mum's situation differently – 'slaves' waiting on her hand and foot, washing and feeding her!

Mum had always been so giving, now it was her turn to be cared for. But rather than slaves they were angels. The staff who spent their lives taking care of people's loved ones were angels who should be on a politician's salary.

***

Without Mum, Dad was lost. He landed in hospital numerous times. I took him to look at places he might think of moving to, places where he might have a chance of living. I knew he wanted to die without Mum, but he didn't.

Our relationship was still difficult but at least I was old enough to know now he was not an easy person. I didn't have to blame myself anymore. He was ridiculously stubborn and grouchy and self-centred, it felt like the only thanks or compliments he gave were backhanded. Still, he was my father.

I took him for coffee in Woollahra, where the cafe owner asked after Mum. We looked in the window of Lesley McKay's bookshop, the last familiar remnants of our old neighbourhood. Out the front of the bustling cafe I sat with him, watching the busy people go about their days.

'Dad,' I said, 'I've got some news … I'm pregnant.'

I'd booked a termination when I found out. Charlotte had just started school, I'd long ago gotten rid of all the baby things and was feeling like I was getting my life back on track. Tim and I had been working at building our printing business back up again and were starting to see results. But as the day of the appointment drew near I'd started waking up in a panic. The loss of Mum was so enormous, and it was my children who got me through, meeting their needs day after day, whether I wanted to or not. The rawness of their emotions had taught me not to be afraid of my own. I couldn't go through with it.

Part 3

When Charlotte was born, before we knew Mum was sick, before Paddington was sold, when my parents were still consumed with working on stage plays and scripts, instead of congratulating me Dad had said, 'Now Katie, no more babies for a while.' I'd told Kate McDonald, who'd nearly died laughing. It was so funny we'd started ending each phone conversation by telling each other, 'No more babies for a while!'

Dad sipped his coffee. There was a long silence and I started to think maybe he hadn't heard me, then finally he said, 'Your mother had a termination once, before you were born. It was silly really ... You weren't supposed to have a baby back then until you were married. Then we had you and she couldn't fall pregnant again. She always wanted another baby.'

How different my life would have been with a sibling – someone to share the top floor of Paddington with, someone to take the heat when I didn't fit the mould, someone to share the loss of losing Mum.

* * *

At long last Dad took my advice and moved into an assisted care residence. I knew he'd been depressed, but the state of his unit still shocked me when I started clearing it out. The pantry was filled with moths, the refrigerator with moulding half-eaten food. The plants on the balcony were long dead, and there were no sheets on the bed, no cover on the doona. The mattress and carpets were stained.

Six months of my life was swallowed up emptying the place out. Besides the unit there was a double garage full of boxes that hadn't been opened since the move from Paddington, filthy and full of cockroach droppings.

'If it were me I'd take it all to the dump!' Tim said, but I couldn't do that – somewhere in those boxes were two silver Logies, a gold, and an Order Of Australia medal.

I got stuck into clearing the place out, sorting things to keep and things to auction. At times it was overwhelming. Dad's cleaner had knocked on the door and told me he'd had his eye on the large elephant god statue my parents had carried back from India.

'Ganesh is the remover of obstacles!' I shouted before slamming the door shut, 'And I've got *a lot of obstacles!*'

The monkey coat and Dad's antiques were taken to auction, barely making the money back from moving it all. The screens he'd always been so damned protective of, the antique bowls and that bloody white china vase he'd always been terrified I would break – none of it was worth the newspaper it was wrapped in. The French velvet couches that Dad hadn't allowed the kids to sit on went to the woman who clipped my dogs – they made terrific beds for her Great Danes, she said.

I contacted the national museums to offer them the pick of Mum's wardrobe – two hundred or more outfits I'd laid out in the garage. The National Film and Sound Archive took one, a man with red-framed glasses from the Sydney Powerhouse Museum looked through a pile of scrapbooks and said, 'Oh, was your mother on television?' Fame had taken my mother away from me for most of my life yet within months of her being out of the public eye she was already forgotten.

Clearing out my parents' belongings was endless. I'd make good, solid progress only to stumble on something that would dissolve me to tears again. A little china blackbird Mum had put in her homemade chicken pies when I was little, the steam would rise from its beak as Mum sang 'Sing a Song of Sixpence'. The earrings and dress from her wedding day. Her false eyelashes, still stuck with eyelash glue. Her handbag, inside, a freshly ironed handkerchief – she always carried a hankie! – and little notes with names on them, some of my parents' closest friends. I realised at moments like these how much trouble Mum had been having alone before any of us even knew what was happening, how confusing that must have been, I thought. It broke my heart.

Friends and neighbours came to my aid, dropping round bags of hand-me-down baby clothes, boxes of toys and home-cooked meals. A friend whose mother owned a dress shop in Chatswood sent over a bootload of clothes for me. Their generosity filled me with hope.

My friend Sally came round to the unit. 'My god,' she said looking at the mess. 'This is enormous! This is too much for one person!'

I laughed. She hadn't seen the double garage yet, and I'd just found out from the caretaker that there was another storage cage filled with yet more things! She rolled her sleeves up and helped me through the final push to clear out the unit.

The gold Logie was finally recovered in the bottom of a box I'd thought was empty apart from newspaper. The Order of Australia was amongst phone directories over ten years old – my parents hadn't thrown out anything in forty years and the removalist company had even moved the rubbish! The silver Logies never turned up.

Several mini-skips were taken away. It took three removalists, after the first two quit. I kept more things than I should have and without knowing what else to do with them, I brought my mother's wardrobe of clothes home.

'What is all this stuff?' Tim kept asking.

Finally, the unit was empty, the carpet and walls marked with the faint outlines of Dad's furniture and antiques. The balcony doors were open and a cold breeze stirred a few pieces of newspaper left on the carpet. One final enormous pile of garbage bags were heaped in a corner waiting to be picked up, there was only one thing left to move.

On the floor of the kitchen was an old stained rug, I rolled it up and under the corner I found a note. Mum's loopy handwriting, across the top the date, Thursday 29 January 2009.

'Strangely my daughter and my husband are taking me to a doctor who asks me to copy some shapes … He takes my shoes off and my feet are tapped a few times. I wonder whatever for. I used to be able to walk along the street but I don't get the chance. The old gentleman taps my feet and asks me what the date is. I was still wondering what is it all about? Then I was told that pills will give me a means of perhaps "how I used to be" but sadly my whole life is ruined, it's kind of like being in jail. Barry is very generous. Even Katie my daughter doesn't tell me what's it all about. My friend Colin asks me "Why don't they let you out?" and smiles.'

SING A SONG OF SIXPENCE

Tim's away on another photography tour. He's somewhere hideously exotic this time – Patagonia or Norway, I've lost track. I've been on set with Tom the past couple of days and I've laughed as I've told friends Tom's selling cars. In the ad he sings Cole Porter along with a banjo. How proud Mum would be, I think, hearing his strong, clear voice filling the cavernous studio!

I've underquoted on a sticker-printing job just to pull in a new client. I'm on my hands and knees on the hard tile floor running scissors through thick sheets of vinyl, questioning again why I've taken this job on. I need a new career. Clients are getting the bigger jobs printed in China, they're using designers sourced through the internet for two dollars an hour. As Scarlett O'Hara would say, I'll think about it tomorrow!

I have to leave to pick the kids up soon and when I get them home I'll go back to working on the outfit I'm wearing on *The Morning Show* next week. I'm going to dress up as a sandwich to get my point across: 'I'm one of the "sandwich generation!"' I'll say, 'Stuck between looking after young children and ageing parents!' I'll make a headband with a giant pickle and cocktail onion stuck on my head – I'm sick of being asked on TV only to talk about depressing things. I want to make people laugh, like Mum!

My mobile rings, awkwardly I wedge it between my ear and shoulder and keep cutting. It's Dad. I'm hoping he's not ringing to tell me he needs me to cut his fingernails again, or worse, that he's had an accident and needs me to come over and clean him up.

I've been bribing little Hunter with Smarties to get him out of nappies right when my father, if he wasn't so stubborn should be going into them! Just like Hunter, Dad calls me when he's had an accident.

But it's neither of these things, it's worse. Much worse.

'Guess how much our old house in Paddington just sold for?' he says sounding rather smug. The house he sold only a few years previously has changed hands again.

'How much?' I ask.

'Just short of ten million,' he says.

'Are you joking?' I say. 'You sold that house for a fraction of what it was worth. You sold the only thing that was worth keeping and left me with nothing.'

In 2018, ten years after diagnosis, my mother Jeanne Little is still alive. She is one of an estimated almost 50 million people worldwide 'living with dementia'. It is now the leading cause of death among Australian females.[1]
There is currently no cure.

If you are concerned about your memory or someone you love, you can phone the confidential National Dementia Helpline on 1800 100 500.

Katie M Little is patron of the Jeanne Little Alzheimer's Research Fund

To contribute to important research please visit
https://foundation.neura.edu.au/appeal/jeanne-little

---

[1] Australian Bureau of Statistics (2017) Causes of Death, Australia, 2016 (cat. no. 3303.0)

ACKNOWLEDGEMENTS

Firstly I would like to thank my parents for this book. If they were not such interesting people I'd have had nothing to write about – and my life would have been interminably average! If my father had not struggled with writing his own book for so many years, never finishing it, I would not have been so determined to finish my own, no matter how hard the journey became.

I'd like to thank Stephen Moriarty who, contrary to what people might assume, is actually quite a bashful type preferring to keep his name out of things. Either that or he's trying to outrun a chequered past! Stephen has a talent for mining B-list celebs like panning for gold, picking up cast off reality faces and hand-me-down forgotten stars who would otherwise go unnoticed, giving them a polish and a second life. It was Stephen who took the time to take me for coffee after the media had picked over the bones of my mother's illness, interested to know what I had to offer the world, and when he said, 'You should write a book about growing up with your mother,' it was nothing short of a lightbulb moment. Thank you Stephen, and Ben for having the grit to stand by me and never give up believing in my dream, and to Fiona Schultz at New Holland Publishers for taking a chance on me!

To my soulmate Timothy Poulton, twenty-five years together for better or worse and not one second has been dull. Writing by its nature is a solitary, selfish pursuit and writers painfully complicated individuals. Mind you, photographers are generally egotistical and opinionated – we're a perfect match. Thank you for supporting me. And to our kids: Tom, La La and Hunter, my beautiful children, for understanding my obsessive need to write and for making my life always far more entertaining than fiction.

Thank you to the stars of the story: Sally Dingle Wall, Dan and Mel Cope, Nicole Burton, Tiffany Farrington and Kate McDonald – thank god we grew up in the 80s before the internet!

When life gets tough you really find out who your friends are. Thank you so much to the following people for your astounding generosity, steadfast encouragement and love: Craig Bennett and Craig Murchie, Angie and Richard Farrington, Amelia Allan and Helen Winter, Barbara Whitnall and Vivienne Cable at Image By Design, Maria Venuti, Desleigh and Ray White, Leandra Coffey, Natalie Hawkins, Lalirra Doube, Michelle and Andreas Johansson, Denise Love, Tanya Ikonomou, Ali and John Huckle, Amanda Barnier, Narelle Hammond, Beth Derbyshire-Sloan, Louise Howlett, Jo McCulloch, Samantha Bennett, Suzan Wills, Sarah Olencewicz, Nina Johnson, Julia O'Reilly, Lisa Sestito, Darren McAlister, Meena Chaudhuri, Andy Rigby and Eliza Giddy, Katrina Lindsay and Alex Gould, Edwina Gould, Rachael Preobrajenki, Zoe Emanuel, Cybele Brown, Katia Michell, Georgiana Mentis, Rebecca Pascoe, Martine Folden, Lorena Iezzi, Jamie Zarzycki and Bree Mankin, Sky Shayne-Innes, Orin and Da Ben, Moira Marien, Katherine Perrott, Mark Murphy, Stephen Allkins, Jason Ross and Helen Raadts, Laura Sparkes, Mike Hammond, Bruce Macdonald at Toot Hairdressing, and the wonderful Hannah and Michelle at Starfish Kids. Also, Ms Denise at The Children's House Montessori, Badrunnesa and Wei Hua at GOCC, Mrs Smith and Miss Hristofski at all the staff at BPPS, and Hunters Hill Preschool for being more like family than teachers to my children and me at times. My husband's family in Brisbane, my neighbours Petra and Brad Kleengraefe and Jo and Geoff Curnow and the Boronia Park community for not burning me at the stake yet! And the township of Bellingen and Camp Creative, my spiritual home!

Writing would suck without coffee. Thank you to the gorgeous boys at Dachshund Coffee, Georgie Cwikel at Unwritten (please can we change the name of your cafe to Written now??), and the lovely ladies at Boronia Bakehouse.

Thank you to Amanda Hampson my cool headed mentor, Rob Sessions who solved the puzzle of a name for the book, Liz Hardy my editor at New Holland, and Writing NSW.

Thank you so much to Evol Ferguson at Bauer Media Group, *New Idea*, Ross Coffey, David Hahn, Sue Smethurst, Dianne Edwards at Hayden Orpheum, Bernina Sewing Machines and Newspix for allowing me to use photos! Also, the NFSA and Arts Centre Melbourne. Thank you also to Neuroscience Research Australia (NeuRA) and Dementia Australia. Plus, Nora Hunter and the wonderful team at Channel 7, Susie Smither and the Australian Ladies' Variety Association.

Acknowledgements

Thank you to my online circle of friends, I cannot tell you how important you are. You have been there through thick and thin, offering encouragement and keeping me focused, helping me over the roughest bumps in the road such as that annual kick in the shins, Mother's Day. Our open-hearted discussions on Facebook have kept me company, made me laugh and also made me cry. Thank you from the bottom of my heart to all of you, but especially Deb Hornby, John Considine, Robert Waite, Val Smith, Mia Middonte, Phill Stephens, Gary Bradley, Pat O'Connor, Linda Gee, Margarette Millard, Caitlin Kirkpatrick, Mark Kristian, Michelle Poulton, Sean Glassford, Margo Thatcher, Craig Guild, Chris King, Val Smith, Suzi Hammond, Sarah Guinevere Heald, Mel Sinclair, Richard Stanton, Lawrence Arbon, Mandy Langlois, Vicki Souter, Jason Dann, Maxine Townsend, Lawrence Arbon, Katherine Bright, Jodie Harkness, Tony Papworth, John Mimlich, Geoff Da Chef, Suzie Q Scott, Nic Wallace, Luke Jackson, Alexander Brittan, Debora Krizak, Rina Gill, Vicki Fletcher, Gordon Brown, Debra Shelton, Kieran Carroll, Caroline Ferguson, Mary Gregory Bradford, Belinda Raeburn, Brooke Hammer, David Misulti, Dan Graham and Eve Wheeler Crawford.

And to the people who look after Mum – the staff at St Luke's and Ashburn House – and the people who look after Dad – Sabina Donnolley, Dale Shaddock, Angela Fenwick and The Lodge at Hunters Hill – thank you from the bottom of my heart for the work you do.

ABOUT THE AUTHOR

Katie M Little is a writer, designer and stage mother. Her work has been published in Adbusters, her style compared to memoirist heavyweight Clive James, and acclaimed philosopher Daniel Pinchbeck once commended her blog as 'similar to my own thinking'.

She writes about the precarious mental balancing act of living in the Anthropocene and promises after reading her stuff, 'You'll start to feel better about life, either that or you won't feel quite so alone.' She uses black humour to cut through people's preconceived ideas, and loves challenging accepted norms of behaviour.

Katie lives in Sydney with her three children, Tom, La La and Hunter and is grateful they are nearly all old enough to understand sarcasm. Occasionally she also lives with her husband, landscape photographer Timothy Poulton, but they keep their laundry separate.

Like her mother, Australian icon Jeanne Little, who inherited the family 'gift' for tealeaf reading, Katie is obsessed with numerology, which she has nicknamed 'human sudoku', and moonlights as a tarot reader in her spare time.

You can follow Katie M Little and her family at *LittleFamily.com.au*

Join her conversations on Facebook or Twitter @LittleFamilyOz

First published in 2019 by New Holland Publishers
Sydney

Level 1, 178 Fox Valley Road, Wahroonga, NSW 2076, Australia

newhollandpublishers.com

Copyright © 2019 New Holland Publishers
Copyright © 2019 in text: Katie M Little
Copyright © 2019 in images: Katie M Little, except where noted

All rights reserved. No part of this publication may be reproduced, stored in a retrieval system or transmitted, in any form or by any means, electronic, mechanical, photocopying, recording or otherwise, without the prior written permission of the publishers and copyright holders.

A record of this book is held at the National Library of Australia.

ISBN 9781760790578

Managing Director: Fiona Schultz
Publisher: Fiona Schultz
Project Editor: Liz Hardy
Designer: Sara Lindberg
Production Director: Arlene Gippert

Keep up with New Holland Publishers:
NewHollandPublishers
@newhollandpublishers

www.ingramcontent.com/pod-product-compliance
Lightning Source LLC
Chambersburg PA
CBHW081202240426
43669CB00039B/2755